ONE EARTH MANY RELIGIONS

Multifaith Dialogue and Global Responsibility

Paul F. Knitter

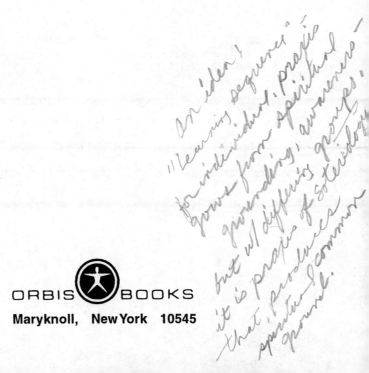

ORBIS ⊕ BOOKS

Maryknoll, New York 10545

The Catholic Foreign Mission Society of America (Maryknoll) recruits and trains people for overseas missionary service. Through Orbis Books, Maryknoll aims to foster the international dialogue that is essential to mission. The books published, however, reflect the opinions of their authors and are not meant to represent the official position of the society.

Library of Congress Cataloging in Publication Data

Knitter, Paul F.
    One earth many religions : multifaith dialogue and global
responsibility / Paul F. Knitter.
        p.   cm.
    Includes bibliographical references and index.
    ISBN 1-57075-037-8
    1. Religions—Relations.   2. Human ecology—Religious aspects.
3. Knitter, Paul F.   4. Christianity and other religions.
I. Title.
BL410.K55   1995
291.1'72—dc20
                                                            95-35187
                                                               CIP

For June Pullinsi,
mama mia italiana

CONTENTS

FOREWORD

Hans Küng

There are two reasons why I am happy to write this foreword to the new book by my friend and colleague Paul Knitter. First, I value the openness and honesty that I have always felt in our relationship. In this book, Knitter is not at all silent about the theological differences that exist between us—differences that we have on occasion expressed publicly. I have always maintained that a Christian theologian, even in dialogue with followers of other religions, must defend the normativity and finality of Jesus Christ as God's revelatory event for Christians—without, however, making any arrogant claims of superiority over other religions. In my view, I am better serving the cause of interreligious dialogue by holding firm to the conviction—as I have done in all my books from *On Being a Christian* (1974) to *Global Responsibility* (1991)—that Christians can accept the truth-claims of other religions only "conditionally" (that is, conditioned by the norm of Jesus Christ), just as followers of other religions can accept the truth-claims of Christianity only conditionally. Knitter, however, argues that at this point, we must cross a theological "Rubicon." When I note these differences between us, I am not at all diminishing the solidarity that I feel with a friend and colleague. On the contrary, I am expressing the honesty and openness that are indispensable for friendship.

But the specific question of the "uniqueness" of Jesus does not form part of the central content of this book. Knitter tells us that he will take up this question more carefully in a coming book—and we can all look forward to it. So in reviewing the content and intent of *One Earth Many Religions*, I find that it elicits my full support. This is the second and the most important reason why I am happy to write this foreword.

There is something immediately evident about this book: this is not a sterile ivory-tower theology. In developing his theoretical groundwork, in taking issue with the proposals of other theologians, in following the procedures of the theological academy, Knitter also makes it clear that this book was written as part of a personal, spiritual "odyssey," by someone who has been existentially shaken by the horrible sufferings of millions of human beings. The book makes for thoroughly engaging reading as Knitter describes both his personal struggle to find his own way and the persons/events who have contributed to and guided that struggle. Both these ingredients go together: only the person who is continuously "on the way" is able really to be affected by the sufferings of others; only the person who is not yet "finished" with his or her own life can be responsive to the incompleteness, the ruptures, and the pitfalls in the biographies of other persons.

Knitter was therefore well-advised to begin this book with an autobiographical introduction. It offers the reader a clearer sense of who this man is. His path is representative of the path that numerous Christian theologians all over the world have followed. Many theologians of Knitter's generation felt themselves confined in a medieval, counter-reformational, anti-modernist model of mission theology. They were led to view the non-Christian world exclusively as a massive assembly of unconverted heathen who would be tripping off to hell if someone didn't baptize them before they died and so introduce them to the only medium of salvation, the Catholic church. Knitter engagingly describes his early steps as a member of a missionary congregation and the painful disintegration of the missionary paradigm that once motivated him. On this issue, the Second Vatican Council made a 180 degree turn and proposed a new paradigm: it recognized the possibilities of salvation in the religious paths that others were following and affirmed the "truth" and "holiness," the value and virtues, of the non-Christian religions. Knitter took this new theological paradigm seriously, and developed, as a young American theologian studying in Germany, a decisive critique of all types of Catholic or Protestant theology that, directly or indirectly, are still caught in an exclusivistic theology of mission.

But Knitter moved on. He soon realized that he could not simply develop a theology about other religions but had to carry on the theological task in a personal encounter with them. His path makes it impressively clear that anyone engaged in interreligious dialogue nowadays will encounter dialogue partners who not only follow different religious and cultural paths but who are also immersed in very different socio-economic conditions. This is especially true of Asia, and Knitter's interreligious experiences have been taking place primarily in India and Sri Lanka.

Such encounters led this academic theologian to a salutary conversion. He realized that when interreligious dialogue takes place "on the spot" in the context of Asia and when it becomes a very concrete encounter, indeed confrontation, with the living conditions of particular human beings, then these living conditions cannot remain external to the dialogue. Dialogue loses all moral credibility if it remains only on the level of the intellectual or spiritual, detached from the social misery and the physical and psychic sufferings of so many millions of persons. The great merit of this book is the impassioned way it makes us aware of this. Interreligious dialogue presupposes more than an intellectual-academic interest in what Hinduism or Buddhism or Islam has to say about particular theological or anthropological issues. Certainly, careful scientific research and vigorous academic analysis are essential to interreligious dialogue; but the dialogue has a totally different foundation and motivation when it arises out of the recognition of the sufferings of millions of underprivileged, marginalized people who have been denied even minimum human rights and dignity. The victims of political or social conditions must indeed, as Knitter claims, have "a privileged voice in interfaith dialogue."

So the high point of this book is found precisely in its final chapter, in which Knitter describes his concrete experiences of interreligious dialogue in India—a land which he rightly calls a "laboratory for dialogue." The reader will indeed find this part of the book particularly engaging, not only because of the important information it provides on ashrams, base communities, dialogue centers, and action groups of all kinds, but also because it offers a priceless "source of enlightenment and inspiration." Interreligious dialogue that is carried out as a "dialogue of action" and a "dialogue of life" takes on very concrete reality for concrete people in concrete places. Here we find genuine signs of hope, indispensable in a book that contains such indictments of massive human and environmental suffering. Here, too, Knitter was well-advised to end his book with descriptions of particular dialogue projects and action programs, for the book's emphasis on the reality and persistence of suffering might easily have paralyzed the reader. This danger is avoided by the encouragement and hope that his final pages communicate; solutions can be found for even the most deeply entrenched social problems.

I share Paul Knitter's conviction that the dialogue among religions must take up the question of a "Global Ethic" and of "Global Responsibility," as the World Parliament of Religions in Chicago in 1993 did in its final "Declaration for a World Ethic." The world can achieve greater peace and justice only if the religious communities of the world can come together to recognize a minimal basis of shared values, norms, fundamental principles, and ideals. The religions of the world, instead of drawing dividing lines between each other (and so making room for fundamentalists and fanatics), must affirm their responsibility to work together for a more comprehensive justice, a deeper peace, and a more sustainable relationship with the eco-system. In my own theological endeavors, in my own way, I try to do this, without holding up, as Knitter does, the reality of suffering as the exclusive foundation and legitimation for interreligious dialogue. The main proponents of liberation theology have also recognized and are seeking to balance the one-sidedness of the "preferential option for the poor" and are trying to give greater attention to the entire cultural context in their theological method. But in such matters, every theologian will have his or her particular emphasis. Differing perspectives complement each other when they share a common goal: to embrace the one world, in which the many religions, while affirming their own truth-claims, will also affirm their individual responsibilities to work toward a shared global ethic. For this reason, I hope that Paul Knitter's book will find many responsive readers.

PREFACE

To chant my thank yous to all the people who stand behind and within these pages would be for the reader, I'm afraid, as inspiring and as tiring as making it through the Litany of All Saints. So rather than list all the holy men and women of God who have helped me with this book, let me mention just a representative or two of the varied categories of "doctors, confessors, and martyrs" who in their different ways have aided me in formulating, clarifying, and correcting this book's vision of a correlational, globally responsible dialogue of religions.

Perhaps my heftiest debt of gratitude is owed to my students, who have a wonderful ability to show both their boredom with theological talk that is unclear or unreal and their zest for affirming and extending religious ideas that touch and challenge their lives. I'm thinking especially of Sarah Hambrook, David Shurna, and the Xavier Scholars Seminar on Religions and Eco-Justice, who wrestled with the first drafts of this book; graduate student Don Kunkel, who did likewise in a directed studies course; and Leslie Heyboer, Paul Nagano, and the other students of my summer course at the Graduate Theological Union in Berkeley, who encouraged me and took me to task for either unclarity or timidity. I received similar encouragement from colleagues in the academy who read early forms of this book, both from those like Joe Bracken, S.J., and Roger Haight, S.J., who urged me along, and from those like Gavin D'Costa and Karl-Josef Kuschel, who worried about the direction or speed I was taking. To Hans Küng I am multiply grateful—for his pioneer work in calling religions to global responsibility, for his introduction to this book, and for a friendship that has grown deeper not despite but because of our differences.

Mother India speaks in the last chapter, but she is present throughout this book as she has been present in my life since my first visit in 1991. I am indebted to many people who introduced me to her and then guided me in my growing love-fear relationship with her, especially the students and faculty at United Theological College (UTC, Bangalore), where my family and I received hospitality, and at Vidyajyoti (Delhi), Tamilnadu Theological Seminary (TTS, Madurai), Gurukul Lutheran Seminary (Madras), and Dharmaram College (Bangalore) where I had extended visits. Individuals whose wisdom and warnings represent the cautious yet genuinely dialogical reception I found almost everywhere in India are Stanley Samartha (UTC), Samuel Rayan, S.J. (Vidyajyoti), Jyoti Sahi (Bangalore), S. Gangadaran and

Israel Selvanayagam (TTS), V. Devasahayam (Gurukul), Ignatius Puthiadam, S.J. (Maitri Bhavan, Banares), Ignatius Hirudayam, S.J. (Aikiya Alayam, Madras)—and in Sri Lanka, Aloysius Pieris, S.J. Doctoral students Roger Gaikwad and Kiran Sebastian were marvelously patient and savvy guides into the beneath-the-surface aspects of the cultural, ethnic, and religious diversity of India.

Finally, my litany of thank yous includes many personal friends whose presence in my day-to-day life guided the growth of this book: my co-activists in CRISPAZ (Christians for Peace in El Salvador) and the Faith and Justice Community of Bellarmine Parish, who helped my "praxis" support my "theory"; Dave Callan and Karol King, who told me honestly how my writing came across to the "educated, interested" layperson; Bill Burrows, Managing Editor at Orbis Books, whose warm, hard-nosed support was always only a phone call away; and of course, my family—Cathy, John, and Moira—who have taught me more about "theological method" than I ever could imagine.

1

MY DIALOGICAL ODYSSEY

An Autobiographical Introduction

Back in 1985, in the opening sentence to the Preface for *No Other Name? A Critical Survey of Christian Attitudes toward World Religions*, I wrote: "All theology, we are told, is rooted in biography." I could well have used the same words to begin this book. Once again, and even more so, I can stand back in happy awe at the way my theological ploddings have followed the flow of what has been going on in my life. My work as a Christian theologian—that is, my efforts to help my community mediate between our Christian tradition and our culture(s)—has been surprisingly, painfully, usually fruitfully, affected by the people and the events that either have been invited or have broken into my life. Certainly I have drawn up my own plans and made my own decisions—but always those plans and choices have been occasioned, stimulated, limited, or reversed by people who meant something to me or events that challenged my mind or touched my heart. There have been particular people and events that have especially shaken and directed me over the past ten years since *No Other Name?* In this first chapter, I want to describe them briefly in order to make clear what I hope to do in this book, and why.

I realize that these past ten years are both piece and product of a larger picture—or better, of a larger journey that has been going on in my life since my high school years, back in the '50s, when I entered what was then called a minor seminary. It's been a movement that can best be described as a "journey with the other" or a "dialogical odyssey." Of course, everyone's life can be so depicted. As relational beings, we've all had "significant others" brightening and bending our lives. When I say "other" to describe my journey, I mean the *really different*, the unexpected, the unthought, the surprising, the jolting. I'm talking about people or events that didn't seem to fit into the world that I had experienced and understood. My life, especially as a Christian and theologian, has been enriched, disturbed, redirected by people who have encountered or embraced me with their differences, or by situations or events that I never dreamed could be or happen. These people and events have crossed over the patrolled borders of my life and made my world different from what it had been.

As I look back over the past decades, it seems there have been two primary Others who have so affected my life and my theology: the *religious Other* and the *suffering Other*. Up until the early '80s, the most significant Other in my social and theological life had been the religious persons from other traditions who challenged or upset many of my spiritual and theological categories and expectations. It was the impact of their entry into and settlement in my life that I reported on and responded to in *No Other Name?* But as I will elaborate below, the flow of world and personal events during the '80s took me into a different and bigger neighborhood of others. The Central American refugees who invaded the southern borders of the United States fleeing economic injustice and oppression represent these new others who have entered redemptively (though illegally, according to my government) into my life: the wide numbers of people throughout the world who are suffering horribly, unjustly, unnecessarily. More recently, I have come to understand, even feel, the suffering not only of humans but of all sentient beings, including our mother Earth. Human and ecological suffering has become an Other who has disturbed my life even more than the religious Other.

Happily, though often painfully, I have been invited, even forced, into conversation with these Others. I say this as a human being, but also as a Christian and a theologian. And so I have felt, ever more strongly and apprehensively, that I must speak with the religious and the suffering Others *as* a Christian and a theologian. If I can't make sense of my Christian experience and beliefs, if I can't carry on my theological task, in dialogue and in a life-giving encounter with *both* of these two Others, then my faith is not authentic and my theology is a distraction.

STAGES IN THE ODYSSEY

From the vantage point of hindsight, as I look back over the decades and milestones of my journey with the Other, I can detect in my own life a mini-recapitulation of what has been the journey and the struggle of many Christian churches who have opened themselves to the genuinely other. The signposts, or stages, in my journey correspond roughly to what have been called the "models" for Christian efforts to develop a theology of and dialogue with other religious traditions. Nowadays many theologians and pastoral practitioners speak and argue about the *exclusivist* or *inclusivist* or *pluralist* approaches to persons of other religious ways (see Race 1983).[1] As with all models and with all technical jargon, there are dangers of defining things too tightly and of stuffing people into pigeon holes they only half fit. I hope to avoid such dangers in the following pages, as I evaluate these models and advocate new ones. Still, these three general perspectives do reflect widespread and differing Christian views of other religions. For me, as I look back over my life, these models are not simply intellectual constructs or academic playthings. Rather, they represent personal and spiritual struggles as I felt my beliefs and my practices shaken by the entrance of the religious and the suffering Others into my life. Before I was even acquainted with the technical terms of "exclusivism, inclusivism, pluralism," I was wrestling with the realities that those terms try to indicate; in my Christian, theological journey I found myself moving—or being forced—from one perspective or model to another.

What follows is a brief account of that journey. In its meanderings and in the direction of its movement, I suspect that it will reflect the journey many of my fellow Christians are making. Whether that's true or not, this is the personal story that has brought me to the writing of this book; I'm hoping that the book may clarify and give better direction to the story—both mine and others'.

MISSIONARY BEGINNINGS: EXCLUSIVISM

My dialogical odyssey began pretty much as a monologue. Other religious persons interested me not so much because I wanted to converse with them, but because I wanted to convert them. I wanted to be a missionary. In 1958, after four years of seminary high school and two rigorous years of novitiate "boot camp," I officially joined the ranks of the Divine Word Missionaries (the "SVDs" or *Societas Verbi Divini*). Though ambiguous in many ways, that decision was one of the most fruitful of my life. It was really my first step toward the religious Other.

Although this step was motivated by concern, even love, for others, it was the kind of concern and love that exists, not between friends, but between a doctor and his or her ailing patient. Five times a day, in our seminary prayers, we stormed heaven with the invocation: "May the darkness of sin and the night of heathenism vanish before the light of the Word and the Spirit of grace." *We* had the Word and Spirit; *they* had sin and heathenism. We were the loving doctors; they were the suffering patients.

In those years of seminary training—late '50s, early '60s—there was much talk about "accommodation" or "missionary adaptation." This was an indirect, though still real, recognition that there wasn't total darkness in the world of other religions. As some German theologians of the time put it, there were also *Anknüpfungspunkte* within other traditions—points of contact where Christians could insert their saving word. Actually, "missionary adaptation" was somewhat equivalent to "getting a foot in the door"—recognizing where other religious believers resembled us Christians and where their transformation into Christians could begin. This was a small, self-interested step toward recognizing positive values in other traditions. For me, it was a first step.

Once I got my foot in the door of other religions, I discovered more than I expected. Here was the first phase in which the religious Other actually intruded into my life. During those seminary years, there was a constant flow of missionaries returning home on furlough and passing through the various SVD houses to give talks to us future missionaries. In their slide lectures, in their colorful, often moving stories of encounters with Hindus, Buddhists, primal religious believers, I gradually realized that the SVDs were not really practicing or experiencing what they were praying about; these missionaries talked much more about the beauty of Hinduism, or the insights of the New Guinea Highlanders, or about the rich depths of Buddhist art and meditation than about their pervasive and perverse "darkness and sin."

I especially remember how moved and bewildered I was at the Indian dance team Father George Proksh, S.V.D., directed; it presented not just Christian beliefs decked in Hindu dance forms but also the beauty and mystery of the Hindu sense of the Divine. Added to this were the discoveries I made as a member of our college Japan Study Club; we were all expected to select one of the SVD "mission countries" in order to study its history, culture, and religion. It was my first taste of Buddhism, my first acquaintance with the history of Zen, the rigor of its practice, the claimed illumination and peace of the satori experience. There was much I couldn't fit into my Christian categories; there was much I liked.

As I finished my college studies in 1962 and tucked away my bachelor's degree in philosophy, I had the uneasy but distinct sense that the old exclusivist model of Christianity as light and other religions as darkness didn't fit the facts. What to do about that became clearer for me when I was sent to finish my theological studies in Rome.

VATICAN II AND KARL RAHNER: INCLUSIVISM

I arrived in Rome to begin my studies at the Pontifical Gregorian University just two weeks before the Second Vatican Council began on October 11, 1962. It was an exhilarating, hope-filled time to be in Rome. Pope John XXIII was not just opening long-locked windows in the Roman church, he was knocking through walls and indirectly calling for reconstruction of old models and practices! Part of the general opening of the Catholic church to the modern world was a recognition of other cultures and religions. I remember well the enthusiasm of the twenty-four SVD missionary bishops who were staying with us while they attended the Council when they discovered that there would be a statement about the church's relationship not just with Judaism but also with other religions. I shared their enthusiasm when one of the bishops, a veteran of decades in New Guinea whose Latin had grown more than rusty, asked me to help him read the text of the *sub secreto* (confidential) document on the "Declaration on the Relationship of the Church to Non-Christian Religions." Here were positive statements about the truth and values of Hinduism, Buddhism, Islam that had never before graced an official church document; here, I realized, was a turning point in Roman Catholic theology of religions.

At the same time the Council fathers were meeting, I was taking courses at the Gregorianum about and by one of the theologians who offered decisive help in opening the Catholic church's windows to other believers: the theology of Karl Rahner figured into many of the courses taught by his brother Jesuits. In 1965 Rahner himself came to "the Greg" as a guest professor. Listening to him, I realized clearly how, with his carefully crafted doctrinal arguments, he had laid the theological foundations for Vatican II's new, positive view of other religions. Even more than the Council's terse but revolutionary recognition of truth and goodness in the world religions, Rahner's theologically honed case that Christians not only can but *must* look upon other religions as "legitimate" and as "ways of salvation" was a breath of fresh, liberating air for me. It enabled me both to make sense of what I had been seeing in the religious world beyond Christianity and to shake free of what I felt was the ungrounded hubris of Christian claims to be the only authentic religion.

So after earning my licentiate in theology in Rome, I decided to move to the University of Münster, Germany, to write a thesis under Karl Rahner on Catholic attitudes toward other religions. After working with him for about a half year, however, I discovered, to my shock, that someone else, back in Rome, had just published a dissertation on the very same topic. Back in Rome to resolve my dissertational doldrums, I sought counsel with Monsignor Piero Rossano, then Secretary for the Vatican's Secretariate for Non-Christian Religions. He helped transform my setback into a new opportunity when he suggested that I do with contemporary Protestant theology what I had hoped to do with Catholic theology.

His suggestion turned out to be an opportunity for the religious Other to knock again on my door—or better, I on its! I moved from my familiar Roman Catholic world of Rome and Münster to the University of Marburg and to a Department of Protestant Theology founded under the Reformers. Here, under the direction of Professor Carl Heinz Ratschow, I wrote a dissertation entitled "Toward a Protestant Theology of Religions." Though I was the first Roman Catholic ever admitted into the doctoral program of Marburg's Department of Protestant Theology, I had the Roman audacity to criticize contemporary Protestant thinkers (even my own "Doctor-Father" Ratschow!) for not going far enough in their efforts to overcome the exclusivism of Karl Barth's neo-orthodox attitude toward religion. In their efforts to recognize the value of other religions, Protestant theologians, I claimed, were stymied by the Reformational insistence on "faith alone" through "Christ alone" (see Knitter 1975). Protestants such as Paul Althaus, Emil Brunner, and even Wolfhart Pannenberg could recognize "revelation" in other faiths, but never "salvation." This was, I concluded, to go only halfway in their efforts to reach out to other religious believers.

But my criticism of Protestant theologians was thoroughly based on, and limited by, my Rahnerian Catholic perspective. I was criticizing the Protestants for not having made the move that Rahner made with his new theology of religions, often epitomized in his theory of "anonymous Christians" (that is, non-Christians are "saved" by the grace and presence of Christ working anonymously within their religions). Yet if I could chide the Protestants for not being able to admit that there is saving grace mediated through other religions, I myself was not able to imagine that such wisdom and grace in other traditions could be anything else but "reflections" of the fullness of truth and grace incarnated in Jesus the Christ. Such reflections, I took for granted, could be brought to full light only in the gospel. Thus, while Rahner's theology of religions constituted for me a giant, liberating step forward, I did not realize at the time of finishing my doctorate that it was for me but the *first* step in a broader, even more liberating, process of reaching into the world of the religious Other.

EXPLORING THE OTHER SIDE: PLURALISM

In an image used by John Hick, Rahner turned out to be for me not a new paradigm, but a bridge (Hick 1980, 180-81). I first began to suspect that I might have to get off that bridge and onto the other side when, during my doctoral studies in Germany, I met Rahim. From Pakistan, Rahim was a bright, friendly, fun-loving, and caring fellow-student majoring in chemistry. He was also a devout Muslim who prayed five times a day and ordered apple juice when the rest of us called for beer. We became close friends and often discussed religion. I began to realize clearly what I could not explain theologically, even with Rahner's help. Personally, Rahim was entirely content with his Muslim faith; ethically, he surpassed most Christians I knew. In discussing our faiths, we learned much from each other. But if I were to speak about Rahim's need of being "fulfilled" through Christianity, it would have to be in the same sense that I needed fulfillment through Islam. Theologically, I could say that Rahim was saved; I could not call him an anonymous Christian. Rahner's bridge was shaking.

It shook even more when I returned to Chicago to begin my teaching career at Catholic Theological Union in 1972. Besides offering courses on theologies of religions and interreligious dialogue, I also began a serious study of other faiths by teaching courses on them, especially Hinduism and Buddhism. Strongly influenced by the method of "passing over" that John Dunne laid out in his *The Way of All the Earth* (1972), I tried, amid many limitations and frustrations, to lead myself and my students into a study of other religious ways that was both intellectual-historical and personal-experiential. When I moved to Xavier University in 1975 (having left the Society of the Divine Word) and continued teaching these same courses with the same methodology, I gradually realized that I had slid, unawares, off Rahner's bridge and was exploring, with a sense of excitement and apprehension, new religious territory. And I further realized that the new territory would eventually call for new theological maps.

Among my most trustworthy yet bold guides in this exploration were Raimon Panikkar, both in his theoretical directives (*The Intra-Religious Dialogue*, 1978) and in the way he passed over to Hinduism (*The Vedic Experience*, 1977), and Thomas Merton, in the way he brought Zen Buddhism to life and meaning (*Zen and the Birds of Appetite*, 1968). I also became more engaged in actual dialogue with Hindu and especially Buddhist practitioners. In the midst of, or because of, all this, I found myself returning, after years of neglect, to a daily practice of meditation, only now it was in the form of zazen. From such study, conversations, and practice, I realized that a dialogue of discovery and theological insight was unfolding—sometimes exploding—within me. There were particular experiences and insights that shook and then rearranged my theological perspectives: when I realized that perhaps the Hindu claim of nondualism between Brahman and Atman was not just an analog, but perhaps a more coherent expression, of what Rahner was trying to articulate with his notion of the supernatural existential[2]; or when I realized that the Buddhist experience of *Anatta* (no-self), as much as I had understood and felt it, enabled me to better understand and live Paul's claim that "it is now no longer I who live but Christ who lives in me" (Gal 2:20).

The theological conclusions from all this exploration and discovery came to an initial focus for me when I read Hans Küng's *On Being a Christian* (1976). With his staunch criticism of the theory of anonymous Christianity, Küng became for me another prophetic prod to get off Rahner's bridge. But when I came to the bottom line of his treatment of other faiths, which in my estimation both misrepresented and unduly subordinated them to what Küng termed the "finality" of the Christ event, I realized that moving off the bridge would require a bigger move than Küng, at that time, was able to make (Knitter 1978). (Since then, Küng has taken his own further steps without, however, loosening his hold on the finality of Christ.) In order to figure out for myself just how this bigger move might be made and what it would entail, I decided, not to hie off to an Indian ashram or Japanese Zen monastery, but to write a book (a more practical decision since I now was a husband and father). Before engaging in deeper dialogue, I wanted to try to sort out, for myself and others, the past efforts and the inherent potential of Christian theology to interpret the so-called new experience of religious pluralism.

No Other Name? (1985) was billed as a "critical survey of Christian attitudes." After the survey and drawing from it, I attempted to assemble a theological case that would convince myself and fellow Christians that one is not at all abandoning the Christian witness contained in scripture and tradition, but rather understanding it more deeply and thus preserving it, when one sublates (which does not mean leaves behind!) the given christocentric approach to other believers with one that is theocentric. Though we Christians claim Jesus the Christ as our necessary and happy starting point and focus for understanding ourselves and other peoples, we must also remind ourselves that the Divine Mystery we know in Jesus and call *Theos* or God, is ever greater than the reality and message of Jesus. Thus we are open to the *possibility* (and that's all I was arguing for in *No Other Name?*) that other religions may have their own valid views of and responses to this Mystery; thus, they would not have to be unilaterally "included" in Christianity. Rather, *all* the religions could be, perhaps need to be, included in—that is, related to—each other as all of them continue their efforts to discover or be faithful to the inexhaustible Mystery or Truth. I had, indeed, moved off the bridge, from inclusivism to some form of pluralism. I was now exploring "the other side." And though I want to clarify and correct particular arguments in *No Other Name?* (and will do so in the following pages), I have continued to move in the direction it set for me.

PLURALISM AND LIBERATION

In 1986, in order both to ascertain how widespread this pluralist turn was among Christian theologians and to expose it to further criticism, John Hick and I assembled a group of theologians who were moving, each in different ways, in this general direction. The results of that conference were presented to the broader Christian and theological community in *The Myth of Christian Uniqueness: Toward a Pluralistic Theology of Religions* (1987). In writing my own contribution to that volume, I came to realize that my pluralist turn had taken a new twist. Again, it was a case of theology following biography. There were some new events and new people in my life. Since the early '70s, I had been trying to follow the developments of the new liberation theology coming out of Latin America. My interest was fueled initially by my desire to be methodologically up to date. Then in 1983 I met in

Cincinnati two Salvadoran students; they were refugees because they had spoken up for human rights and were being pursued by their Salvadoran government, which was supported by my United States government. Since that fortuitous encounter, my life, as they say, has not been the same.

The following year my wife Cathy and I became active members of the local Sanctuary Movement—a loose ecumenical bonding of churches and synagogues who, in defiance of U.S. government policy, were publicly providing shelter and support to Central American refugees fleeing the poverty and dangers of U.S.-sponsored wars in their countries. This led to summer visits to El Salvador and Nicaragua over the next five years. Through these experiences—through working with refugee families in Cincinnati, meeting with base Christian communities in Central America, collaborating with Jon Sobrino and Lutheran Bishop Medardo Gomez in El Salvador, experiencing the pain of Salvadoran friends picked up by security forces and tortured—liberation theology became for me not just a "new method" but a matter of making sense of religion and of being a faithful disciple of Jesus. I experienced the fundamental option for the oppressed to be not simply an option but a demand. It affected the way I do theology to the point that I could no longer go about a theology of religions unless it was, somehow, connected with a theology of liberation. And so my contribution to *The Myth* collection bore the strange title "Toward a Liberation Theology of Religions."

Since then, the suffering Other has continued to accompany and challenge my spiritual and theological journey. Their voices and their cries for justice remain with me not only through my continuing contacts with the people and churches of El Salvador as a member of the Board of Directors of CRISPAZ (Christians for Peace in El Salvador), but also through my participation in local peace and justice groups in Cincinnati.[3] One of the staunchest and most encouraging confirmations of the need for dialogue to include both the religious and the suffering Others came for me during my five month sabbatical in India, July to December 1991. With my family, I found myself immersed in a land of incredible, sometimes overwhelming, religious richness— a land, also, in which a diversity of religions have lived and dialogued (on the practical level) for centuries. But at the same time, India is also a land of incredible, and always overwhelming, poverty. If there was ever a country which housed, so graphically and tensely, the "many religions" and the "many poor," it is India. During my months there, the voices of the religious Other and of the suffering Other, though distinct and sometimes at odds, merged and spoke to me with new urgency and with new hope.

The urgency came both from those who have long been involved in the Hindu-Christian dialogue (e.g., Bede Griffiths, Ignatius Hirudayam,

Ignatius Puthiadam) and from those committed to the liberation of the Dalits or oppressed classes/castes (e.g., Swami Agnivesh, Samuel Rayan, K. C. Abrahams). From both sides, despite their differences in procedure and strategy, I was told that in India "dialogue" and "liberation" must be two facets of the same agenda. To have one without the other is to live outside the Indian reality. Despite the difficulties of such a "liberative dialogue" in a country where religion is being used with horrible success to foster "communalism" or factionalism, my hopes were nurtured by the examples I did find of Hindus, Christians, and Muslims coming together to struggle against oppression or communalism, and to learn from each other in their common struggle. (I will report on some of these examples in chapter 9.)

But as I already indicated, I have come to realize, especially during the last half of the '80s, that the suffering Other includes not just humans but also earthlings, indeed the Earth herself. And just as human suffering and ecological suffering have common causes, they will have common solutions. To speak of justice and liberation, therefore, one must intend eco-human justice and liberation. Intellectually and logically such a statement has become clear and convincing for me through the books and studies on the environmental crisis that have filled our bookstores and our awareness over the past decade. But personally and in the fibers of my feelings, the Earth has become an object of love and concern through my encounters with particular religious Others— Native Americans. I am thinking especially of my meeting with elders and spokespersons from various North American nations in June 1993 at a conference on "The Land and the Human Presence" sponsored by Bucknell University. As we sat and talked around the circle in the woods or around the fire, in their stories, statements, and especially rituals, my Native American sisters and brothers enabled me to pass over to the sense of the Sacred they find in the Earth and all its inhabitants. More clearly and intensely than ever, I saw that dialogue must include liberation and that liberation must include the Earth, for here was a people who could not talk about the Sacred without talking about the Earth and who could not talk about the horrid sufferings they themselves have endured without talking about the sufferings of Earth and animals. For me, this has become a paradigm for all interreligious encounters.

I received further and encouraging support for such a paradigm from my more academic conversations with friend and colleague Hans Küng. Though we have had our differences on theological aspects of Christian dialogue with other believers,[4] his recent project for a global ethics resonates with and expands my own sense that a concern for dialogue must be wed with a concern for justice. For Küng, and for the many who have endorsed his proposal, the avalanche of dangers that is forming on the slopes of economic injustice, environmental devastation, and military build-up will not be stayed unless the nations of the world come together to formulate and endorse some kind of shared ethical convictions and guidelines; such a task will not be accomplished, however, unless the religions of the world, in dialogue, make their contribution. In other words, interreligious conversations must take as their most pressing agenda the ethical issues behind the mounting sufferings of humans and Earth. That Küng's project received international endorsement from the World Parliament of Religions in Chicago in September 1993 is an indication that he is speaking to "the signs of the times." Despite my reservations about *how* Küng is going about the implementation of his project (as I explain in chapter 4), I want to step to his side in calling upon all religious persons to cooperate in promoting eco-human justice and well-being. So I have drawn the subtitle of this book from the title of the book in which Küng announced his project: "global responsibility" must be part of all interreligious conversations (Küng 1991).

NECESSITY BECOMES OPPORTUNITY

So people and events in my life have led me, sometimes lured me, to what has become for me a moral obligation to join "pluralism and liberation" or "dialogue and global responsibility." The two somehow have to go together. I have to speak with and learn from both the voice of the religious Other and of the suffering Other. If this isn't possible, if I can't listen to both, if I can't link my concern for interreligious dialogue with my concern for eco-human justice, then I have to make a choice. Were such a choice necessary, I would have to abandon dialogue and pursue justice and the alleviation of suffering. Fortunately, however, my experiences both in theological conversations and in dialogical encounters (especially in India, Sri Lanka, and Thailand) have assured me that such a choice need not be made. Indeed, I have gradually became aware that what I felt to be a necessity was also an opportunity.

My own limited dialogical experiences, and especially the experiences and reflections of my friend and mentor Aloysius Pieris, S.J., have brought me to the strong suspicion, if not conviction, that the *necessity* of linking interreligious dialogue with global responsibility provides the *opportunity* not only for a different kind of dialogue but also for an effectively better dialogue. (In chapter 9 I describe how Pieris is creatively combining dialogue and liberation in his work in Sri Lanka.) The voices of the suffering Other, in other words, have informed and made more comprehensible to me the voices of the religious Other. The immediacy and urgency that are contained in the presence of the suffering Other have been an occasion and means for me to enter into and appreciate the mysterious depths of the religious Other. That's quite an assertion. Let me try to explain.

The longer I have tried to engage in interreligious dialogue, the more clearly I have realized how difficult it is. The reason for this, I suspect, is that the more one seeks to enter the world of another religious tradition, through personal encounters and through textual studies, the more one bounces up against the wall of differences that are, finally, incomprehensible. While similarities in religious experience and expression abound, the differences are even more abundant—and many of them are incommensurable. To describe who the religious Other has been for me, and how it has affected me, I find Rudolf Otto's expression most fitting: they have been a *mysterium tremendum et fascinosum*— a mystery both frightening and fascinating. I have been unsettled, confused, often put off by what the religious Other makes known to me, but at the same time (or soon thereafter) I just as often find myself touched, lured, persuaded by the very strangeness that frightened me.

This is true of my experience of the other in my long-standing dialogue with Buddhists, as it is of my meetings with Hindus during travels through India; it is even more true, surprisingly, of my more recent experience of three-way dialogue among Jews, Muslims, and Christians. In trying to pass over, for example, to the Buddhists' experience of impermanence or to the Zen insistence on non-attachment even to God, and in trying to understand and appreciate the centrality of Halakhah for Jews or their sense of uniqueness and their wariness about dialogue, I have found myself trembling before the utter, or "frightening," Mystery of difference. It is a difference that I cannot comprehend, that sometimes threatens me, that chides or even laughs at my theories. I have thus experienced the religious Other as the *totaliter aliter*—the utterly other, the incommensurable, the incomprehensible. And so I have been experientially convinced that "common essence" or "common experience" are gossamer theories spun out by academicians who most likely have never felt the hard, obstructing reality of otherness. Confronting the religious Other as the utterly Other or overwhelming Mystery, I must bow in silence.

But at the same time, in a paradoxical process that I cannot explain, the religious Other, precisely by being an overwhelming Mystery, has more often than not become a "fascinating," inviting Mystery. What was so utterly different that I could not comprehend it also engaged me, beckoned me, held forth the promise of enriching me. This is a process that can, I think, only be experienced, not proven or clearly analyzed. In the interaction of mutual presence, in speaking and listening, in witnessing the commitments, the values, the rituals of others— the incommensurable, incomprehensible, utterly Other *has become* for me the possible, the imaginable, the attractive. I cannot simply bow in silent respect before other believers; I must also learn from them, speak to them, somehow find myself in them. The cocoon of silence becomes the birth place of the fragile but inquisitive butterfly of conversation.

Having experienced total, mysterious otherness, I find myself experiencing relatedness, even though I cannot explain such relatedness or say where it will lead. This is where Panikkar's notion of "cosmic trust" becomes real—I find myself trusting that despite or because of our differences, we can and we must talk to, and learn from, and be changed by each other.

For me, the suffering Other has provided help and guidance in coming to feel that the frightening otherness in my dialogue partner is an inviting other. When religious persons *together* listen to the voices of the suffering and oppressed, when they attempt *together* to respond to those needs, I have found that they are able to trust each other and to feel the truth and the power in each other's strangeness. The suffering Other becomes mediator, as it were, or conduit of trust and comprehension, between differing religious worlds. As I acted together with Jews and Buddhists in the Sanctuary Movement, as I prayed or meditated with them before the Federal Building in Cincinnati to protest U.S. aid to the Salvadoran military, as I heard their witness about why they were engaging in these activities of protest and concern, I felt that their strangeness was an inviting and affirming strangeness, one from which I could learn.

And so my image of the religious Other as a frightening and fascinating Mystery has been complemented by an image of them as *fellow travelers*. By this I do not mean that we are traveling toward some kind of eschatological or other-worldly realization of truth or fulfillment. Rather, my experience—and my trust—is that as followers of various religious paths, we all can and do experience a common concern and a common responsibility to respond, *as* religious persons, to the widespread human and ecological suffering and injustice that are threatening our species and our planet. I am not saying that all religious persons are concerned about such this-worldly suffering and crisis. But I can say, from my own experience and from reading about the experience of others, that a growing number of believers from most religious paths *are* so concerned—and *are* experiencing themselves as fellow travelers and fellow actors with persons from other faiths.

THIS BOOK: CONTINUING THE ODYSSEY

This book is both the product and the continuation of the dialogical odyssey I have just described. In it, I want to clarify the journey I have been on and at the same time give it both more solid substance and clearer direction. And I want to do so in conversation with others who are also searching for truth and values—primarily with members of my own religious community, Christianity, but also with brothers and sisters of other religious paths, in the hope that what I am talking about and proposing will enlighten and guide their own journeys. My suspicion is that persons in a variety of religious traditions are growing ever more sharply aware that to understand and live their faith-lives in our present-day world, they must be in a conversation both with other religious believers *and* with the suffering ones of this Earth.

To speak in Christian terms and especially to my fellow Christians, in this book I will try to bring together the concerns of a theology of religions and a theology of liberation—or the concerns of a dialogue of religions and a dialogue of liberation. Edward Schillebeeckx has described the twofold challenge facing all Christians (I would say, all religious persons): "The 'standpoint' from which we, as Christians . . . begin to think is increasingly the ecumene of the world religions and the ecumene of humankind . . . really and finally the ecumene of suffering mankind" (Schillebeeckx 1990, 189). These words summarize what my dialogical odyssey has told me—that unless I allow the religious and suffering Others to enter into my life, unless I am responding to them from the center of my human and religious values, I am less a human being, less a religious believer, less a Christian.

That many Christians have felt these same challenges is indicated in two of the most significant developments within Christian theology over the past half century: the *theology of liberation* and the *theology of religions*. Each movement has responded to one of the two Others who have, willy-nilly, intruded upon and challenged the composure and security of the Christian churches. While each of these theologies has contributed disruptively and creatively to Christian clarity and conviction regarding the gospel, they have not, especially in the Western churches, had much to do with each other. Liberation theologians and theologians of religions or interreligious dialogue have been working in different corners of the Christian vineyard.

In this book I will try to represent and develop the efforts of those theologians who, in both North and South, have over the past decade been attempting to build bridges between Christian efforts to respond to the religious Other and to the suffering Other. These efforts grow out of the mounting and ever-clarifying conviction that although the suffering Other may speak to Christians with a more urgent and immediate voice, even though the removal of suffering has a priority over the promotion of dialogue, still there is the clear and strong sense that an effective, enduring, really transformative dialogue with the suffering of this world will have to include a dialogue with the world religions. If the unnecessary sufferings of humanity and of the Earth are truly to be addressed and removed, the religions are going to have to make a combined, cooperative, dialogical contribution (see chapter 4). To be effective, a theology of liberation must also be a theology of interreligious dialogue. To be meaningful, an interreligious dialogue or theology must include a theology of liberation. In the following pages, I hope to lay the foundation—and maybe the first few floors—of a theology of religions that will be liberative, that is, a theology that will grow out of and contribute to the salvation and well-being of suffering humanity and Earth; and of a theology of liberation that will be dialogical, that is, a theology that is able to embrace and learn from the potential of many religions for promoting human and planetary life.

A GLOBALLY RESPONSIBLE, CORRELATIONAL DIALOGUE AMONG RELIGIONS

In the language of current Christian theology, the purpose of this book is to urge a *pluralistic, liberative dialogue of religions.* But precisely because such terms have been so battered and blurred by academicians and politicians, I'm wary of using them. Despite admonishing clarifications, "liberative" or "liberation" is felt by many to mean primarily if not exclusively a Latin American brand of theology based on a particular economic theory (usually Marxist) and limited to social or political reform. "Pluralistic" is suggestive to many of an approach to religions that sees them all as equal and as differently colored containers of a homogenous mystical experience; pluralist theologians, for many, want to pile all religions on a happy syncretistic bandwagon. In the popular mind, and in many theological minds, all "liberation" or "pluralist" theologians are stuffed into the same drawer, even though there are distinctive, sometimes opposing, differences among them. So even though I will be using the terms "liberative" or "liberation" and "pluralist" or "pluralism" in order to be understood in the theological conversation, I will also adopt, even prefer, other clarifying, distinguishing designations.

I prefer to call the approach or model I am exploring in this book a *globally responsible, correlational dialogue of religions.* I'll be explaining these terms more expansively in the next chapter, but as a introductory statement of purpose, let me say here that in proposing a model for a "globally responsible" dialogue or theology of religions, I will be urging that religious persons seek to understand and speak with each other on the basis of a common commitment to human and ecological well-being. Global responsibility therefore includes the notion of liberation intended by traditional liberation theologians but goes beyond it in seeking not just social justice but eco-human justice and well-being; it does so aware that such a project, in order truly to attend to the needs of all the globe, must be an effort by the entire globe and all its nations and religions. A globally responsible dialogue is one that is aware that any interfaith encounter is incomplete, perhaps even dangerous, if it does not include, somehow, a concern for and an attempt to resolve the human and ecological suffering prevalent throughout the world.

A "correlational" dialogue of religions affirms the plurality of religions, not because plurality is good in itself but because it is a fact of

life and the stuff of relationship. A correlational model seeks to promote authentic, truly mutual dialogical relationships among the religious communities of the world, analogous to the kind of human relationships we seek to nurture among our friends and colleagues. These
are relationships in which persons speak honestly with each other and
listen authentically. Far from requiring that everyone be the same, a
correlational dialogue presumes that the religions are truly diverse;
without genuine diversity, dialogue becomes talking to oneself in the
mirror. Participants will witness to what makes them distinct, trying
to show and convince others of the values they have found in their
tradition. But at the same time they will be truly, courageously, open
to the witness to truth that others make. This is a mutual, back and
forth *co-relationship*, of speaking and listening, teaching and learning,
witnessing and being witnessed to.

For such a correlational dialogue to take place, the dialogical encounter will have to be carried out in an *egalitarian*, not a hierarchical,
community. Though all religious participants will speak their mind
and make truth claims to each other, none of them will do so from a
theological position that claims that theirs is the religion meant to
dominate or absorb or stand in judgment over all others. A correlational dialogue cannot begin with one religion claiming to hold all the
cards, or to be superior in all respects to the others, or to have the final
norm that will exclude all other norms. Just as a relationship between
two human beings cannot thrive if one of them claims, before the relationship even begins, to be superior or to always have the final word,
so too is the relationship constitutive of interfaith dialogue doomed to
failure if one religion claims, a priori, general superiority over all others to the extent that it is not willing or able to learn from them. If
women are correct in insisting that life-giving relationships between
women and men are impossible in a rigid patriarchy that subordinates
women to men, it is also true that a dialogical relationship between
religions is impossible in a religious hierarchy that insists that all other
religions are to be subordinated and fulfilled in only one of them. In
the dialogue a particular religious belief or practice may be corrected
or fulfilled in another; but that will happen *as a result of the dialogue,*
not because it is dictated by a theological master plan.

In trying to bring together the voices of the religious and the suffering Others, and in mapping out a theology and dialogue of religions
that link global responsibility with religious pluralism, I am furthering
the project I laid out back in 1985 in *No Other Name?* Even though
I'm uncomfortable with the name, I am still a pluralist—though a chastened one. Since then, and also since the publication of *The Myth of
Christian Uniqueness* (1987), a dark though life-giving cloud of critics
has followed the project for a so-called pluralist (I prefer correlational)
theology of religions. I hope these pages will make clear that I have
tried to take seriously the danger signals or dead-end signs these critics

have raised alongside this project's path. I believe that the best way to respond to the many criticisms about the way I am calling religious persons into a correlational dialogue is to include suffering persons and the suffering Earth in that dialogue. Simply stated, this book will try to show that the most effective way to carry on a correlational dialogue among religions is to make it a globally responsible dialogue.

Although this book is still sailing toward the same destination as *No Other Name?*—that is, an authentic, fruitful dialogue among religions—it also marks a change in course. In *No Other Name?* I ended up proposing a "non-normative, *theocentric*" approach to dialogue based on the common ground of shared religious experience. To unwrap that theological language: I was seeking a dialogue in which God, and not the church or Jesus, would be in the center, and in which Christians would no longer insist that in Jesus they have the only or the final norm for all religious truth; let all religious people come together on the basis of their different experiences of the one Ultimate Reality or God. Having been shaken by the voices of the suffering and by the voices of theological critics both from within Christian communities and the academy, I would now like to plot the course, in this book, of what might be called a "multi-normed, *soteriocentric*" (salvation-centered) approach to dialogue based on the common ground of global responsibility for eco-human well-being.

Rather than searching for the common God dwelling within different religious communities (since the "indweller" usually turns out to be *my* God), and rather than presupposing a common core for all our individually wrapped religious experiences (since we can never really discard the wrappings), I am now following the lead of those who hold up the "salvation" or "well-being" of humans and Earth as the starting point and common ground for our efforts to share and understand our religious experiences and notions of the Ultimately Important. In such a dialogue, especially when suffering and its remedy are at stake and when concrete decisions and actions must be taken, norms are necessary. Religious persons will speak their convictions and make claims regarding what will or will not remove suffering and promote life, about what must or must not be done. But such norms will be multiple, correctable, expandable—and always established within the dialogue. What this means and how this might work, I will be exploring in the pages ahead. Doing so, I trust that it will be clear that this soteriocentric or globally responsible model for a theology of religions is *not* a rejection but rather a revision and a reaffirmation of the "God-centeredness" and "Christ-centeredness" that are essential to the way Christians live and talk about their religious faith.

STILL A MISSIONARY

After reviewing my dialogical odyssey and after formulating what I would like to do in this book, I have to admit, to myself and to my readers, that in a sense I've come full circle. I'm still a missionary. In this book I have something I want to "preach," something I want to persuade people about—yes, convert them to. Both intellectually and morally I am convinced that I and other religious persons can and must open our minds and our hearts to the many religious others and the many suffering others who dwell and toil upon this Earth. Because I believe this deeply, I want others to believe it deeply too. Thus, in this book I will consciously, sometimes unapologetically, be indulging in apologetics, in advocacy, in an agenda. For traditional denizens of the academy, such conduct has been considered a blight on proper scholarly conduct. Research and publication are to be value-free, entirely objective, scrupulously neutral: "The facts, only the facts." Nowadays, I am not alone in recognizing that such value-free objectivity or facts-without-advocacy are *always* impossible and *often* immoral. So I want to be straightforward about the values, convictions, and agenda that motivate me.

But though a missionary, I remain a theologian. It is my intention that my missionary élan will always be embodied in and tempered by reasoned and researched arguments showing that what I am urging is consistent with both the tradition of my religious community and the insights and needs of our contemporary context. Fueled sometimes by passion, my case for a globally responsible, correlational dialogue of religions will also be sustained by reasonability and coherence and by a knowledge of what's going on in the community of scholars. As already noted, my theological and philosophical peers have greeted this so-called pluralist project with a baptism of fire; they have laid bare what they think are its scriptural, doctrinal, cultural, philosophical, even political soft spots and dangers. I would not be honoring their concerns and talents, nor would I be properly carrying on the always-communal task of theology, if I did not take these warnings and criticisms seriously and respond to them as adequately as I can. I hope, therefore, that though I am clearly and strongly advocating something in this book, I will also be making a case that will be taken seriously by my theological comrades.

Missionary and theologian, I am also a Christian and Westerner. I have to bear those last two aspects of my identity in mind insofar as in this book I also will be addressing and trying to persuade persons who are neither Christian nor Western. Contrary to the culturally correct canons of the scholarly community, I will be making universal truth claims. Although my immediate conversation partners are my fellow Christians and theologians, I also want to direct my reasoning and preaching to members of other traditions and cultures. I suspect and hope that the way *I* see things is the way *we* might see things. I am hopeful, if not convinced, that we can speak to each other and persuade each other across our cultural and religious divides. But as I try to do that, I have to remind myself at every step and every word along the way, that what I propose as *clear* for everyone to see, or as *imperative* for the welfare of all, or as *globally* responsible will always be seen, understood, articulated within my Christian-Western (also, my white, male, middle-class) categories and limitations. We always make universal claims from particular perspectives. Some would say our perspectives are so particular that they can never be universal. I don't believe that. Yet I must remember that all my universal statements are also particular. That means I have to make them carefully, recognizing the limitations of my particular viewpoint and seeking, through conversation, to link my particulars with those of non-Christians to see if our differing particulars might resonate with a universal reality.

The way I will try to make my case for a globally responsible dialogue of religions that is globally acceptable to differing religions will embody, I hope, the way such a dialogue itself should proceed: from our individual perspectives we make our universal assertions, not authoritatively or one-sidedly, but *dialogically* or *correlationally*, in conversation, hoping that what we feel is true for all but grasped in our own way will be recognizable, in the back and forth of conversation, as true also by the other. In such a process, we also realize that our own perspectives often have to be not only clarified and expanded but sometimes adjusted and corrected before all sides can reach agreement on universal validity. So I am proposing a model for interreligious dialogue I am convinced can be true for all religions; if I'm right, though, I'll never be entirely right, for as this proposal is tossed back and forth in the dialogue itself, it will most likely be adjusted to the point of transformation before it finds universal consensus. That's how dialogue works. That's how one is right in dialogue—by hardly ever being entirely right.

Finally, a word about the primary audience that I hope to address in this book. Though I certainly want to speak to and be taken seriously by my theological friends and foes, the main (and bigger) public I want to talk with and be heard by are the many Christian women and men who are struggling to make sense of their religious heritage in a world of so many other religious heritages and so many human and ecological problems. I state the obvious in pointing to the many Christians who are painfully engaged in, and often overwhelmed by, the effort to reconcile what they hear and do in their parishes with what they see and feel in the wider world. Among their most tangled questions are the ones dealing with how to put together traditional Christian claims of being the one true (or the best) religion with the apparent truth in other faiths, and how to relate their religious values to sociopolitical issues like poverty or ecological devastation. I want to address such Christians with such concerns. If they can't hear me, and if what I have to say does not elicit some kind of positive (though critical) response, then there's something wrong with the way I'm plying my theological trade. Theologians have to be in a fruitful conversation with their theological community, but even more so with their religious community—with what Christians call "the sense of the faithful." So while I'm concerned that this book be taken seriously at the University of Chicago, I'm even more concerned that it have something helpful to say to St. Robert Bellarmine Parish, my base Christian community, and my undergraduate students at Xavier University.

Given what this book is all about, I cannot carry on my theological conversation only within Christian confines. As already suggested, I also want to address women and men of other religious communities, as well as non-theistic persons who are asking themselves how differing cultures and religions might listen to and learn from each other and cooperate in confronting our planet's human and ecological problems. So while I will be talking in this book mainly to and for my fellow Christians, I hope that other religious and even nonreligious persons will be able to eavesdrop and appreciate what they hear.

To address my intended diversified audience successfully, I'm going to have to walk a stylistic tightrope. In order to be part of the so-called theological conversation and be understood and taken seriously by my peers, I'm going to have to speak "theologese." A certain amount of technical terminology and jargon will be unavoidable. But I intend to minimize such theological shop-talk and, when I use it, to explain it. This book may presume some theological interest in readers, but it does not presume that they be professional theologians. So while I want to keep the language technically precise, I also want it to be clear and engaging. As for differing opinions and schools within the theological community, certainly I will have to mark off differences and "respond to critics," and so the nonprofessional reader will be invited to join the theological debate. But when the debate takes up academic niceties or bickering, I will try to avoid it or confine it to footnotes. I'm more and more concerned that we theologians spend too much time talking to ourselves, in a language foreign to most people. We have to discuss the really important issues in a manner and language that will allow non-theologians to understand and have their say. I hope I can do that in this book.

A PREVIEW

A snap-shot of each of the following chapters can serve as a preview of how I will make my case for a dialogue of religions that will listen both to the voices of the religious Other and to those of the suffering Other and so will be both correlational/pluralistic and at the same time globally responsible/liberative:

- Chapter 2 sets the stage and provides the props for the ensuing discussion. In it I will lay out, as concisely as possible, the main

ingredients of a multifaith dialogue that is correlational and globally responsible—what such a dialogue presumes and intends, and
what it does not presume and intend.

- In chapter 3 I review the "problems and pitfalls" that theologians
  and philosophers of religion have identified in recent proposals
  for a pluralistic or a globally responsible approach to religious
  diversity. The gist of these criticisms is that because such an approach does not really respect diversity, it cannot really promote
  dialogue. To a great extent I will develop the proposal contained
  in this book in a careful and grateful conversation with these critics.
- Chapters 4 and 5 make up the heart of the book. In chapter 4 I try
  to show why concern for the widespread suffering that grips humanity and threatens the planet can and must be the "common
  cause" for all religions. This is the message contained in recent proposals that a "global ethic" be made the top item on the agenda for
  international and interreligious discussions.
- Chapter 5 responds explicitly to postmodern criticisms and attempts
  to show why shared global responsibility provides the most promising terrain on which religions can discover or fashion the common
  ground of dialogue. To do this, the dialogue will have to be rooted
  in liberative praxis and will have to provide a preferential place for
  the voices of victims.
- In chapter 6 I try to respond to one of the knottiest objections to a
  globally responsible dialogue—the claim that not all religions are
  concerned about well-being in this world, and even if they were,
  they would understand it differently. Judging from what one sees in
  the history and present life of differing religions, it seems that most
  religious communities contain a prophetic tradition that involves
  them in this world. Indeed, involvement in the world and struggling
  for eco-human justice can become, I suggest, a shared context for
  religious or mystical experience.
- Chapter 7 carries forward the movement of chapter 6 and suggests
  how the Earth, with its mysteries and with its travails, might serve
  as a broader story in which to understand and connect our diverse
  religious stories. Within this broader story, with its promise of and
  demands for eco-human well-being, we can work toward interreligious criteria for truth.
- Chapter 8 is more practical, suggesting how religious individuals
  might actually engage in a correlational, globally responsible dialogue. I propose a dialogical circle of praxis and theory—shared
  actions toward eco-human well-being leading to shared reflection
  on each other's religious experiences and beliefs. The circle can turn
  only if all the participants go about their praxis and reflection with
  a shared commitment to nonviolence.

- The last chapter offers both concrete examples of and encouragement for a globally responsible, correlational dialogue. It describes and analyzes instances of this kind of dialogue already taking place, especially in what have been called basic human communities in India and Sri Lanka.

•

I do not think I am overdramatizing or romanticizing when I express the conviction that as humanity steps into a new millennium, the religious traditions of the world find themselves at a turning point. Up until now, for the most part, religious communities have understood themselves from within the circle of their own experience and tradition; as this century slips into the next, they are being challenged to expand their ways of knowing who they are by allowing their circles to touch and overlap with others. That's how I have understood my own Christian religious identity and story; I have come to know more clearly and meaningfully who I am by talking and acting with other religious persons. Both the nature of our intercommunicative world and of the crises this world faces offer and require such a dialogical, correlational manner of religious self-understanding.

It is my hope that this book will further such a coming together of religions and the cultures they represent and that as more and more religious persons travel and act together to confront and overcome the suffering and oppression that so threaten human and planetary life today, they will be better able to recognize and respect the real differences that exist between them and, at the same time, turn these differences into opportunities for mutual transformation of themselves and of the world.

2

TALKING ABOUT WHAT REALLY MATTERS

A Correlational and Globally Responsible Model for Dialogue

In this chapter I hope to provide a broad but clear overview of what in the last chapter we called a correlational, globally responsible model for interreligious dialogue. The emphasis will be on "correlational," since the rest of the book will lay out the "globally responsible" part of the model. What we're talking about is the so-called pluralist turn in Christian approaches to other traditions. My dialogical journey, as described in the previous chapter, has brought me to the personal and theological imperative of having to recognize and embrace the plurality of religions more honestly and thoroughly than I have in the past. As is the case with many of my fellow Christian pilgrims, my deepening acquaintance with the reality of other religious persons and histories has pushed me in a pluralist direction. To state just what this "turn" means, and to describe the pluralist or correlational model that directs it, is not easy.

Part of the problem has to do with the incompleteness of the turn. The correlational model is still being built, and the job is being carried out by a variety of builders, many of them with differing blueprints and construction materials. What one particular proponent of a pluralist theology of religions presents may differ sharply, sometimes embarrassingly, from that of a fellow-pluralist. So to speak about a new, pluralist or correlational model for a Christian understanding of and approach to other religious traditions is to speak of a project that is not yet complete and that has various proposed versions.[1]

This makes for the deeper problem indicated in the previous chapter—the stereotyped image that the term *pluralist model* or *pluralistic theology* of religions has assumed over the past decade. Because there is a "plurality of pluralists" and because the model is still being constructed (which means corrected), there's ample room for misunderstanding or misrepresentation. Some critics have taken statements of

23

certain pluralist theologians and held them up as representative for all the others; often such statements are not sufficiently nuanced, or taken out of context, or later clarified or corrected by the author; or they are representative of only a minority perspective within the pluralist movement.[2] Thus the pluralist model for a dialogue or theology of religions is all too often depicted as an irenic, warm-hearted attitude that views all religions as differing but equally valid versions of the same mystical experience and that therefore wants to do away with all apologetics or argumentation among religions. No doubt there are theologians or philosophers of religions who might affirm such a relativizing perspective; but to rank all pluralist theologians among them does not do justice to what many, if not most, so-called pluralist Christians are searching for.

Therefore the subtitle of this chapter: "*A Correlational and Globally Responsible Model for Dialogue.*" Given the variety of pluralists and recognizing that many of them would not want me to speak for them (nor would I want them to do so for me!) I offer this general description as one version of the new model many Christians are searching for in their approach to people of other faiths. Though it is my own rendition, I do believe that it represents the *intent* of almost all so-called pluralists and the *content* of the views of many of them. I speak for myself, but I speak within and for a community of Christian believers who have a general sense of where they want to go but are in the midst of plotting the course for getting there.

And given the loaded connotations of the term *pluralism*, while I will be using the word, I don't want to be limited or defined by it. As already indicated in the previous chapter and as announced in the title of this one, for me and for many of my colleagues, a pluralist model is one that seeks to promote a truly *correlational* dialogue among religions—a dialogue in which all sides are able to hear and be challenged by the others and at the same time to speak to and challenge in return. If the pluralist model calls for a dialogue among religions that is correlational, it also proposes a theology within each religion that is *comparative*. The theological task of interpreting and understanding one's own religious tradition must be done in conversations with others.[3] So I deeply resonate with David Tracy's declaration that "genuine conversation with the religions . . . is needed from the very beginning of theology to the end" (Tracy 1987b, 145). The goal of a pluralist model (and I think that almost all pluralist theologians would agree with this) is to further a genuinely correlational dialogue among religions and a comparative theology among Christians.

As the bulk of this book will try to make clear, I'm convinced that one of the most effective ways to foster an interreligious dialogue that is pluralist/correlational and a Christian theology that is pluralist/comparative is to make sure that such a dialogue and theology are *globally responsible.*

So in this chapter I want to offer a basic outline of the model that the rest of the book will be developing and defending. The outline will consist of a summary of the main ingredients or central contents of a pluralist approach that is correlational and globally responsible. In what follows, I want to describe as accurately as possible, but I also want to correct or balance the overly generalized or simplified stereotypes of the pluralist model.

THE CURRENT MODELS

To be properly understood and evaluated, the following overview of the pluralist approach first needs to be contextualized in the panorama of other Christian ways of understanding the many religions. When one looks out over the landscape of Christian attitudes toward other religious ways, a variety of shapes and forms is immediately evident; how to classify them is a problem. Here again we face the difficulties of terms that are either too ambiguous or too strictly defined, and of models that blur differences or simplify complexities.

- In *No Other Name?* I adopted rather cumbersome confessional tags for describing Christian views of others: conservative evangelical ("Christianity is the one true religion"), mainline Protestant ("other religions contain revelation but no salvation"), Roman Catholic ("other religions may be true and good but need fulfillment in Christ), and theocentric ("there are many ways to the one Divine Center").
- These same categories might be sorted out according to their ecclesiocentric (church-centered), or christocentric (Jesus-centered), or theocentric (God-centered) starting points or criteria.
- From a christological perspective, Christian models for evaluating other religions can be described as "Christ against the religions" (as one who negates the value of other religions) or "Christ within the religions" (as a universal saving presence), "Christ above the religions" (not within them as cause of salvation but ahead of them as the fullest embodiment of salvation), or "Christ together with the religions" (as one among many possible saving figures and manifestations of Truth).

This all can become rather confusing.[4] Thus it seems better to sacrifice precision to clarity and to follow the neat classification, first provided I believe by Alan Race (1983), of exclusivism, inclusivism, and pluralism. Certainly, the same problems arising from "defining" the pluralist camp and then assigning someone to it can accrue to definitions of exclusivism or inclusivism. A number of theologians have complained that the rigidity or simplicity of these three models obscures a broader variety of perspectives or predetermines the flow of theological conversation (Markham 1993; Barnes 1989; DiNoia 1992). Still, if we recognize the limitations of all models, if we are always open to modifying and expanding our models, it seems to me that these three classifications represent in broad lines the differing presuppositions and approaches within recent Christian efforts to make sense of the many religions. Such models are limited, possibly dangerous, but also useful. They provide a workable framework that can direct, but not restrict, the discussion (D'Costa 1993). So let me suggest how the big basket of Christian perspectives on other religions might sift out into the three general types of exclusivism, inclusivism, and pluralism:

Exclusivism	Conservative Evangelical Mainline Protestant[5] Ecclesiocentric Christ against the Religions
Inclusivism	Mainline Protestant Roman Catholic Christocentric Christ within the Religions Christ above the Religions
Pluralism	Theocentric Christ together with the Religions

Descriptive and persuasive presentations of exclusivism and inclusivism have been given elsewhere and at length.[6] To provide the context for our discussion of the pluralist perspective, let me offer here only a sketchy review of these two other models.

Exclusivism

Representing the historically dominant Christian view of other religious individuals who do not know or are not interested in Christ, *exclusivism* is still very much alive and active within the borders of worldwide Christianity. Its deep convictions about and often heroic commitment to what God has done in Jesus Christ are found especially within the so-called fundamentalist or evangelical or pentecostal churches. For them, although God is clearly a Parent who loves and wishes to embrace all God's children, this loving Parent has chosen to make the possibility of salvation—that is, of knowing and responding to the divine offer of love—available and impelling *only* through the historical reality of Jesus Christ and through the community in which his saving message and power are kept alive: the Christian church.

Thus for the exclusivists, any recognition of the truth or saving power of other religions or religious figures is a slap in the face of God; it denigrates what God has done in Jesus. While exclusivist churches may advocate a dialogue with persons of other ways, this dialogue is understood as an often necessary instrument in working for the conversion of these peoples. God's intent therefore is to gather and transform the profuse religious diversity in our world into a unity grounded in and made possible by the God-man Jesus Christ. Here on Earth, within history as we know it, God wills that all Hindus, Buddhists, Muslims, primal religious believers, and yes, Jews, become Christians. There is to be one religion.

If that is not yet the case, after some two thousand years of the powerful presence of the resurrected Christ within history, it is not God's fault; rather, it is due to lack of missionary élan or prowess on the part of Christians. Asked about the salvation of the millions before and after Jesus who through no fault of their own have never heard of him, the exclusivists will not, generally, affirm their perdition—but neither will they affirm their salvation. That's God business, they will say, perhaps to be carried out in a transhistorical realm; in the meantime, here in earthly history, it is the business of Christians to roll up their sleeves and make other Christians (Demarest 1992; VanderWerff 1992; Phillips 1992).

INCLUSIVISM

Within the so-called mainline Christian churches, *inclusivism*, in a variety of forms, describes the dominant attitude toward followers of other religious paths. Challenged by the deepening and more human encounters with people of other cultures and religions, sobered by the truth, beauty, and lack of Christian presence evident among non-Christian religions, and stimulated by the more positive Roman Catholic views of other faiths (planted already in the sixteenth-century Council of Trent and showing first fruits in the Second Vatican Council), these churches have come to recognize and even celebrate the self-manifesting and saving presence of God throughout history, and therefore within other religions. If God's love reaches out to all people, then it must be made concretely, actually, available to all peoples. Evidently, the religions of the world—despite their corruption and because of the evident fruits of the Spirit among them—will be the vehicles of God's love and presence.[7]

The theological grounding for the inclusivist model is found in its christology—the way these Christian communities understand Jesus Christ. Some will hold that in view of the New Testament witness, Jesus is *constitutive* of salvation; that is, God's offer of truth and saving grace has been brought about, or made possible, by the historical life, death, and resurrection of Jesus. Therefore, whatever truth or presence of the Spirit is found in other faiths is in some way "anonymously

Christian"—Christian without a name—caused by and directed toward fulfillment in Jesus and his community. Other inclusivists look upon Jesus as *representative* of God's saving love and truth. He does not cause God's love, for love is part of the fabric of God's being, but he does embody and manifest and thus represent God's saving love as fully as is possible in the human condition. Although these "representative" inclusivists shy away from any talk of Buddhists as anonymous Christians, they tend to term Buddhists "potential Christians"; that is, what the Buddhists already have by way of transformative truth is best represented by, and therefore is to be fulfilled in, Jesus Christ. Both christological perspectives, constitutive or representative, end up agreeing that other religions, for all their truth and goodness, are intended by God to find their final fulfillment and identity in Jesus the Christ. In this sense, as Schubert Ogden has pointed out, both exclusivists *and* inclusivists are what can be called salvational "monists"; both hold that God's gift of salvation is found clearly, adequately, fully, only in Jesus Christ (Ogden 1992, 80-81).[8]

Inclusivists will also argue that there are sound philosophical reasons for their position; in other words, their insistence on Christ as a final norm makes good sense. They remind us that this is the way that *all* religious persons experience and live religious truth. Indeed, it's the way any human being knows and affirms truth. We don't experience truth in general, or in the abstract; it is always delivered to us and made attractive and persuasive for us, through some concrete mediation or form. It is through *a* particular manifestation of truth that we know *the* truth. Therefore, this particular expression is *decisive* or *normative* for us. We cannot help but encounter and evaluate all other claims for truth through the particular decisive form in which we have been convinced of truth or goodness in the first place.

This, according to the inclusivists, is what Christ is for Christians— the decisive truth by which they live their lives and the guiding norm by which they step into the arena of other truths. To deny this is to deny the way we function as human beings. All religions, therefore, have their "jealousies"—their claims for universal, normative truth (Taylor 1981). All religions, in other words, want to *include* other religions in their own understanding of truth. This is what gives dialogue its substance, excitement, and value. To remove normative, decisive, final claims for truth is to rob dialogue of its muscle and to fill it with hot, innocuous air (see D'Costa 1987; DiNoia 1992; Newbigin 1990).

KEY INGREDIENTS IN A CORRELATIONAL, GLOBALLY RESPONSIBLE MODEL

Proposals for a correlational or pluralistic dialogue of religions have been made elaborately and diversely over the past decade or so.[9] Such a theology is still very much a growing, changing, often ambiguous phenomenon. What I offer here is a distillation of what I think are the main ingredients in this relatively new theological mix. Although I trust that most of the theologians involved in formulating the pluralist recipe would agree with my list of what is, and what is not, to be included, let me repeat that I make no claims of presenting *the* pluralist model. What follows is *my* view of a movement—called pluralistic, correlational, globally responsible— that I have detected in myself and in Christian communities around the world.

IN GENERAL

In general, the *negative* reasons why many Christians are searching for a new, more correlational approach to other religions include their desire to move away from and correct the excesses of the exclusivist model and to clarify or resolve the good intentions but lingering ambiguities of the inclusivist perspective. Simply stated, as a pluralist I believe that given our present encounters with the religious and suffering Others of this world, as well as our understanding of the original witness and history of the Christian communities, neither the exclusivists nor the inclusivists are being faithful to what God is revealing in Jesus Christ *and* in the world around us.

The *positive* reasons and energy moving Christian communities to search for a different, more correlational approach to other believers flow from the growing conviction that *dialogue* among religions and nations is necessary for the survival of our species and planet. Thus, one of the highest goods Christians can strive for is to promote an authentic, interreligious, intercultural dialogue that will enable all partners genuinely to search for and discover Truth in its inexhaustible richness and to cooperate ever more effectively in removing the suffering, human and ecological, that is devastating our globe. What promotes such revelatory, liberative dialogue is true and good; what does not, is, at the least, suspect.

Therefore, a correlational approach to other believers wants to avoid the "absolutist" language that has for so long colored Christian consciousness and witness; this approach avoids claims that Christians are in possession of the God-given final word on all truth. In a pluralist perspective Christians reject or shy away from adjectives such as "one and only," "definitive," "superior," "absolute," "final," "unsurpassable," "total" to describe the truth they have found in the gospel of Jesus the Christ. Without claiming that all religions are *equal*, Christians with a correlational mentality hold that at the outset of dialogue every partner in the conversation should recognize the *equal rights* within the dialogue of all religious believers. This means that each religious believer has the full right to speak out, or to make a claim, and that all the other participants have the *duty* to open their minds and hearts to the truth, the very new truth, that may be confronting them in the Other.

Furthermore, without holding that there is a "common essence" or a "common experience" within all religions, pluralists acknowledge what has been called a "rough parity" (Gilkey 1987) among religions. Such rough parity means, not that all religions deep down are saying "the same thing," but that *because of* their differences from Christianity, other religions *may be* just as effective and successful in bringing their followers to truth, and peace, and well-being with God as Christianity has been for Christians; also, that these other religions, again because they are so different from Christianity, may have just as important a message and vision for all peoples as Christianity does. In other words, with a correlational theology, Christians insist on the *possibility,* and urge the *probability,* that the Source of truth and transformation that they have called the God of Jesus Christ may have more truth and other forms of transformation to reveal than have been made manifest in Jesus.

Only if Christians are truly open to the possibility (which, I will argue below, is for Christians a probability bordering on a necessity) that there *are* many true, saving religions and that Christianity is one among the ways in which God has touched and transformed our world—only then can authentic dialogue take place. Only then can Christians enter the forum of interreligious encounter and both witness mightily to what God has done in Jesus and at the same time listen humbly to what God may be doing elsewhere.

Out of such dialogue, my pluralist instincts tell me, there will not result a final unity in which the many finally become one. Absolute, final oneness does not seem, philosophically, what the world is heading for, or, theologically, what God intends for creation. Rather, through the dialogue and encounter of religions, there will be greater unity, yes, but it will produce ever more and exciting diversity. Through the transformative interaction of dialogue, each religious partner will be changed and thus will have more to offer for the ongoing process of communication and cooperation. As Alfred North Whitehead put it, the "many become one and are increased by one" (Whitehead 1957, 26). The dialogue will produce both unity and ever more splendid diversity.

With the broader vision of a pluralistic or correlational theology in focus, let us look, again briefly, at the particular pieces that hold this vision together: its understanding of other religions, of the uniqueness of Christ, and of the basis and goal of dialogue.

OTHER RELIGIONS

As we shall see in greater detail in the next chapter, one of the gravest concerns that many people have about the new proposals for a more open, pluralistic theology of religions is that the real diversity among religions becomes submerged in a placid sea of sameness; differences don't really matter, for they are but varying cultural reflections of the same common essence that shines like a hidden diamond within the heart of every religion. Such concerns about the new pluralist model are not without foundation. In their revolt against the exclusivism that marks so much of their past and in their desire to affirm the value of other religions, some Christians and theologians have swung toward a facile universalism. They have too hastily or neatly talked about the "one God" or "the Transcendent" or the "Really Real" as the self-evident content or goal of all religious history; or they have too glibly or naively announced a common ground or a basic unity that holds all religions in a dynamic relatedness.[10]

Such dangers and excesses in exploring new models for Christian openness to other religions can be recognized and avoided; they are neither components nor necessary by-products of the model for a correlational dialogue and comparative theology that I am trying to propose. Today, chastened by criticism and by the interreligious dialogue itself, I am more aware that whatever might be the "common ground" for dialogue, it is not immediately at hand or prepackaged by any one dialogical partner. Also, in most of the Christians I know who are trying to foster a more correlational dialogue with other believers, there is an awareness and an abhorrence of relativism; they are conscious of the dangers of sliding down those oft-cited slippery slopes into a quicksand in which it is either not possible or not important to take strong stands on what one believes is false or immoral.

Regarding other religions, then, the pluralist or correlational theology I'm talking about will, first of all, recognize, affirm, embrace, and wrestle with the patent and real *differences* between religious traditions. In their views of the Ultimate, of this world, of life after death, of human conduct, of ritual and worship—religious communities clearly and often incommensurably differ. Anyone who would hold that the religions are really saying the same thing reveals that he or she has only begun to study or enter into a relationship with other religious believers. It is like two people in love: in the beginning they feel that they have everything in common and see the world as one; only as the relationship grows over the years do they realize, sometimes frighteningly, how different they are from each other and how difficult it is to build and nurture unity out of their differences. It's much the same with interreligious relationships: the deeper and longer I am involved with another religious person or community, the more evident it becomes that many of our differences are irremovable and that our relationship is as difficult as it is rewarding.

Yet in recognizing the stark, even incommensurable, differences between the religions, the correlational model I'm exploring will affirm the *value and validity* of this world of differences. Other religions are not only genuinely different, they can also be genuinely valuable. This is what I referred to above as the "rough parity" among traditions.

In making such a statement about the world of religions, however, one must be careful. Schubert Ogden has perceptively pointed out that many of the Christians espousing a pluralist model for dialogue are much too hasty in declaring that "there *are* many true religions." What they can and must say, Ogden counsels, is that it is *possible* that other religions are true; whether they *actually* are is something we can know only by careful examination. Ogden's admonitions are appropriate and, I hope, well-taken. Sweeping generalizations that "all religions are true and saving" are as untidy and perhaps dangerous as declarations that "all Americans are democratic." Especially in the historical light of how religions have been used as tools of manipulation and exploitation, one should always demand "evidence" before declaring a religious belief or practice to be good and valuable.[11]

So a correlational, pluralist model for a dialogue of religions will begin, cautiously, by affirming the *possible* value of other religions besides Christianity. And yet, even though it might appear to outsiders as a minimalist, excessively careful statement, it is a giant step in Christian consciousness and theology. For most of its history, Christian theology has denied even the *possibility* that God might be making use of other religious traditions to communicate divine truth and grace.[12] Today, those Christians who hold to an exclusivist attitude toward other believers continue to deny the possibility that there can be other true religions in which people are "saved." And inclusivists, while admitting that other religions can be valid and saving, deny the possibility that there can be other saving manifestations of God as valid and as effective as that given in Jesus Christ; in other words, they deny the possibility that other religions might be as true as Christianity.

But as significant as this "giant step" of recognizing the *possibility* of other true, valid religions is, a pluralist-correlational model can and does say more. There is "evidence" and good reasons for Christians to open themselves not only to the possibility but to the *probability*, indeed the *actuality*, that they will discover genuine truth and spiritual power in other communities. Such evidence is both theological and empirical.

Theologically, Christians say they believe in a God who truly wishes to save all people; this is the God of Jesus Christ, a God of "pure unbounded love," who embraces all beings and wishes all of them to have life and salvation. But as Karl Rahner has pointed out in his theology of religions, such a belief and assertion is effete and unreal unless we recognize and affirm the means by which this divine love is operative in the human condition. God's love, in other words, must be embodied; it must take historical shape and flesh if it is to be real in a person's or culture's life. And as Rahner concluded, among the many vehicles that God's loving presence can take, we would expect the religions to figure prominently (Rahner 1966). Our Christian experience of the God of love revealed in Jesus Christ tells us that despite our own sinfulness, despite the corruptions in our church, this God has embraced us in and through the ecclesial community. It seems to me that if I doubt that God can do the same thing for other people through other communities, I have reason to doubt that God has really done so for me. A loving God who loves only some people or who can overcome sinfulness and corruption in only some religions is somehow not a trustworthy God of love (Gilkey 1987, 38-39). Therefore, Christians can and must approach other religions expecting not just that they might *possibly* find much that is true and good but that they *probably* will.

There is empirical data to conclude that this probability is a *reality*. Here I am referring to volumes of data, stored in books and in human hearts, that Christians have gathered from the actual experience of dialogue with other religious communities, especially since Pope John XXIII opened the windows of the Catholic church in the Second Vatican Council. For many of us, the fruits of the Holy Spirit are evident and verdant in the lives of other religious persons and in the beliefs and practices of their communities. By their fruits you shall know them. Where we find the fruits of holiness, love, and perseverance, we find the actuality of the saving Spirit of Truth.

Thus, a pluralistic-correlational model for a theology of religions affirms not just the possibility but the reality of other authentic religious believers and therefore of other true religions. Such a statement is based on "evidence." It is not a blanket endorsement of all that goes on within the walls of religion, but it does affirm that much of what we will encounter in the lives and worlds of other religious persons will be true and meaningful and challenging not just for them but also for us. To what extent this is so, or how the truth of one tradition will compare with that of another, can be known only in the actual dialogue.

And so we move to a third affirmation that a pluralist approach makes of other religions, which flows from the first two: because the *diversity* of the many religions must be recognized and maintained, and because this diversity is held up to be potentially *valuable and important* for all persons, then the many valuable contents of the religions must be shared, communicated. The religions of the world must *dialogue*. If I recognize that you are really different from me, and if I also recognize that what is different can also be true and valuable, I cannot ignore you. At least curiosity, if not integrity, will compel me to explore whether what is true for you might also, though in different ways and degrees, be true for me. The correlational model I am urging, therefore, also affirms the relational or dialogical nature of religions. Religions are in need of talking and acting together. While this model insists on the radical and inextricable differences and particularity of religions, it also recognizes the relatedness-to-others stemming from the incompleteness-in-themselves of all religions. And as we shall explore below, the necessity of dialogue inherent in the nature of religions becomes all the more compelling when we look at the state and the needs of our divided, suffering world.

THE UNIQUENESS OF CHRIST AND CHRISTIANITY

One of the most delicate and explosive aspects of the pluralist-correlational theology of religions that I am trying to formulate is the way it apparently questions, or even does away with, traditional understandings of the uniqueness of Christ and Christianity. I will be examining more carefully and extensively the importance and complexity of this issue in the companion volume to this book.[13] Here, I offer only a sketch of how Christians can understand and affirm the uniqueness of Jesus in a way that will promote a truly correlational dialogue with other religious ways.

In their efforts to *reinterpret* such traditional claims as "there is salvation *in no other name* but that of Jesus" (Acts 12:4), Christians are carrying on a task that began during the church's fledgling years in Palestine and Asia Minor and extends to the present growing pains of churches in Asia and Africa: how to understand and live out the meaning and power contained in the person and work of Jesus the Christ. That's the task of christology. To invoke a cliché, the job of christology is never done. It continues in its dynamism and diversity still today, which means that the issue of Jesus' uniqueness is still open to new understandings.

In the new interpretations proposed by what has been called a pluralistic christology (Knitter 1983), the core content of the early kerygma or proclamation about Jesus is maintained: that he is divine, that he is risen and with us, that he is savior for all. Contrary to the attestations of some critics,[14] none of these central assertions about Jesus needs to be denied by Christians who are searching for more correlational ways of relating to other faiths. Even John Hick's unsettling and provocative reassessment of the "Myth of Incarnation" need not, and should not, be read as a denial of the divinity or the saving power of Jesus; rather, it is intended as a way of reinterpreting what it means to call Jesus divine in such a way that Christians can understand the role of Jesus more clearly and follow him more resolutely.[15] Nor is a pluralist christology suggesting in any way that there are no significant, vitally important differences between Jesus and other religious figures of history. Jesus is not simply "one of the boys"—blending into the line-up of archetypal figures who have animated and redirected the human project. Jesus is different—wondrously and consequentially different—from Buddha, and Muhammad, and Krishna, and Lao Tzu.

Perhaps the most incisive way of stating what the pluralist model is and is not saying about the uniqueness of Christ is to put it in terms of adverbs. Christians can continue to affirm and announce to the world that Jesus is *truly* divine and savior, but they no longer need to insist that he *solely* is divine and savior. "Verily, but not only"—this I think catches the new efforts to affirm the significance of Jesus in a world of many religions. *Theologically*, this means that while Christians can and must continue to announce Jesus of Nazareth as one in whom the reality and saving power of God is incarnate and available, they will also be open to the possibility/probability that there are others whom Christians can recognize as son or daughter of God. *Personally*, such a pluralistic christology allows and requires Christians to be committed fully to Christ but at the same time genuinely open to others who may be carrying out similar and equally important roles. *Ecclesially*, this means that the churches will go forth into the whole world with a message that is universally relevant and urgent, but at the same time will be ready to hear other messages from very different sources that may also be universally meaningful and important.[16]

A pluralistic christology, therefore, does not at all question *whether* Jesus is unique but only *how*.

BASIS AND GOAL OF DIALOGUE

I am suggesting that the new model for a Christian understanding of other religions be not only "pluralistic or correlational" but also "globally responsible or liberative." Over the past decade or two the bonding of these two issues has been a central concern for a number of theologians searching for new models of dialogue (Pieris 1988a; Knitter 1987, 1988; Suchocki 1987). This concern represents not a shift in the direction of a pluralistic theology of religions but rather a new avenue of approach and a more clearly defined destination. The basic content and intent of this book is to promote a theology or dialogue of religions that will be not only pluralistic but globally responsible—or better, that will be more effectively pluralistic by being globally responsible. In this overview chapter I paint only the broad lines of what a globally responsible dialogue of religions means. The rest of the book will make the case for its specific contents and its value and urgency.

A globally responsible dialogue of religions seeks to draw out the *opportunity* that is inherent in an experienced *necessity*. The necessity I am speaking about is rooted in what was said earlier about the obligation many Christians feel today to respond to the overwhelming and frightening suffering that is afflicting—better, is being inflicted upon—so many people and upon this planet Earth. A liberative theology and dialogue of religions arises out of the urgency or the moral obligation to respond, as Christians and as humans, to the suffering Other *and* to the religious Other.

For such Christians, dialogue with the religious Other simply cannot be divorced from a concern for the suffering Other. More precisely and more controversially, this means that global responsibility or a concerned effort to promote human and planetary well-being can and must be the primary *context*, or *basis*, or *starting point*, or *goal* of all multifaith dialogue. (I'm really not sure which of these terms is most appropriate.) I even want to say, in terminology that may be offensive to many scholars today, that a concern for *soteria* (salvation) or eco-human well-being and justice can and must provide the "common ground" for interreligious dialogue in our global village, which has become a threatened village. There are untold complexities to that last statement, I know; we will explore and respond to many of them in the next two chapters. But the main message of this book is this: dialogue *must* be globally responsible.

I also want to show that *if* dialogue is globally responsible, it can be more effective, rewarding, and transformative than it has been in the past. This is where the necessity becomes an opportunity. Global responsibility can provide both a *theological key* to hear and understand the gospel in a more dialogical openness to other religions, and it can provide a *hermeneutical key* to hear and understand the otherness and genuine differences in other spiritual paths. The rest of the book will try to make clear that with a liberative perspective, a pluralistic theology can be authentically Christian and a pluralistic interreligious dialogue can be more hermeneutically sensitive and effective in bridging the gaps of cross-cultural communication.

This focal concern for human and ecological well-being represents for me, and I think for many Christians, a clear progression or growth in trying to work out a viable theology of religions. As I mentioned in chapter 1, in my own life and in the lives of many of my fellow Christians, there has been a cumulative movement from an *ecclesiocentric* (church-centered) theology of religions to one that is *christocentric*, and then to a *theocentric* (God-centered) way of approaching religious history and interreligious encounter. Now, I suggest, the movement is continuing toward a *soteriocentric* or salvation-centered focus.[17] The movement has been motivated or necessitated by both the value as well as the inadequacies of previous phases.

The church-centered model rightly perceived the need for a community that would carry on the vision and the Spirit of Jesus through the course of history, but it improperly exaggerated the role of that community to the exclusion of others and to its own self-aggrandizement. The Christ-centered model rightly experienced and announced the universal, saving relevance and necessity of what had happened in the life-death-resurrection of Jesus of Nazareth; but it erred in so stressing that universality as to exclude, denigrate, or manipulate the particularity of other religious figures and communities. The God-centered model rightly perceived the priority that must always be given to the Divine Mystery, to which, as Paul tells us, even Christ Jesus must hand over all things (1 Cor 15: 28), but it offended in often presupposing to know who that God was and in imposing such a God on others (often on religious traditions that had no notion of a Divine Being). As I hope to show in subsequent chapters, a soteriocentric or globally responsible approach to a theology and dialogue of religions suggests how the inadequacies of each of the other models might be addressed without jettisoning or watering down their values.

In other words, this evolution of stages or models in Christian attitudes toward other believers has been *cumulative* not *disjunctive*; it does not simply reject but rather clarifies and preserves what went before. A Christ-centered theology continues to stress the necessity of the church, but in relation to Christ; a God-centered view of other religions continues to press the necessity of Christ, but within the trinitarian nature and activity of God. And a salvation-centered approach preserves the value and the necessity[18] of church, Christ, and God as it holds up *soteria* or human and ecological well-being as the context and criterion for a theology and dialogue of religions.

3

PROBLEMS AND PITFALLS

The Critics Weigh In

In this chapter I do not want to indulge in the scholarly game of "responding to the critics"—the game of showing how much academic dust one has stirred up and how misguided or misunderstanding one's critics are. The caveats and objections that we will consider in this chapter are coming from colleagues and fellow Christians, many of them my personal friends, who care about dialogue and global responsibility as much as I do and who are concerned not just about academic or theoretical niceties but about genuine respect for others and commitment to their own religious identity. These are matters that must be significant for every Christian and scholar. I want to take these warnings as seriously as I can.

As we shall see, the critics of the so-called pluralist model for interreligious dialogue form a large chorus, and they sing in a variety of voices. But they seem to follow a common melody: the advocates of a pluralist or correlational approach to dialogue understand the *plurality* of religions in such a way that they neglect or violate the *diversity* of religions. Pluralists either do not take plurality seriously enough and therefore miss the ineradicable differences among religions, or they are so swept up by the desire to dialogue and get along that they gloss over or play down what is unique in each religion. Enchanted by the beauty of the symphony, pluralists miss the distinctiveness of each of the musical instruments.

In other words, the critics we now will hear from—whether they are speaking from the perspective of cultural anthropology, or hermeneutical theory (the science of interpretation), or political theory—warn pluralist scholars and Christians that they are not really pluralists. Pluralists may preach a fine sermon about the value of manyness and the need to embrace it in authentic dialogue, but they don't necessarily practice what they preach. The roots of these warning are to be found, to a great extent, in what is called our contemporary *postmodern* consciousness.

THE POSTMODERN PERSPECTIVE:
THE DOMINANCE OF DIVERSITY

Postmodernism (*Postmodernity*) is a catch-all term that points to but does not define a widespread cultural awareness (at least in the West) about the drastic limitations of "modernity." Found in a variety of forms, raising its flag in a diversity of disciplines, applying its muscle more in admonition and opposition than in definition and commitment, notoriously difficult to define, postmodernity seeks to signal and then move beyond the limitations of the Enlightenment and the dangerous modern world that has derived from it: an excessive confidence in reason, an authoritative appeal to empirical data, a close-minded exclusion of the mythical-mystical, and a naive endorsement of universal truths or methods.[1] It is especially this last aspect that motivates and fuels what we are summarizing as the postmodern critique of the pluralist-correlational model for a theology and dialogue of religions.

The central pillar of this postmodern criticism is its insistence on *the dominance of diversity*. Whether they are speaking as philosophers, anthropologists, historians, literary or art theorists, ethicists, or natural scientists—postmodernists affirm and try to embrace the vast variety and astounding differences that make up the world they are trying to comprehend. The reasons for this affirmation of diversity can, I think, be stated quite simply in two insights into the human condition that have become much clearer today than they were for the architects of the Enlightenment: 1) all human experience/knowledge is filtered; and 2) the filters are incredibly diverse.

In acknowledging the "time-bound," "situational," "linguistic," "theory-laden," "hermeneutical," "constructed" filters with which we experience and comprehend our world, postmodernists are really deepening and drawing out the content of what has been called historical consciousness. We are radically and irreducibly historical beings, and that means that we look out upon our world from one particular historical situation or perspective. We can never really grasp the world as it is, but only as we see it through our particular historical filters.

Frederick Nietzsche realized and vigorously announced that all our declarations of truth are not really derived from what we see but from what we ourselves have created and imposed on what is before us; thus he believed we can never reach any kind of objective reality that can measure our truth. Truth itself, which means God as the source of truth, is beyond reach and therefore, practically, nonexistent. Heidegger deepened this sense of confronting the world through historical filters when he depicted our "being-ness" (*Dasein*) as a "thrown-ness" (*Geworfensein*) into the inextricable net of our historical situation. Wittgenstein went on to portray these historical filters as linguistic filters: language is not just a means by which we speak of what we know; it determines or at least limits what we know and can speak about. We are always caught in our "language games," which enables us to enjoy the game but reminds us that it is only one game among many others.

If it is the philosophers who have argued, in a variety of ways, that we are always wearing historical-cultural glasses and can never experience the world without them, it is the cultural anthropologists who have made clear both how many glasses exist and how well each of them works. Each society has its own filter, its own worldview, and if we could only enter into that culture we would realize that it functions much more effectively and adequately than we on the outside can imagine. Each filter must be judged within its own context, according to the needs of its own world; we cannot use the filter of one culture to evaluate—or to denigrate—another. To hold up some universal standard of reason or logic by which we can judge all cultures is to think, naively and dangerously, that we can have a "filterless take" on the world.[2] Thus, the diversity of filters wins out over the possibility of a universal filter.

But what about the natural sciences? Is not this one area where the dominance of diverse opinions or perspectives has to give way to universally accepted methods that can yield universally recognized truths? Scientific method, nurturing joint research projects, seems to transcend cultural-historical filters. Yet even a cursory reading of contemporary philosophers of science will indicate that the winds of postmodernity have also shaken the adamantine towers of science. Despite the efforts of Karl Popper, with his appeal to principles of falsifiability that can apply anywhere, and of Imre Lakatos, with his efforts to describe research projects that can yield universally recognized results, the unpleasant admission that more and more scientists are making is that every scientific method, and even every scientific model or system (such as evolution or quantum mechanics), depends on certain assumptions or starting points that are either tacitly assumed by, or grounded in, the model or system itself (Popper 1959; Lakatos 1978).

Thomas Kuhn's pioneering work on the fallibility and the potential diversity of scientific paradigms, as well as Paul Feyerabend's sobering admonitions about the imperialism lurking within scientific method as practiced today, have shown that scientists, too, are working out of filters that they have either chosen or been given (Kuhn 1970; Feyerabend 1978). Harvard philosopher Willard Van Orman Quinn's whimsical observation packs a sobering reality: He compared the question "Which sentences in physical theory are definitions?" to the question "Which places in Ohio are starting places?" (In Placher 1989, 33). Our starting places are not determined purely and simply by universally recognizable data but by the "filter" or "worldview" in which we stand. Wittgenstein's trenchant observation applies also to science: "When we find the foundations, it turns out they are being held up by the rest of the house."[3]

But can we find any kind of common foundation for all the houses—one that would provide security to them all and enable them to communicate among themselves? Here we are pushing on the edges of postmodernity. Many so-called postmodern spokespersons would answer our question with a perhaps reluctant but still resolute "no." In fact, Jean-Francois Lyotard defines postmodernity as a worldview based on "incredulity toward metanarratives"—one that does not allow any universal stories or truths (Lyotard 1984, 3ff).

Whatever one thinks of the "anything goes" relativism lurking in the "anti-foundational" proclamations of Richard Rorty, however frightening are the anarchical implications of Jacques Derrida's "deconstructionism," still they signal what many of us are aware of but afraid to recognize: there is no one foundation for, or expression of, or criterion for truth which is, as it were, given to us from outside the diversity of historical filters. There is no universal perspective hovering over these filters to which we can appeal for our grasp of truth. There is no one reserve of common ground which is protected from the limitations of history or culture where all the different cultures or religions can meet to agree on truth and resolve their differences. Therefore, any attempt to establish such an ahistorical common ground, or such a universal foundation, must be resolutely, bravely, deconstructed or exposed for what it is: an effort to find a direct access to truth that circumvents the messiness of historical diversity and limitation. Diversity cannot be reduced to one foundation.

But this lack of a universal, singular foundation for experience and knowledge has further implications. It means not only that there is an incorrigible diversity, but it also suggests an obstinate *incommensurability* among the cultures and religions of the world. This, too, is a challenge for any theology or dialogue of religions: because we are so limited by the historical glasses through which we view the world (and God!), because we cannot really know and evaluate another religion unless we put on its glasses (but that would mean putting off our own, or wearing two pair of glasses at the same time), because there does not seem to be any one prescription for a set of glasses that we all need and could all wear—therefore one culture or religion cannot really, truly, in depth, be "measured" by another. Yes, some understanding is always possible, and sometimes that understanding can grasp even the deeper convictions of a religion. But there will always be a space, usually at the heart of a religion, that will remain a mystery to the outsider. "It is but a half truth that the nearer we get to their centers, the more the variant faiths become alike; the complementary truth is that there is a turning about incommensurable centers. . . . We are more locked out of each other's intimacies than the ecumenically inclined interpreters among us like to admit" (Rolston 1985, 181, 215).

The postmodern suspicion that there is an irreducible diversity among cultural-historical perspectives and an obstinate incommensurability between them has been seeping, slowly but consistently, into the awareness of Christian theologians. They are critical of the relativizing or the compartmentalizing consequences of antifoundational or deconstructionist viewpoints, yet they are admitting that such viewpoints cannot be simplistically dismissed.[4] A theologian who has taken postmodernity seriously but responded to it creatively and who, in the process, has neatly embodied the warnings that postmodern awareness offers to a pluralistic theology of religions is George Lindbeck. Taking seriously the postmodern awareness of the historical filters that determine what we can know, Lindbeck rejects a *propositional-cognitive* understanding of religion, according to which truth is something in front of us or given to us by God which we can grasp with our reason and then express in our religion. Pluralists would agree with him here. But they would grow uneasy as Lindbeck goes on to reject what he terms an *experiential-expressive* notion of religion, which holds that we first have an inner experience of, or an "inner word" from Divinity, which we then display in our religious beliefs and practices. Such an experiential understanding of religion leads to the position that deep within all religions there is a common originating experience that binds them together despite or through their differences. Evidence for this, says Lindbeck, is slim.

In line with postmodern sensitivities, Lindbeck advances what he terms a *cultural-linguistic* approach to religion, which raises serious problems for the pluralists' call for a correlational dialogue. As learned cultural-linguistic systems, Lindbeck maintains, religions are more like languages that form and determine experience than experiences in search of language.

> A religion can be viewed as a kind of cultural and/or linguistic framework or medium that shapes the entirety of life and thought. . . . Like a culture or language, it is a communal phenomenon that shapes the subjectivities of individuals rather than being primarily a manifestation of those subjectivities. . . . A religion is above all an external word, a *verbum externum*, that molds and shapes the self and its world, rather than an expression or thematization of a preexisting self or of preconceptual experience (Lindbeck 1984, 33-34).

Understanding religions as filters that determine experience rather than as pictures that express experience, Lindbeck draws conclusions that no pluralist can ignore: there cannot therefore be

> an inner experience of God common to all human beings and all religions. There can be no experiential core because, so the argument goes, the experiences that religions evoke and mold are as varied as the interpretative schemes they embody. Adherents of different religions do not diversely thematize the same experience, rather they have different experiences (Lindbeck 1984, 40).

PLURALISTS BECOME IMPERIALISTS

In light of the postmodern awareness just described, proponents of a correlational model for interreligious dialogue have to ask themselves whether they are really taking seriously the dominance of diversity among religions and the incommensurable uniqueness at the heart of each tradition. William Placher puts it kindly but pointedly: "Many contemporary theologians and philosophers of religions seem extraordinarily uncomfortable with genuine religious pluralism. They cannot accept the possibility that there may be just different, even conflicting, religions and no point from which to evaluate them except from within some one tradition or another" (Placher 1989, 144).

The way pluralists view the diversity of religions and the way in which they call all these religions to dialogue might be, warn the critics, something like a group of baseball coaches from the United States who call together international athletes in order to form a globally elite baseball team. These are "pluralist" coaches who affirm the universality of athletic prowess and the valuable contributions that each of these athletes can make to this team. What they don't realize is that those athletes who play the game of baseball at home (e.g., Japan, Cuba, Nicaragua) may do so by significantly *different rules* and may not wish to submit to USA rules; more drastically, the coaches do not realize that most of these athletes are committed to *different games* and have no interest in playing baseball. They are, and want to be, athletes in totally different ways. In their efforts to promote one game, or one dialogue, the coaches impose not only their own rules but their own game.

With their pluralist or correlational model for dialogue, Christians might be doing the same thing in the world of religions. Because they are not sufficiently aware, or respectful, of the genuine diversity and incommensurability of religions, they can end up imposing their own rules and definitions. They might become the adversary they were struggling against: religious imperialism.

The criticisms I am reviewing in this chapter indicate two general ways in which good-intentioned pluralists can nonetheless become dangerous imperialists: 1) they too quickly presuppose or describe the common ground that establishes unity among religions, and 2) they too easily draw up common guidelines for dialogue among the religions.

The problem, according to the critics, has to do with the various ways in which the correlational model posits a "common something" that is at the heart of each religion, or that is beckoning each religion, or that makes for the family resemblances among all religions. Despite the clear differences among apples, oranges, and bananas, there's something that makes them all fruit. Likewise, according to the pluralists, with the religions: there is a common something that makes them all religions. In the so-called theocentric models for a theology of religions, this common ground has been called God, the Absolute, or Reality itself (Knitter 1985, chap. 8; Hick 1989, part 4).

This sounds good. But what these theologians or philosophers fail to realize, the critics warn, is that they are envisioning this God or this Reality itself through their own filters. They think they are talking in universal, non-biased terms, but they are not. They can't! "Pluralists substitute religiously indeterminate concepts like Reality and Mystery for otherwise distinctively conceived religious objects" (DiNoia 1990, 128). But in doing so, in thinking that they can speak universally, for everyone, they end up speaking individually, for themselves. In failing to realize that the Universal can be grasped only through the particular, pluralists end up imposing their own particularity on others. Lesslie Newbigin is uncomfortably to the point: "Every proposal for human unity which does not specify the center has the self as its unacknowledged center" (Newbigin 1990, 139). S. Mark Heim states this same warning more concretely: "If 'only God is absolute' is to mean anything, it must have some reference point. If God is not decisively known anywhere in particular, then this 'God' who is absolute is only what I make God to be, according to my definition. Thus, in fact, it is myself or my group that I make absolute" (Heim 1985, 144).[5]

The critical warnings point out further that even the generous, affirmative statement that "many religions are true because there is one God within them all," can be a cover-up for the imposition of one's own views on others, for such a statement implies that one has some normative conception of religion or of God by which one can know that another religion is true and to be affirmed—or, that it is false and to be rejected. But, the critics ask, whose criterion is being used? Usually, one's own! (See Ogden 1992, 70-72). Therefore, Thomas Dean can identify what he thinks is a "theocentric foundationalism" within the new pluralistic approaches to other religions: one's own understanding of God, or Reality itself, becomes the foundation for the unity of all religions (Dean 1987).[6]

The postmodern warning continues: Christians embracing a pluralist model for dialogue can be transformed, usually unwittingly, into imperialists or manipulators not only in the way they talk about "the one God" within all religions but also in the way they talk about the one dialogue that must occupy all religions. The general notion of dialogue contained in the pluralist model sounds noble and egalitarian: a dialogue from which no one is to be excluded and in which everyone wants to learn and improve, and most important, a dialogue which no one enters with absolute, final, exclusive, superior claims. Pluralists are quite eloquent and precise in drawing up principles, or guidelines, or a "decalogue for dialogue," which they presuppose all sincere, right-minded religious persons will readily embrace (Knitter 1985, 207-13; Knitter 1990, 20-25; Swidler 1990, 42-46).[7]

Are proponents of such programs for dialogue sufficiently aware of how much their understanding of dialogue is filtered through their own view of the world, their own philosophical convictions, their own Christian agenda? Some critics point out, for instance, that to require others to give up their claims to absolute truth—that is, truth that is normative for all peoples— is to disrespect, even violate, them. Most if not all religions necessarily come equipped with certain convictions or projects or "jealousies" that they can never abandon; if another religion contradicts such convictions, they believe, it is not only different, it is *wrong*! For Buddhists, according to Joseph DiNoia, whatever truth may exist outside of Buddhism has to agree with the Dharma preached by Lord Buddha (DiNoia 1990, 120ff; John Taylor 1981).

William Placher reminds his pluralist friends that by insisting on nonabsolute positions they can become quite absolutist, and by insisting on all-inclusion they can end up being exclusive. The danger is that pluralists will close themselves to those who close themselves to others. They end up with a seemingly smug viewpoint: "I announce that I am willing to take your point of view seriously. If you are not willing to do the same, then I am 'open' and you are 'closed,' so it turns out that I do not have to take your point of view seriously" (Placher 1989, 64). Is there not a danger, ask the critics, that in the end, the grandiose vision of a universal pluralistic dialogue among religions shrivels to the proportions of a club of Western intellectuals or do-gooders? "Hick and many other contemporary philosophers of religion claim to want to foster a universal religious dialogue, but it turns out that evangelical Christians, Hasidic Jews, traditional Muslims, and so on are not really eligible to join that dialogue, because they will be unwilling to accept the proposed rules of the game, rules that seem to emerge from a modern, Western, academic tradition" (Placher 1989, 146).

These are serious admonitions: because those who embrace a pluralist approach to religions don't recognize how diverse the world of religions really is and because they don't recognize how limited their own universal projects really are, they can end up as half-baked pluralists who have become anonymous imperialists.

WHOSE JUSTICE? WHAT SALVATION?

These warnings of imperialism or self-interest are also directed at the most altruistic or good-intentioned efforts of the model I outlined in the previous chapter—its commitment to global responsibility, to justice, to eco-human well-being as the basis or "common ground" for interreligious dialogue. Even the liberation-centered or soteriocentric model for a correlational theology of religions, admonish the critics, can be exploitative or manipulative. The axis of this warning is summarized neatly in the title of Alasdair MacIntyre's book *Whose Justice?* (1988) and is rooted in the postmodern affirmation of the dominance, or the precedence, of the diverse over the universal. "Justice," "salvation," "human well-being," or even "global responsibility" are not universal terms, clear to everyone (Milbank 1990, 185-88); such noble ideals are vacuous in themselves and can be filled with meaning only through the filters of *diverse* religious or cultural traditions. "Hence, promoting human welfare is an unhelpful common denominator [for interreligious dialogue] as it specifies nothing in particular until each tradition addresses itself to what is meant by 'human' and the 'welfare' of human beings. . . . The 'kingdom of God and its justice' is a vacuous phrase if it is not given some normative content, be it Christian, Jungian, or Buddhist" (D'Costa 1990, 57, 59).

Once these terms are given some "normative content" in the diverse religions, the result may well be not a nicely arranged basket of different fruits but a bucket of utterly different objects. William Placher warns theologians who take a liberation-centered approach to dialogue that when they talk about "liberation and *moksha* and *mukti* and *nirvana*" in the same breath they are not speaking about different roads to the same destination, but rather "radically *different* goals" (Placher 1989, 152). John Milbank holds that the notion of justice, as it has developed in the West from its Jewish-Christian roots, is such a distinctively Western vision that to use it as the context of interreligious encounter is to westernize the entire conversation (Milbank 1990).[8]

The critics we are listening to in this section see striking similarities between the call to base interreligious dialogue on a shared concern for liberation or justice and the efforts of John Rawls to propose a notion of justice that could transcend and thus be acceptable to all cultures. Recognizing the actual diversity in the way different cultures construct their systems of proper order, Rawls calls everyone back to what he terms their "original position"—that is, their pristine feeling for things before they were conditioned by their particular cultural or religious and political persuasions. From this bedrock original position, Rawls holds, all peoples would see justice as essentially the call to give everyone a fair chance.[9]

Here, again, warnings are voiced: such an appeal to a universal description of and commitment to justice, for all its noble intents, turns out to bear two bitter if not poisonous fruits. It boils off distinctive identities in the pot of universal agreement, failing to realize that there is no common essence or "original position" where all can neatly agree. "Justice is an essentially contested concept and every theory of justice arises within and expresses a particular moral and political perspective" (Lukas 1977, 170-71). Or, Rawls's efforts to prune away our cultural-religious conditionings so that we can agree leads to the unanimity of the bland or the indifferent. With Rawls's notion of justice or well-being, people basically agree to be nice to each other, or better, to leave each other alone. We can agree on only this minimum of justice—to give everyone a chance; we do not engage in the further, messier dialogue about what constitutes the common good. A minimal agreement on justice opens the door to individualism. A dialogue based on such a minimal, universal notion of justice will not lead to "a family or a *communitas* but [to] a well-regulated marketplace" (Placher 1989, 85).[10]

According to the critics, those who call for a globally responsible dialogue based on a shared commitment to justice are exposed to similar dangers. Either they operate with a universal notion of justice that is so bland and malleable that it becomes innocuous. Or, Christian liberation-centered theologians *do* give justice a concrete, normative content that has muscle in the struggle for transforming this world—but the content is their own! Really, it is the content provided by the gospel—by the person and message of Jesus Christ. The ideals of "justice" or "salvation" or "human well-being" held up by Christian pluralists as the common ground or common starting point for dialogue are really the justice and the salvation envisioned in Jesus' notion of the Reign of God.

So a further question for the pluralist globally responsible model follows: Isn't this the same kind of christocentrism and inclusivism that the model is trying to overcome? Just as one cannot have "God" in the center of dialogue unless one in some way gives content to that center, so one cannot have justice or *soteria* as the foundation for dialogue unless one offers some kind of definition of what *justice* means. And as soon as Christians do that, they are being christocentric—that is, operating out of Christian convictions and vision. But that means they are imposing this vision on others. So I cannot evade Schubert Ogden's uncomfortable observation: "Whereas the inclusivists appeal to the salvation constituted by the event of Jesus Christ, Knitter appeals to the salvation to be realized by following the historical Jesus in his service of God's kingdom, and thus in promoting liberation and transforming the world. In both cases, however, the norms appealed to are provided by some one specific religion or philosophy, which is thereby made normative for all the others" (Ogden 1992, 76).[11]

Even more seriously, as John Cobb has pointed out, the call to place *soteria* or eco-human well-being in the center of the dialogue may not be agreeable to all religious believers.[12] There are religious traditions which are not that concerned about the state of humanity or of the world, for they understand their ultimate and meaningful goal to be beyond this world in some other realm, or away from this world within the confines of the human heart. To hold up justice or a concern for this world as the centerpiece—or even just as a necessary element—for the dialogue would seem to exclude such religions from the conversation. When the pluralist model insists so centrally on global responsibility and justice, it can end up more exclusive than plural.

POLITICAL CRITICISM: PLURALISTS "UNDER THE MCDONALD'S ARCH"

The warnings and critiques we have reviewed so far flow out of the cultural or philosophical mainstream of what is called postmodern consciousness: an awareness that all knowledge is historically filtered, that diversity has precedence or dominance over unity, that it is extremely difficult if not impossible to find common ground. There are other critics with even more unsettling warnings about the dangers of pluralism; their perspectives or concerns derive from a political-economic analysis of the world and of the political structures and agenda that influence all our knowing and all our academic as well as religious pursuits.

Their central concern focuses on how easily the correlational model for dialogue can be or has been coopted and used by the dominant power-holders of the world in order to maintain their control. The trite but telling image used by one of these critics is the McDonald's hamburger. Although the "Big Mac" can serve as a symbol of universality, literally present to and embracing all cultures, it is also, in the view of many, a manifestation of—and a tasty distraction from—an economic system that dominates and exploits the world. In the same way, the recognition of pluralism and the call to dialogue appear as generous affirmations of universality when, really, they may be instruments of the dominant economic power-blocs. Kenneth Surin minces no words:

> The McDonald's hamburger is the first universal food, but the people—be they from LaPaz, Bombay, Cairo, or Brisbane—who eat the McDonald's hamburger also consume the American way of life with it. Equally, the adherents of the world ecumenism canvassed by the religious pluralists align themselves with a movement that is universal, but they too consume a certain way of life. . . . To resist the cultural encroachment represented by the McDonald's hamburger, therefore, is of a piece with resisting the similar depredation constituted by the world ecumenism [i.e. the pluralistic model for interreligious dialogue] (Surin 1990, 201).

The reason Surin and others consider the pluralist model for dialogue a "depredation" has to do with further insights they offer on the nature and use of language. We have just seen how the philosophical contingent of postmodernity reminds us of the way our language and knowledge is filtered and conditioned by our historical context; the political expression of postmodern awareness stresses what we can call the *political* or *ideological* nature and intent of all language. Stated simply, our language and our truth claims are not only limited by our filters, they are also conditioned—or better, *motivated*—by our political or economic or social position in society, and by our desire to either maintain that position or to better it. We don't have to endorse a Marxist perspective on language to recognize that although our pursuit of truth cannot be reduced to a "materialist" basis (as some Marxists would have it), still what we hold to be true and the way we talk about it can be influenced mightily by "what's in it for us." This is simply a statement about the human condition that both a Marxist and a Christian could make. Thus, to understand the words another, or we ourselves, are using, we have to ask questions about our socio-political situatedness.[13]

Michel Foucault pushes this political nature of language further, and again we don't have to agree with him fully in order to learn from him. His basic claim is that truth is tied to power—that which society holds up to be normal or sane or good or noble is not determined by any objective pursuit of truth but rather by the power-structures in the given society (Foucault 1980; Rabinow 1984). Although Foucault, toward the end of his life, admitted that knowledge and power cannot be simply equated (Placher 1989, 103; Foucault 1984, 18), his central claim remains: we are always playing with power when we make assertions about what is really true, praiseworthy, beneficial for all members of society. If we don't sufficiently take this into account, we can easily turn what is truth for us into chains for others.

This is the caveat that proponents of a pluralistic-liberative approach to dialogue must bear in mind—that because they are not sufficiently aware of how all truth claims are political and "power-full," their program for plurality and dialogue can become, whether they are aware of it or not, oppressive of others. This process of oppression works basically the same way it does in what is called "civil discourse" within or between nations; in fact, interreligious dialogue, some would say, has been sucked into and made part of the oppression and manipulation that so often hides beneath the cloak of civil discourse. What the critics are getting at here can be captured in a sentence from Toni Morrison's novel *Beloved:* "[He was] clever, but school teacher beat him anyway, to show that definitions belonged to the definers—not the defined" (Morrison 1987, 190). Or in the traditional proverb: "'Every man for himself and God for all' said the elephant as he danced among the chickens" (Lindsey 1992, 50).

Behind all the pretty, inspiring words about the beauty of plurality, the necessity of dialogue, and the challenge of communicative praxis there can lurk a process or program which sets the agenda in order to control, mollify, and dilute anyone whose voice might upset the status quo. Many pluralist theologians, critics warn, seem to think that there is something like Adam Smith's "magic hand" guiding their call for open-ended, all-inclusive dialogue and assuring that its results will benefit all; to forget the ever-intruding realities of economic, national, class, gender, and racial interests is as naive and dangerous within the interreligious dialogue as it is within the capitalist (or socialist) system. "Modernity contains demonic forces operating under the name of freedom; in the name of free discourse and pluralism, these forces may operate to impose a consensus that is actually domination of the many by the few" (Lindsey 1992, 67).[14]

Raymond Williams sounds a warning that should be announced around the world before every interreligious dialogue:

> A primary means by which privileged groups mask their hegemony is via a language of common contribution and co-operative shaping; to the extent that such groups can convince all partners in public dialogue that each voice contributes equally, to that extent does the conversation deflect attention from the unequal distribution of power underlying it (Williams 1977, 112).

Here is the danger: advocates of a correlational-liberative model for a theology and dialogue of religions do not seem to be sufficiently aware of the "unequal distribution of power" that underlies their dialogue. And so they can be coopted by these structures of power. There is much talk about the "global village" in which we all must acknowledge and jointly exercise, in Hans Küng's terms, "global responsibility" based on a "world ethic." Küng speaks about the demise of Eurocentrism and the coming to be of a "post-colonial," "post-capitalist" economy that will be part of the aborning "multi-confessional ecumenical world society" (Küng 1991, 19-20). Unity, peace, cooperation—these, according to proponents of a globally responsible dialogue, are the possibilities now within reach if nations and religions would only endorse and carry out this program of global discourse! Yet here, according to the critics, is where the pluralists, because they are not doing their political-economic analysis, can so easily be swallowed up and used by the powers that be. They are not aware, as Surin points out, that the Eurocentric/Western-centric powers of domination have not been dismantled; rather, they have been disguised. The stark, horrible inequalities between rich and poor, North and South, that continue to produce massive human and ecological suffering are still there; indeed, they are increasing rather than diminishing.[15]

The critics press their case: Why are not the pluralists, in all their glowing language about dialogue and well-being, talking about this? More so, why are they not talking about the political and economic structures that continue to maintain and produce these inequalities? We are not in a post-colonial but a neo-colonial world. The so-called new world order is the old world order cleaned up, focused, given a new face (Nelson-Pallmeyer 1992). The pluralists don't seem to recognize that "the rise and dominance of the West has been metamorphosed, or been 'sublated' into a 'new' project, that of the rise and dominance of the global" (Surin 1990, 196). But the global or new world order is being determined by those with the economic and military power.

Because the pluralists do not seem to be aware of these political realities, they can speak "the language of the angels" and condemn the horrible evils of racism, poverty, sexism, ecological devastation; they can summon all religious believers to assume "global responsibility" and "a new world ethic"—but they do so without becoming too specific, without raising the uncomfortable questions that would challenge the basic structures of power and the economic system. Surin is specific in this criticism: "European colonialism is condemned, but the neocolonialism into which it has been largely transmuted is again not positioned in their discourse. Thus David Livingstone and the East India Company will be rightly criticized, but not the United Fruit Company, or the Union Carbide Corporation or the International Monetary Fund or the World Bank" (Surin 1990, 207).

Again we see, this time from the perspective of political analysis and awareness, how well-intentioned pluralists can become perpetrators or pawns for the oppression or mistreatment of others. Such warnings have to be taken with utter seriousness.

AN ALTERNATE MODEL:
POSTLIBERAL "GOOD NEIGHBOR POLICY"

In light of our postmodern awareness of how much we are contained in our own historical-cultural locations, of how difficult it is to find common ground between locations, and how easily we slip into power plays every time we try to do so, the pluralist globally responsible model for understanding other religions seems riddled with either defects or hidden weapons. So a number of Christian theologians have been proposing a new model for a theology of religions that will sidestep the thorns and the land mines of both the traditional exclusive-inclusive and the recent pluralist approaches. Proposed by committed Christian thinkers such as George Lindbeck (1984), Stanley Hauerwas

(1985), Hans Frei (1974, 1975), Paul Griffiths (1991), and William Placher (1989), it has been called a postliberal model in that it draws on the insights of postmodernity in order to step beyond either liberal or conservative limitations.

The centerpiece of this postliberal perspective is that Christians—really, all religious believers—should for the most part stay in their own backyards. This is where they have grown up, where they have been formed, where they have learned and lived a story that is the filter which determines, not just colors, their world. Or, in Lindbeck's more philosophical terms, their backyard is their cultural-linguistic system which provides the beliefs or rules by which life makes sense (Griffiths 1990, 162-65). The religious or cultural neighborhood, for the postliberals, consists of backyards; there is no "commons" which all the households share.

Postliberals are therefore wary of venturing out of their own backyards to find some kind of common ground for mutual understanding; this wariness stems not only from the fear, described above, of doing harm to others by imposing one's own views on them, but also from the fear of doing harm to *themselves* by losing their own identities and distinctiveness in the effort to find the commonalities necessary for dialogue. To search for "public criteria" or "common human experience" which will enable us to speak with others all too often means "cutting and trimming the gospel to fit it to the categories and assumptions of a particular philosophical or cultural position." And "that inevitably distorts the faith" (Placher 1989, 160, 20). What our mixed-up, suffering world needs from Christians today is not a voice that fits in but a voice that disturbs and offers an alternative vision (Hauerwas 1985, 11-12; Placher 1989, 19).

But the postliberals will also add that although we are to stick mainly to our own backyards, we still should not ignore our neighbors. This is where the postliberal viewpoint contains what I would call a "good neighbor policy" toward other religions. Our neighbors are there; we must live with them in peace, help them, and cooperate with them where we can. This will mean, first of all, *not* that we try to search for some method or foundation on which we can understand each other, but, rather, that we let them know who we are. "Christian self-description" not correlation with universal "human, cultural quests for ultimate meaning" is the primary task of the Christian community (Placher 1989, 19, quoting Frei). Let them see who we are, understand as they may, and respond as they will—this, for postliberals, is the primary responsibility toward persons of other faiths.

But there are other responsibilities in being a good neighbor. We must converse with them, not out of any intrinsic or general need to do so, but as the need for conversation arises. Although no given common ground for dialogue exists, there do arise little plots where we can stand and talk to each other over our backyard fences. This is what some postliberals call "ad hoc apologetics"—provisional opportunities to give and receive witness. "All that we ever have is the common ground that *happens to exist* [emphasis mine] among different particular traditions. By 'ad hoc apologetics' . . . [is meant] that we should let the common ground we share with a given conversation partner set the starting point for the particular conversation, not looking for any *universal* rules or assumptions for human conversation generally" (Placher 1989, 167-68; Werpehowski 1986).[16]

Paul Griffiths stresses even more the need for "apologetics" in these ad hoc encounters. Recognizing that they all have grown up in their own backyards and see things differently, religions must try to convince each other of the truth they have discovered or been given; they must argue with each other, carefully, nonviolently, with an openness to learn from the other. But the main task is to stand firmly in one's own identity and to give hard witness (Griffiths 1991). For such an apologetic approach to dialogue, one should not have to apologize; thus, Placher's title, *An Unapologetic Theology.*

The postliberal model, therefore, presents itself as both more adequate to postmodern awareness and more appropriate to Christian convictions than is the pluralistic-correlational model.

•

The problems and pitfalls pointed out by the critics we have reviewed in this chapter are real. They have to be taken seriously by anyone who is trying to plot a pluralistic or correlational course in approaching the reality of the many religions. But I think that the warning signs that these critics are setting up should read "Danger Ahead" rather than "Road Blocked." The dangers are real, but they can be avoided, sometimes by careful plotting, sometimes by detours. For if the road to genuine dialogue between differing cultures, nations, religions is really blocked, so is humanity's future.

In the remaining chapters, I will try to give substance and persuasion to my suspicion (bordering on a conviction) that if we can better relate the "many religions" to the "one world," if we can better—that means more carefully, more humbly, more persistently—integrate interfaith dialogue with global responsibility, then most if not all criticisms we have reviewed can be removed, mitigated, or at least discussed further in a more fruitful way. The following chapters will attempt a revision, but at the same time an affirmation, of a pluralist globally responsible approach to a theology and dialogue of religions.

4

GLOBAL SUFFERING CALLING
FOR GLOBAL RESPONSIBILITY

The Pain of the World as a Religious Challenge

So far, we have heard the case both for and against a correlational globally responsible model for interreligious dialogue. After I retraced in chapter 1 my autobiographical journey toward such an approach to persons of other faiths, I presented in chapter 2 a digest of the main ingredients of an encounter among religions that would be both *correlational*, recognizing the equal rights and possible universal validity of all religions, and *globally responsible*, affirming a commitment to eco-human well-being as the ground for dialogue. In chapter 3, I tried to replay and rehear the voices of those who warn that a dialogue that so extols a common conversation based on a commitment to this world ends up diminishing or destroying particularity and therefore the possibility of genuine interchange.

In the remaining chapters I will attempt, especially by taking these warnings seriously, to clarify, revise, and reaffirm a pluralistic globally responsible model for interreligious dialogue and theology. The centerpiece—or the guiding light—for this revision and reaffirmation will be a commitment to *soteria* or *eco-human well-being.* By showing how a shared commitment to global responsibility *must* and *can* work in interreligious encounters, I hope both to respond to the critics and to strengthen the case for an authentically pluralistic embrace of our religious world.

SUFFERING AS A COMMON GROUND AND COMMON CAUSE

I have to admit that my first reaction to the warnings of the so-called postmodernists or deconstructionists or postliberals is more a matter of the heart than the head; I cannot reconcile what they tell me with what I see in the world. On the one hand, I hear their admonitions that there can be no common ground for intercultural discourse, no universal truths, no "metanarratives" but only diverse perspectives, individual constructs, ad hoc themes for conversation. On the other hand, I see and hear a world in agony, torn by starvation, dehumanizing living conditions, unjust distribution of wealth, ecological deterioration—a world that calls for global, coordinated action based on commonly recognized values and truths. I cannot put the insights and admonitions of postmodern awareness together with the reality and the moral requirements of the world as it is.

Yes, I know that these postmodern warnings embody sincere and valid concerns; I tried to state and empathize with those concerns in the previous chapter. But on the other hand, I am also convinced that if such reservations become a reason to abandon or even diminish our efforts to bring about a cooperative, coordinated response from many nations and religions to the reality of human suffering and ecological peril, then there is something intrinsically wrong with all these objections. If not in their internal coherence, then at least in their timing, they are inappropriate.

To insist on the dominance of diversity and on the impossibility of finding any common ground on which we can make common ethical decisions can all too easily lead to a moral lethargy or quietism. Thus I would agree with David Tracy when he criticizes his own extolling of diversity:

> whenever any affirmation of pluralism, including my own, past and present, becomes simply a passive response to more and more possibilities, none of which shall ever be *practiced*, then pluralism demands suspicion. That kind is, as Simone de Beauvoir insisted, the perfect ideology for the modern bourgeois mind. Such a pluralism masks a general confusion in which one tries to enjoy the pleasures of difference without ever *committing to any particular vision of resistance and hope* (Tracy 1987a, 90, emphasis mine).

A further danger in the contemporary insistence that every truth claim is only a limited, particular "construct" is that such particular constructs become *absolutes*! They have absolute power over all other sources of truth and value. Everything is captured in the construct; nothing can break out of it. If I claim, for instance, that nature or the Earth or the plight of the poor is telling me something that applies to all peoples or is a universal value, such a claim will be immediately locked into a particular cell; its universal call will be incarcerated. Such an absolutizing of human constructs leads, as Charlene Spretnak warns, to a type of individualism in which each person or each culture/religion is a "lone cowboy" that has to tough it out alone (Spretnak 1991, 125-27; 218-19, 245-46).[1]

The obsession of so many contemporaries with preserving diversity at all costs, with not wanting to impose any kind of a common agenda or seek after common criteria by which we can decide what is true or false (or right or wrong) can easily lead to what David Krieger has called, with a typical theological penchant for tongue-twisting terms, a "relativist agonistics." What he means is simple and frightening: if we have no common agenda, if there are no common criteria to be discovered or fashioned by nonviolent consensus, then ultimately what is "true" will be decided by power—by who has the money or the guns. A refusal to recognize the possibility of a common agenda for dialogue that will both require and lead to common criteria for determining the true and the ethical really is an affirmation not of "to each his/her own truth" but "to each his/her own power" (Krieger 1990, 227).[2] And as we know today, power is not shared equally in this world. The nations and races that have more of it than others will decide the criteria for truth and value. To avoid making the pursuit of truth a pursuit of power, we must be able to agree among ourselves that there *is*—or better, *can be*—common ground on which we can come to common convictions, criteria, and action.[3]

The common cause out of which we can fashion our common ground is all around us in the sufferings that rack and endanger our species and planet. Our world is such that moral discernment and moral commitment are simply unavoidable. There are issues and dangers and a spectrum of suffering on which we must take stands. And we must do so, not individually, each in our own perspectival tower or armed turret, but together, in a manner which will lead to common discernment and common commitment. So David Tracy is, I believe, right when he describes "the great pluralists of religion" as those who not only "so affirm plurality that they fundamentally trust it" but also "do not shirk their responsibility to develop criteria of assessment" by which the diversity can be evaluated and directed toward common commitments (Tracy 1987a, 91). Anyone who will not allow for the possibility and necessity of developing such shared "criteria of assessment" is, I believe, an enemy to us all. While we must treasure our diversity, we must also discern what can unite us in common concern and action for the sufferings of our fellow beings and planet.

THE COMMON HUMAN EXPERIENCE OF SUFFERING

What I am saying, then, is not that there is a common essence or a common religious experience or even a precisely defined common goal within all religions. Rather, I am pointing to what I think is starkly and painfully obvious when one looks at and tries to live in the world as it is: there is a common *context* that contains a common complex of *problems*. This context calls for a common *agenda* for all the religions of the world as they try to come together to understand and make sense of each other. I am talking about realities that are universal, cross-cultural, impinging willy-nilly on all religious believers and demanding a religious response from them. What is common to all these issues and to the context I am referring to is the horrible reality of *suffering*—suffering that is draining the life and imperiling the future of humankind and the planet.

If with William Placher and the neo-liberals we want to speak about an ad hoc issue that we can agree on, it is this—the human and ecological suffering that now menaces our world. Given its universality and its urgency, this ad hoc issue must be part of, if not prior to, all other issues that make up the dialogue. If with David Tracy and Schubert Ogden we want to talk about a "common human experience" to which all religions can respond in order to understand themselves and others, then it is this experience of suffering and the dangers that it brings forth (Tracy 1975, 43-63; Ogden 1972). If with Paul Tillich we wish to speak about an Ultimate Concern that animates all religions, I suggest we find it in a concern for the suffering of others.

There is today a growing awareness among religious persons that their religious identity must somehow be related to these common experiences of suffering and global threat. What might be called a cosmological faith, springing from a cosmological responsibility, is coloring and renewing the religious awareness of people across religious and national boundaries. Gordon Kaufman describes this cosmological faith as a "growing passion":

> It seems to me that, as we have been propelled with greater and greater rapidity into an uncertain future, humans everywhere have increasingly raised the question whether it is a genuinely humane world that we are producing. . . . Throughout the world there appears to be a growing passion to reconstruct the present order into one more truly humane. That is the great aspiration of our time—underlying much of the unrest of our world—whether we are Christians or Buddhists, Americans or members of the so-called third world, communists or adherents to Western-style democracy. How shall we build a new and more human world for all of the peoples of the world? That is our most important question (Kaufman 1981, 181).

What Kaufman goes on to say about Christian theology applies even more compellingly to interreligious dialogue: "A theology [or dialogue] that makes an essential contribution to our humanization is the only sort we can afford today" (1981, 184). Hugo Assmann is even more graphic and compelling: "If the state of domination and dependence in which two-thirds of humanity live, with an annual toll of thirty million dead from starvation and malnutrition,[4] does not become the starting point for *any* Christian theology [read: for any interreligious dialogue], even in the affluent and powerful countries, then theology [dialogue] cannot begin to relate meaningfully to the real situation" (Assmann 1974, 54).

This common context or starting point can be understood as a new hermeneutical kairos for interreligious encounter; that is, a situation that casts both its shadows and its lights on all corners of the globe and in doing so makes a new encounter of religions both *necessary* and *possible*.[5] I call it a "kairos" because it is a unique constellation of events that constitutes both new opportunities and responsibilities; it is "hermeneutical" because, as we shall argue below, it enables followers of different religious paths not just to feel the need for each other but to understand *and* to judge each other. It is a global situation consisting of concerns and questions that transcend differences of culture and religion and so touch all peoples.

THE FACES OF SUFFERING

This world of suffering, which provides the context or kairos for dialogue, is all around us. It is impinging ever more sharply and disruptively on the consciousness and feelings of people throughout the world. This book is not the occasion to describe and analyze this world in detail. And yet at least a few simple cameo shots of this worldwide suffering, in its many faces and in its common roots, are appropriate at this point simply in order to remind our heads and hearts of the reality of the world in which we seek to be human and religious.

1. *Suffering of the Body—Due to Poverty:* If, as Jesus reminded us, the poor are always among us (Matt 26:11), they are with us today in ever greater and staggering numbers and with a presence that insists on having a place in our awareness. Regularly the cries of the poor become a deafening lamentation when countries or regions are decimated by mass starvation, as in Ethiopia in 1984 and Somalia in 1992. Then we cannot close our ears to the death wails or our eyes to the skeletal figures of children. But in the background of these outbursts of starvation is the steady, relentless moan of millions who suffer chronically because they are poor, because they do not have the wherewithal to meet the most basic human needs of themselves and their children.

We know the statistics; they bob up and down in the daily flow of information. All the figures point to an undeniable fact that shatters both intellectual and moral comprehension: "After nearly five decades of unprecedented global economic growth, the world heads toward the twenty-first century with *more than a billion people in poverty*"

(Kennedy 1993, 49). Amid all the progress we have made in this technologically marvelous century, the human family, as a whole, *has grown poorer!* More precisely: "Some 1.5 billion people . . . —more than one out of four human beings alive today—are living in 'absolute poverty.' That is, they do not regularly drink fresh water, eat enough to stay healthy and spend most waking hours gathering firewood for fuel."[6] Forty million persons die each year from hunger or hunger-related causes; fourteen million children die every year before the age of 5, mostly of diseases that are preventable in Europe and North America.[7] More than two million deaths a year are linked to polluted water and poor sanitation. One adult in four in the world is unable to read and write.[8]

Such statistics on the low or inferior economic status of nations or groups do not constitute mere "facts" for us to imbibe with our morning coffee along with the baseball scores. These figures represent, rather, a huge, throbbing mass of human suffering. As the liberation theologians tell us with sobering simplicity: poverty kills, poverty murders, poverty *is* violence.

The poor are "among us" with such proximity that the divisions—the walls?—between us become ever more difficult to maintain. It becomes more and more difficult for North Americans to ignore or not feel threatened by the poverty of their South American neighbors. Throughout the countries of Central and South America, some 180 million people are living in abject poverty—50 million more than in 1982, two out of every five people (Kennedy 1993, 205). Even in the United States, one of the most "developed" nations of the First World, the poor are present in growing numbers and louder voices: in 1991, thirty-six million Americans were classified as poor, the highest number in twenty-seven years (with 40 percent of them in female-headed families); almost one out of every five children under 18 is among these numbers; daily 5.5 million children under 12 suffer from hunger, while six million others suffer from malnutrition.[9]

Even from a purely pragmatic, self-interested perspective, such Earth-strangling poverty must call forth concern from the so-called developed countries. Paul Kennedy, in his cautious, well-researched, middle-of-the-road assessment *Preparing for the Twenty-First Century*, gives one of the principal reasons:

> If the developing world remains caught in its poverty trap, the more developed countries will come under siege from tens of millions of migrants and refugees eager to reside among the prosperous but aging populations of the democracies. Either way, the results are likely to be painful for the richest one-sixth of the earth's population that now enjoys a disproportionate five-sixths of its wealth (Kennedy 1993, 46).

So Kennedy formulates what he sees as a forced option if the world is to move peacefully from one millennium to the next:

> Although few, if any, of our political leaders appear willing to face the fact, the greatest test for human society as it confronts the twenty-first century is how to use "the power of technology" to meet the demands thrown up by "the power of population"; that is, how to find effective global solutions in order to free the poorer three-quarters of humankind from the growing Malthusian trap of malnutrition, starvation, resource depletion, unrest, enforced migration, and armed conflict—developments that will also endanger the richer nations, if less directly" (Kennedy 1993, 12).

But in order to be successful, any pragmatically motivated solution for the "problem of poverty" must be grounded in moral feelings and convictions. The reality and physical proximity of poverty alongside affluence must bring about a moral proximity; the "they" and the "we" must blend into a connected, responsive humanity. *Their* poverty must somehow be *ours*. Unless I respond to the murderous reality of poverty, I am less a human being, certainly less a religious being.

Religious persons, because they are religious, can and must do something about the monster of poverty that continues to stalk the so-called new world order. I am suggesting that the contemporary spectrum of poverty and the suffering that it causes must affect—is affecting— the way people are religious. The awareness of such suffering is calling for a reform, or a renewal, of how we think and act as religious persons.

Whatever their tradition, religious believers are coming to feel that their religion must confront such basic physical needs and sufferings and that whatever salvation or enlightenment or *moksha* may mean, such beliefs have to say something about this kind of suffering. Hindus, Christians, Jews, Muslims, Buddhists are recognizing that if any of their traditional beliefs become the reason or the occasion for ignoring or condoning such human suffering, then such beliefs lose their credibility. Even the most traditionally "other-worldly" religions are showing concern and trying to formulate some kind of response to our world's growing awareness of human suffering. Tables bare of bread and water can become the tables around which the religions of the world gather to talk and act (Knitter 1990, 27-28).

2. *Suffering of the Earth—Due to Abuse:* If humanity is suffering, so is the Earth. One does not have to be a biological mystic and explicitly endorse the Gaia hypothesis that the Earth is a living organism in order to *feel* as much empathy and concern for the suffering Earth as one does for one's suffering fellow human beings. What we are presently doing to this planet in the way we are using and abusing its

resources is a destruction of life, in its actuality and in its potentiality. In the 37.4 million acres of forests that are destroyed every year, in the 13 million acres of land that yearly lose their productive topsoil and are turned into wasteland (Nelson-Pallmeyer 1992, 96), in the 25 percent increase of heat-trapping carbon dioxide in the atmosphere since preindustrial times because of our burning of coal, oil and natural gas[10]—in such destruction or alteration of our eco-system we are both killing the actual life that moves within it and, more frighteningly, depleting to the point of destroying the ability of this system to produce and sustain future life. The precipitous rate of species loss due to our alterations of the environment—to the point that many biologists fear that 25 percent of the world's remaining species will be wiped out within the next fifty years—has become both fact and symbol of what we are doing: we humans are destroying life—plant, animal and our own.[11] To harm the planet is to harm our Mother and it is to harm ourselves. For this we are grieving—and we are frightened.

The realization of our ecological sins, with their attendant fear, has only begun to register on the global consciousness. For some, especially for the most responsible, it is still remote. Lester Brown describes the reality and its avoidance:

> Anyone who regularly reads the financial papers or business weeklies would conclude that the world is in reasonably good shape and that long-term economic trends are promising. . . . Yet on the environmental front, the situation could hardly be worse. Anyone who regularly reads scientific journals has to be concerned with the earth's changing physical condition. Every major indicator shows a deterioration in natural systems: forests are shrinking, deserts are expanding, croplands are losing topsoil, the stratospheric ozone layer continues to thin, greenhouse gases are accumulating, the number of plant and animal species is diminishing, air pollution has reached health-threatening levels in hundred of cities, and damage from acid rain can be seen on every continent.[12]

It is becoming increasingly difficult to keep our heads buried, ostrich-like, in our books or in our banks while our parent-planet literally loses her breath. As was heard loudly and clearly during the United Nations Earth Summit in Rio de Janeiro in June 1992, we can no longer "go about business as usual" and divorce economics from the environment. Concern for the environment must influence the way we do business. We can no longer simply foster development; it must be *sustainable* development; it must meet the crying human needs for food and shelter without destroying the Earth's ability to provide food and shelter. This is another aspect of what Paul Kennedy described as "the

greatest test for human society as it confronts the twenty-first century"—to bring the power of technology and science to address not
just the problem of an impoverished population but also of an impoverished ecosystem.

But if concern for the environment must influence the way we do
business and science, it must also influence the way we are religious. In
fact, the "ecological crisis" is more and more being recognized today
as a religious issue. Religious persons are among the voices calling for
a new kind of relationship between the world of business and the real,
physical world. Thomas Berry, an Earth-prophet and "geologian,"
describes these links: "We come to the essential point of economics as
a religious issue when we consider that the present threat to both economics and religion is from a single source, the disruption of the natural world. If the water is polluted it can neither be drunk nor used for
baptism, for it no longer bears the symbolism of life but death" (Berry
1988, 79-80).

If, as some see it, the Earth Summit of 1992 was the historical turning point when concern for the Earth began to become part of the
common consciousness of nations, the same would have to be said
about ecology and the common consciousness of religions.

> Historians will regard this [the Earth Summit] as a global mo-
> ment when the world began to speak of the failures of earlier
> dreams and began a search for a new relationship between people,
> the Earth, and their economic activities. That search leads quickly
> into the terrain of values and ethics, and raises questions con-
> cerning spiritual realities. At question is whether there is, in fact,
> a path than can lead the world to a future where all people can
> be offered the hope of life, and the Earth can be preserved in its
> capacity to provide that life (Granberg-Michaelson 1992, 31).

UN General Secretary Boutros Boutros-Ghali also called, indirectly,
for an interreligious ecological consciousness when in his closing address to the Earth Summit he joined his usual language of diplomacy
with the language of spirituality; we have been told in the past that we
must love our neighbors, he pointed out, but now we need to hear that
we must love the Earth. To realize both loves, the vision and vigor of
religion will be necessary.[13] Therefore, what Sallie McFague has said
about Christian awareness and theology can be heard and affirmed, I
believe, by followers of other religious traditions: "To feel in the depths
of our being that we are part and parcel of the evolutionary ecosystem
of our cosmos is a prerequisite for contemporary Christian theology
[and dialogue]" (McFague 1987, 9).

3. *Suffering of the Spirit—Victimization:* The horrendous sufferings
of body and Earth that we have pointed to are rendered even more

horrible by a simple fact: they need not be. They are not natural events or chance happenings. I do not think that even the most rigid, unfeeling Darwinian or neo-Darwinian view of biological evolution would affirm or suggest that such widespread human and ecological suffering is the natural result of "nature red in tooth and claw." Nor, I think, would the most hard-core social Darwinian want to attribute such destruction of human and natural life to the natural, unavoidable result of "the fittest" making sure they "survive." And if there are any economists who would appeal to Adam Smith's "magic hand" to explain how such suffering ultimately produces economic gain, then I would have to declare that magic hand and the economic system it guides to be demonic.

No, the cause of the spectrum of human and ecological suffering is both much more simple and complex: it is, for the most part, the result of *human decisions,* the result of what some human beings, those who have the power, decide to do to other human beings. Such decisions do not have human beings as their primary object or intent; they are oriented primarily toward personal gain or advantage, usually economic. Humans beings become part of the mechanism or process for realizing such gain. Human poverty and ecological destruction result, if not intentionally then still necessarily, from these gain or profit-motivated decisions, especially as such decisions are enacted and translated into economic policies, legal systems, and international arrangements.

Such decisions, made by the few but affecting the life and life-giving capacity of peoples and planet, embody the *victimization* of some people by others. This is, perhaps, the most painful form of suffering that a human being—and may I say the Earth spirit—can experience. Not only the body but the spirit, identity, and sense of selfhood are maimed or destroyed. To be a victim is to be an instrument, nothing but an instrument used by another. To be a victim is not to count, to be there purely to be used and then discarded. To be a victim is the horrible, strangling feeling that one cannot dispose of one's own life; the victim is powerless in the face of a greater, consuming power. The feelings of being violated and abused are human feelings. If we can trust the voices of those who speak from a sense of relatedness with the natural world, then we know too that the Earth and its plants and animals are suffering the same victimization.

Victimization means injustice. *Injustice* is the word we use when our minds and hearts respond to a situation of suffering which we know, immediately and certainly, need not be and should not be. There is something wrong, something evil, in decisions and systems that produce so much victimization. They are unjust. They must be resisted. They must be changed.

This injustice and victimization, evident in the faces and voices of the victims, is clearly revealed in general statistics on the distribution of the goods of this Earth. There is something wrong and unjust when the countries of the North, who make up only one-fourth of the world's population, possess five-sixths of its riches.[14] There is something wrong and unjust when the three-fourths of the Earth's peoples who comprise the so-called developing world, can make use of only one-sixth of the world's wealth—or when the richest fifth of the world's population enjoys 150 times the income of the poorest fifth.[15] There is something wrong and unjust when in 1989 peoples of the developing world sent $52 billion more in debt payments to developed countries in the North than they received in new credits, or when in 1990 Latin America's international debt was four times as large as its total annual earnings from exports, or in general when the Third World's debt burden rose from $785 billion at the beginning of the debt crisis to $1.3 trillion in 1992.[16]

Also within the developed world there is something wrong and unjust when in the United States in 1989 the 4 percent of the population at the top of the economic scale earned as much as the bottom 51 percent, or when during the 1980s the increase in total salaries of people earning $20,000 to $50,000 rose 44 percent, while the salaries of those earning $200,000 to $1 million jumped 697 percent (for those earning over a million dollars, income surged 2,184 percent!).[17]

The victimization that dwells within such figures and facts is rendered all the more unsettling and enraging when we recognize that the ranks of the poor and exploited do not represent a cross-cut of the world population and have not been determined by random economic "natural selection." Rather, *race and gender* seem to be selecting factors in determining who will be among advantaged "users" and the disadvantaged "used." Both internationally as we look at the differences between North and South and nationally as we look at income distribution in the United States, people of color outnumber white people among the poor and the victimized. And among the poor, women are clearly poorer and more abused than men. Throughout the world, even in countries that vaunt a growing awareness of sexism and patriarchy, women continue to work more and be paid less than men.[18] The "feminization of poverty" that has been noted in the United States is a global reality. It is clear how much racism and sexism fuel and direct the decisions that lead to victimization.

While one may argue whether there are any more injustices or any more victims in our world today than there ever were, it is incontestable that the awareness of injustice and victimization is keener and more widespread than ever. The reason such awareness is more acutely felt among the community of nations is that it is more acutely felt among the community of victims. What seems to be markedly and hopefully different in our world today is not that there are more victims but that the victims are waking up to and determined to do something about the reality of victimization and injustice. The awareness is coming, not from those in power, but from below, from the "underbelly" of history, from those whose bodies and voices have never counted, or rather, have counted only on the ledgers of factories or armies. There is today a universal thirst and hope for liberation which "defines the spirit of our epoch, of our times in which we live. Modern humankind is in quest of liberation, of a 'liberated' life, which for the poor has to come through the humble sacraments of bread, a roof over their heads, health, and peace" (Boff 1987, 90).[19] And though this awareness of victimization and thirst for liberation has had to overcome new obstacles and refocus its analysis and tactics in light of the restructuring of geo-political realities and powers after the collapse of the Soviet bloc, both the reality and the consciousness of victimization, together with the determination of victims to free themselves, remain unabated.

This consciousness that victimization and injustice form a horrible part of our "world order" is also seeping, slowly but persistently, into the awareness of religious persons, no matter what their tradition. They are awakening to the conviction that unless their religious identity, in its beliefs and practices, embraces and responds to the victims of this world, it is neither authentic to its sources nor relevant to this world. An essential, perhaps prior, part of the response of religions to the reality of victimization and injustice is the realistic, humble, and repentant recognition that religions themselves have played a significant and shameful role in fostering or sanctioning the exploitation of some peoples by others. Religions must first confess to their sins of injustice before they can profess to have a remedy for it. They must first admit that religion has been an opium that has victimized people; only then can they propose religion as an energy to liberate them.

Such confessions and professions are happening, at least to some extent, around the religious world. The faces and voices of victims are making a difference in the way religious believers understand themselves and those of other traditions. From his broad study of religions and experience of dialogue, Hans Küng predicts the future: "Numerous conversations in the Far and Near East have convinced me that in the future all the great religions will foster a vital awareness of the guarantee of human rights, the emancipation of women, the realization of social justice, and the immorality of war" (Küng 1986a, 241). Some might say that Küng's prediction is naive. For me and for many religious persons, unless we can share Küng's "naiveté," we cannot be religious.

4. *Suffering Due to Violence:* The realities of victimization and injustice which nurture the dreadful specter of physical and ecological suffering foster another form of suffering that is just as horrible as an emaciated body or polluted lake. I am talking about the usually indis-

criminate and uncontrolled suffering that results from the violence of armed or military conflict. The 1980s witnessed undulations of military violence throughout the world—faction warring against faction in internal or external wars in El Salvador, Nicaragua, Guatemala, Lebanon, Palestine, South Africa, Angola, Sri Lanka, Kashmir, the Punjab, Northern Ireland, the Philippines. As the Gulf War and the ethnic-regional conflicts in Eastern Europe and the countries of the former Soviet Union indicate, the new world order, despite its dissolution of superpower tensions, does not promise any real change in the violence that racks humanity and the environment or in the arms production and trade that feed such violence. Whether between superpowers or mini-powers, the violence and the suffering continue. And in almost every instance, the violence is incited or justified out of a situation of injustice or victimization in which one side feels it is being used or abused by another.

But such, some will say, has been the state of humanity for all of its evolutionary life. What's so different? Violence is a fact of life; we have to live with it. But that, precisely, is what today is different: if we continue to live with violence, we won't continue to live. The quantity and quality—and therefore, the nature—of armed violence is different today. Given the kind of weaponry we have created, given the vastness of its destructive power and the remoteness of those who press the buttons, warfare today cannot be controlled. Even the Gulf War, with all its precision, computerized weapons, worked incredible (and often hidden) devastation on civilian populations.[20] As moralists and ethicists have been concluding, according to the principles of the just-war theory, modern warfare, it would seem, can never be just.

If this is true of so-called conventional warfare, it is incontestable in regard to nuclear conflict.[21] Even though the Cold War's "MAD" policy of "Mutually Assured Destruction" has been diffused, even though the "nuclear clock" is ticking more slowly, still the clock remains on the geopolitical shelf and it continues to tick! These weapons still exist in numbers sufficient to destroy almost all life and the planet's life-producing capacity. Also, the knowledge and the means to make more of these instruments of death remain.[22] They can still be used if ever the new world order and its smooth functioning are seriously threatened. And as the mini-powers acquire their own nuclear weapons, we can expect situations of nuclear threats and "brinksmanship" to once again multiply.[23]

Besides the actual physical suffering inflicted by the violence of war, besides the psychological suffering resulting from the ever-present thought that humanity now has and threatens to use weapons that can bring about "humanicide," there is also the suffering that is taking place daily when huge sums of money and resources are poured into the maw of the international military machine. The realization that every day the nations of the world spend $1.8 million for the maintenance and creation of instruments of death[24] and that in the United States in 1993, 53 percent of the federal budget was fed into some aspect of the military (twice the amount devoted to human resources),[25] once again stirs the insult and outrage of *victimization*. That so much of the Earth's resources and human production should be devoted to the destruction or threat of life when there are so many humans who cannot provide themselves and their children with what is necessary to live a human life—such realities cry out to the heavens and to the depths of the human heart. There is something fundamentally awry with such a world. It must be changed. We cannot so continue.

Again, I think a case can be made that the religions of the world can and will take this situation to heart and respond to it. Given on the one hand the needs of a world ravaged by violence and on the other the vision of peace and unity lying, in different metaphors and narratives, within the original teachings of all (or at least most) religious traditions, peace can and must become a common commitment and a common ground for conversation and action. We can say that *peace*, understood as the overcoming of military violence and build-up, is a symbol that all religions can share and respond to. As Raimon Panikkar claims, "Peace appears to be emerging as a symbol for our times. No other symbol seems to have the power and universality of peace" (in Rapp 1985, 29).

Peace is a religious symbol because one cannot think of peace and the conditions of its possibility without confronting and dialoguing about religious issues; in planning and hoping for peace we face the necessity—and at the same time, the apparent impossibility—of humanity living and thinking and being radically different than it is today. There can be no peace without a revolution or conversion of our being and thinking. But how can we bring about such a revolution? What is necessary for its realization? These are religious questions, which bond all the religions in a new, common project: to respond to and make real the symbol of peace.

THE NEED FOR A GLOBAL ETHIC—A RELIGIOUS CHALLENGE

In view of the sorry state of our suffering world, in view of the plethora of human and ecological crises confronting all nations, there are those who are calling for the formulation of a global ethic that would ground and guide the kind of concerted, common response needed to resolve these crises. One of the strongest voices for such a program has been that of Hans Küng. He formulates his case in apocalyptic though realistic terms:

The catastrophic economic, social, political, and ecological de-velopments of both the first and the second halves of the century necessitate a world ethic if humankind is to survive on this earth. . . . The one world in which we live has a chance of survival only if there is no longer any room in it for spheres of differing, con-tradictory, even antagonistic ethics. This one world needs one basic ethic (Küng 1991, 25, xvi).

Küng's reasoning is simple and tight: the menacing problems con-fronting humankind today demand concerted, common action, but such action is impossible unless it is based on and directed by general agreement on ethical goals and the ethical means to those goals. With-out some such consensus, diverse groups of people who face common problems simply cannot act together and therefore they cannot live together. "Without a minimal basic consensus on certain values, norms and attitudes, no human society worth living in is possible in either a smaller or larger community" (Küng 1991, 28). Daniel Maguire agrees: "Without a broadly accepted ethic to feed and direct our quest for a livable social existence, chaos ensues" (Maguire 1993, 22).[26]

Küng is proposing that individual nations, as well as the commu-nity of nations, move beyond the traditional "liberal" understanding of the social contract theory formulated by John Locke and elaborated and applied to modern society by John Rawls. According to such an understanding, we agree to allow each other to have the room to be our individual selves; we live our lives so as not to disturb the other; we agree to leave each other alone. Küng is urging much more—that we agree on shared values, common moral ideals and convictions, so that we can not only live and let live but act and act ever more concert-edly. He's after *consensus*, which can come *only through dialogue* and which will not destroy or swallow up the diversity that is part of our multicultural, multireligious world. It will be an ethical "consensus that is not 'strict' or 'total' but 'overlapping'" (Küng 1991, 28). Küng holds that there will be sufficient overlapping to make this consensus a "world ethic"—a moral platform on which nations can formulate com-mon action for common problems.

This world ethic is admittedly general in that it seeks not to formu-late particular programs of action but the basis on which such pro-grams can be mutually formulated, as needs arise, through dialogue; it is also dynamic in that it must be open to new input from differing cultural or national perspectives and ready to change as new problems or pains develop. Leonard Swidler, an ardent promoter of Küng's pro-posal, recognizes this needed elasticity and dynamism:

What is needed is not a full-blown global ethics in great detail—indeed, such would not even be possible—but a global consensus on the fundamental attitude toward good and evil and the basic principles to put it into action. Clearly also, this ethos must be global. It will not be sufficient to have a common ethos for Westerners or Africans or Asians, etc. The destruction, for example, of the ozone layer or the loosing of a destructive gene mutation by any one group will be disastrous for all (Swidler 1991, 2).

Swidler emphasizes the urgency of elaborating such a global ethos: "That the need for a global ethos is most urgent is becoming increasingly apparent to all; humankind no longer has the luxury of letting such an ethos slowly and haphazardly grow by itself. . . . It is vital that there be a conscious focusing of energy on such a development. Immediate action is necessary" (Swidler 1991, 2). Swidler has some practical suggestions on how such immediate action might be taken: the United Nations should strive to formulate a "Universal Declaration of Global Ethics," which would serve as a "minimal ethical standard for humankind to live up to, much as the UN's 1948 Universal Declaration of Human Rights" (Swidler 1991, 2).

The contents of this global ethics, as Küng and Swidler make clear, would have to be formulated in the actual dialogue of nations. Both of them, however, offer suggestions as to what some of these fundamental values, attitudes, or principles might be. They propose that nations and cultures can generally agree on something like the Golden Rule, on the necessity of resolving conflict nonviolently, of overcoming human suffering due to poverty, of protecting those who cannot protect themselves, of basing all socioeconomic development on an ethic of planetary or ecological responsibility (Küng 1991, 28-34, 39-40; Swidler 1991, 3). Admittedly, such objectives or principles are still quite general, but they are specific enough to provide an arena for moral discourse that can lead to moral decisions and common action.

Küng's and Swidler's proposal for a global ethics is inspiring and bold—but maybe also a little too hasty and unguarded. I think they are not sufficiently aware of the warnings that the postmodernists and postliberals (see the preceding chapter) raise for any project that thinks it can isolate or create some kind of common ground out of the diversity of cultural backyards. More seriously, they are not properly tuned to the danger that such international programs become dependent upon and therefore influenced by the financial support—which means the ideological concerns—of countries like Germany and the United States. Thus committees or programs working for a Declaration of Global Ethics have to guard constantly against being subtly or not-so-subtly coopted by the interests of the dominant nations.[27]

Such inadequacies or dangers, however, do not remove or reduce the necessity and the validity of what Küng and others are proposing. They are entirely justified, I believe, and therefore to be commended for proposing an *ethical dialogue* among nations that will lead to an *ethical consensus* of vision and action. Such a dialogue, rife with complexity and possibilities of exploitation though it be, can be endorsed and engaged in by all nations insofar as all nations and peoples have recognized—or are in the process of recognizing—three ethical insights regarding the world in which we live: 1) Human beings, as individuals and as communities, have a *global responsibility*—that is, a responsibility to promote the well-being and life of a threatened humanity and planet; 2) Such a responsibility cannot be *carried out separately* by individuals or individual communities. Disjointed, uncoordinated actions simply are not up to the job. Global responsibility must be communal responsibility; it must be a joint project; and 3) Such a joint, communal project is impossible—here Küng is right—without some kind of *communal agreement or consensus on ethical values*, visions, and guidelines for action. We need global dialogue toward a "global ethics" in order to carry out our global responsibility. I know, this sounds idealistic, grandiose, utopian. But it is also necessary.

The Role of Religions in Formulating a Global Ethic

Küng goes a step further in his proposal. He maintains that the kind of global ethics necessary for sustained global action cannot be achieved without the contribution of religion. And that means the *joint* contribution of religious communities. So, no global ethics without input from a global interreligious dialogue. That's quite a sweeping claim. He grounds it in what, I believe, is an essentially philosophical argument: morality needs a religious foundation.

According to Küng (and Immanuel Kant), when we feel a moral obligation—say, to help a disadvantaged, suffering person—especially when that obligation presses upon us absolutely and despite apparent disadvantages to ourselves, we cannot explain and own such an obligation merely through rational arguments. Our head can't explain what our heart feels. Philosophers and nonreligious persons "cannot give a reason for the absoluteness and universality of ethical obligation" (Küng 1991, 51). What can? Here enters an awareness that is available only through experiences that are classified as religious. The sense of unconditioned, meaningful obligation derives from the deeper sense of the Unconditioned itself. Moral action takes shape and makes its claim as part of a moral universe, which cannot be explained without reference to an absolute moral Ground.

> The categorical quality of ethical demand, the unconditioned nature of the ought, cannot be grounded by human beings, who are conditioned in many ways, but only by that which is unconditional: by an Absolute. . . . That can only be the ultimate, supreme reality, which while it cannot be proved rationally, can be

accepted in a rational trust—regardless of how it is named, understood, and interpreted in the different religions (Küng 1991, 53).

Küng's case that morality requires a religious rooting is, I think, philosophically debatable.[28] More seriously, I believe it vastly understates the role that religious experience and convictions can and do play in giving muscle and clarity to our ethical commitments. The religious experience that one witnesses in the followers of Buddha, Jesus, or Muhammad does not simply confirm an already implanted ethical imperative; rather, it inserts people into a larger story that offers them a new vision and the inspiration to pursue that vision. The story of one's own life becomes enlightened and empowered in this larger story. Religion, then, not only confirms but creates an ethical life; it not only reassures one's ethical commitments, it makes them glow with fire and compulsion. Therefore, if we cannot make a tight philosophical case that religious faith is *necessary* for ethics in general, or for a world ethic in particular, we can show that religion is powerfully *helpful*, *valuable*, *important* for the ideal of a world ethics. For many people, a religious faith makes a determinative difference in regard both to *what* they hold up as their ethical vision and to *how* they go about putting it into practice.

The vitally important, if not determinative, contribution of the religions to a program of global, ethical concern sifts down to two major ingredients: vision and energy.

In vastly different symbols and narratives, religions offer their followers a *vision of hope*—hope that they and their world can be different, transformed, better. Religion stands up to the world as it is, points a finger at its inadequacies (suffering, injustice, sin), and declares that the world and the human condition need not be that way because it *can* be different. Some would hold that all religious traditions are conceived in the confrontation with "negativities" and born in the conviction and determination that such negatives can be overcome (Haight 1990, 196; Haight 1994, 243-44). In chapter 7, I will attempt to show that the various religious visions seem to vibrate sympathetically in a hope that the world we experience to be one of self-seeking, conflictive individualism can be transformed into (or realized to be) one of compassionate, cooperative mutuality.

The religious conviction that this vision of hope can be realized is nourished and vitalized by the *energy* that religion instills to act on this conviction, to give ourselves to it, no matter what. All religion, in infinitely varied forms, brings about *metanoia,* internal change, enlightenment—the results of which are that we act differently and find ourselves doing things that previously seemed beyond both imagination and realization. We are energized to pursue the vision, and it is an energy that sustains us to keep acting even when success is limited or nonexistent, even when our own welfare or life are threatened in the effort.

Here, I believe, is the contribution of vision and energy that religions can—and must—make to formulating and then following a global ethics. Political analyst Richard Falk believes that such a contribution is not coming from the given sources of our postmodern awareness. He argues that in a postmodern world, in which our recognition of *deconstruction* has led to a fervent but often futile longing for *reconstruction*, politics will have to forge new alliances with religion, and religion will have to lend its ethical support to the political task. "A religious grounding deepens and extends struggle, enabling mass forms of resistance that incur risks and accept sacrifice, insist on an agenda of radical structuring, and yet does not abandon normative discipline" (Falk 1988, 387).[29]

Küng's proposal, though it may be much more complex than he realizes, and though it will have to be pursued more cautiously and in different forms than he suggests,[30] is one which, I believe, an ever greater number of persons and nations throughout the world can endorse. We need new forms of ethical cooperation which call for a new ethical dialogue and consensus, and for this, the religions—together, not separately—have a valuable role to play. How that role can call them to a new form of dialogue and cooperation is the concern of the next chapter.

5

GLOBAL RESPONSIBILITY: COMMON GROUND FOR INTERFAITH DIALOGUE

Giving Priority to Praxis and the Voice of Victims

The world realities we reviewed in the previous chapter serve as a counterweight to the concerns and warnings we heard in chapter 3. If, as the critics point out, diversity is a dominant fact in our postmodern world, well, so is responsibility. If our world consists of an irreducible variety of cultures and viewpoints, we have to face the fact that this same world consists, more than it ever has, of dangers and crises that are threatening the very life of the planet and humanity. We therefore have a responsibility to do something about these crises. These two realities—diversity and responsibility—must be affirmed and brought into some kind of moral balance and creative interplay. We cannot assume our responsibility to the world without affirming and engaging the diversity of perspectives about what this responsibility means. But also—and I would say, even more importantly—we cannot allow our affirmation of diversity to become a diversion from or an obstacle to assuming our responsibility.

THE DOMINANCE OF RESPONSIBILITY VS. THE DOMINANCE OF DIVERSITY

In this effort to balance cultural-religious diversity with global responsibility, we have to admit, I suggest, that the two do *not* weigh in equally. Responsibility presses upon us more urgently; responsibility is "more real," or more revealing of the real, than is diversity.[1] Therefore, while we try to be as respectful of diversity as we can, we must transform it from an obstacle into a resource for a genuinely diversified, communal, dialogical responsibility.

I have the impression that the defenders of diversity and the critics of the pluralist model whom we heard from previously would agree that although diversity is dominant, it cannot have the last word. After these critics announce the dominance of diversity, after they identify the walls of incommensurability, after they proclaim the impossibility of finding "one foundation" or a "common ground"—after all this, most of them go on to admit or insist, in differing ways, that *we still have to talk to each other.* What seems impossible must still be ventured. Most of the postmoderns or postliberals we have heard from would affirm that despite the incommensurabilities and lack of common ground, authentic conversation between utterly different cultures or religions is not only good but necessary. They still believe—or trust—that it *is* possible for members of different perspectives to somehow reach across the chasm of difference and particularity and understand each other. If we believe that there is life after death, we can and must also believe that there is dialogue after diversity.

In other words, the critics recognize that there must be a middle way between modernity and postmodernity—or as David Krieger puts it, "a middle way between the unfounded claim to universality characteristic of modernism and the postmodern celebration of pluralism" (Krieger 1990, 240). John Cobb, for all his wariness about proposing any common agendas or preconditions for dialogue, urges religions to seek a middle path between a monolithic "essentialism" and an uncontrollable "conceptual relativism" (Cobb 1990, 86). Even William Placher, after urging each religion to tend its own narrative garden, tries to "muddle through" a path between a "fideism" that keeps us captive in our own gardens and a relativistic natural theology that makes all gardens grow the same produce (Placher 1989, 61, 106-9). Cultural anthropologists, too, who have long been some of the most vocal proponents of total relativism, now are searching for a middle way that will be neither "the relativist abyss nor an absolute haven" (Mark Taylor 1991, 153; also Buck 1991). All these experts are seeking the necessary but elusive goal that Richard Bernstein envisioned for all postmoderns: to move "beyond objectivism and relativism" (Bernstein 1983).

Many are the ways in which the scholars affirm and illustrate the possibility of scaling the walls of incommensurability and enabling authentic conversation between diverse cultures or religions. All of them, it seems to me, never really prove their claims that diversity can become the stuff of dialogue; their cases consist mainly of assertion and trust, *assertion* that cross-cultural or intertextual dialogue is necessary and *trust* that it is possible.

Hans-Georg Gadamer, one of the most influential hermeneutical gurus of our age, recognizes in true postmodern fashion that all knowledge is interpretation and that all interpretation depends on our particular horizon. But he asserts that the different horizons—between text and interpreter, between one religion and another—can *fuse* in a *Horizontverschmelzung:* as my world of meaning melts into the totally different world of meaning of the text or another religion, both meanings are expanded. This fusion takes place through a process in which meaning manifests itself or springs from the text (or the other) and *claims* us. When we feel claimed, we know the fusion has occurred. But just what makes this possible Gadamer does not really say. There is some kind of unity to history or the human condition that renders "effective history" possible; one piece of history, contained in an alien text or alien culture, can affect, and therefore effect, another piece of history. For Gadamer, this unity of history is "given" in the fact that we actually *do* read other texts or communicate between cultures (Gadamer 1982; Guarino 1990, 225-28).[2]

What Gadamer intends with his fusion of horizons, David Tracy pursues with his "analogical imagination." Like so many of his Western contemporaries, Tracy is taken by, often overwhelmed by, diversity. To truly encounter an other, in all his or her difference, is to confront a mystery that is both fascinating and frightening—the *mysterium fascinosum et tremendum.* Refusing facile or subconscious attempts to domesticate the other (attempts he identifies in many pluralist theologies of religions), Tracy wants to allow the other to *be* other and thus to allow himself to be thoroughly fascinated and frightened. Precisely by doing this, communication takes place, the wall of incommensurability becomes a path of communicability. The other becomes, not the familiar and old friend, but the *possible* and the guide to new horizons. As we allow the conversation to take place, as we open ourselves to the genuine otherness of the other,

> we notice that to attend to the other as other, the different as different, is also to understand the different *as* possible. To recognize possibility is to sense some similarity to what we have already experienced or understood. But similarity here must be described as similarity-in-difference, that is, analogy. An imagination trained to that kind of encounter is an analogical imagination. . . . If we could converse with their texts [the texts of other cultures and religions], we also come to understand why otherness and difference rarely becomes sameness or even similarity. Otherness and difference can become, however, genuine possibility: the *as* other, the *as* different becomes the *as* possible (Tracy 1987a, 20-21).

Tracy seeks to bridge the gap of incommensurability between cultures in much the same way that Roman Catholic theologians have traditionally sought to bridge the gap of incomprehensibility between the Divine and the finite: through analogy. Theologians have affirmed—trusted—that there is an *analogia entis*, an analogy of being between God and ourselves by which we can find within ourselves and our nature that which can reflect or vibrate sympathetically with the infinitely other *(totaliter aliter)* nature of God. Tracy is trusting that there is an "analogy of culture" or "analogy of humanity" that makes it possible to make connections of understanding between cultural and religious perspectives that are utterly other *(totaliter aliter)* from our own. That such a ground for analogy exists cannot be established with certainty. It must be trusted and then felt in the act of dialogue.

Tracy's philosophical-hermeneutical description of how the analogical imagination works dovetails with Mark Kline Taylor's description of how cultural anthropologists are attempting to discover or create "intercultural liminality." This is the evasive, chimerical "common ground" between cultures or religions. It is not preexistent; rather, it must be discovered or created together, by both sides, and it must belong to both sides. In order for this to happen both sides must be genuinely open to each other in an attitude of questioning and searching, they must be ready and willing to change and move from where they are, and they must make the attempt to enter into each other's world as thoroughly as possible. With such attitudes and efforts, a "shaky common ground" can take shape. Even though it will always be "fragile and thin," even though it will always be "breaking down" and in need of "being patched up, and re-examined," it will provide a sufficient footing on which both sides can stand and genuinely hear, learn from, and challenge each other (Mark Taylor 1991, 153; Rabinow 1979).

The recognition that such common ground is possible was made also by the master of language whose ideas have been used by others to construct the linguistic or cultural walls of incommensurability. Ludwig Wittgenstein reminds us that every language is distinct and can be judged only by the rules of its own "game." The problem with so many efforts to carry on cross-cultural discourse or global conversation is that one language game is always hearing and judging the others according to its own rules. Each language is a world unto itself.

And yet Wittgenstein said more about these games and their worlds than is often recognized. Without developing the full consequences or demands of what he was saying, he held that language games are not "closed systems." In fact, in his later thinking he came to recognize the impossibility and the danger of private languages. If within every language game we have to function according to the rules of the game, we still have to be able to question and reform these rules. But that is not possible within our own game. The only possibility of testing the soundness, or "rationality," of our own language game is to open ourselves to the "other rationality" of another language game. Language games, for Wittgenstein, not only can but must overlap. He is affirming, or at least presupposing, some kind of common ground on which the overlapping or the conversation between games can take place.[3]

Wittgenstein's later insights and conclusions are confirmed by an analogy with ordinary experience: we can learn to speak other languages besides our mother tongue. Even though it is almost impossible to speak a foreign language as well as we speak our own, even though we can never really achieve in another language that total at-homeness which enables us to have an intimate feeling for the meaning of a word or a particular usage, still we can so steep ourselves in another language-world that we no longer have to translate our thoughts into it but can think and feel in and through it. We can reach a point where speaking and understanding a foreign language enables us to discover, and even feel at home, in a foreign culture. In fact, our contemporary world is such that to move in it comfortably and profitably, we have to be multilingual. "True catholicity and ecumenicity consist of one's ability to speak or at least understand languages other than one's own" (Pieris 1989, 299).[4] As we are not trapped in our languages, we are not trapped in our cultures and religions. Bridges of communication can be built over the chasms of diversity.

But what are these bridges made of? What makes it possible to build them? After all, as we saw in chapter 3, the critics of pluralism—those whom we might call the "postmodern fundamentalists"—make a pretty tight case for the impossibility of any foundation for genuine cross-cultural communication. Now we hear other postmoderns affirming the necessity and therefore the possibility of conversation. The *necessity* is evident. But how explain the *possibility*? As I suggested above, here is where they all seem to make an act of faith or trust. They believe or trust, at least implicitly, that there is something that provides "the conditions for the possibility" of genuine interreligious discourse.

If we would try to name or describe this "something," maybe Panikkar's notion of *Pneuma* or Spirit can provide a focus. After all his ardent reminders that *plurality* is a reality that can never be captured in a system of pluralism and that the incommensurable differences between religions cannot be boiled away, Panikkar affirms that there must be *something* that knits the spaces between religions into some kind of unity or connectedness. This something will transcend our reason. We will not be able to prove it or control it. Rather, we must trust it with a "cosmic confidence" and let it lead us where it will. We cannot "split human ultimate consciousness into incommunicable compartments. On the doctrinal and even intellectual level systems may be incompatible, religions may be incommensurable, but not by bread alone, not by *logos* alone, does Man live. There is also the Spirit enlivening Man—and the universe" (Panikkar 1990, 122). Anyone who attempts the complex task of interreligious or intercultural dialogue trusts in this Spirit—is enlivened by this Spirit—who broods over the abyss of diversity and makes it creative. In Tracy's terms, because of this Spirit, the utterly different *can* becomes the excitingly possible.

Besides affirming the necessity and possibility of reaching across differences in order to communicate, critics of the pluralist approach to other religions also proffer recommendations on how one should go about communicating. While they generally shy away from any suggestions of a common ground or preconditions for dialogue, they do lay out what appear to be certain ground rules or guidelines that are necessary for any kind of conversation to take place. Tracy offers a stripped-down version of these guidelines that is hard to argue with: unless we are ready to speak honestly, listen humbly, and be ready to change our minds, no real conversation will ever take place. Dialogue requires: "a) a self-respect (which includes, of course, a respect for, even a reverence for, one's own tradition or way); b) a self-exposure to the other as other; c) and a willingness to risk all in the questioning and inquiry that constitutes the dialogue itself" (Tracy 1990a, 73).

John Cobb, who soundly chides the pluralists for pre-establishing a normative content or process for dialogue, does admit that some kind of general, normative agreements have to be accepted before the dialogue begins. He suggests a "relatively objective norm" that all the participants can and must admit: they must recognize that the truth is larger than what they know through their own religion and that they might see something of this larger truth by conversing with others. Religious persons who are serious about dialogue must affirm "the belief that there is more truth and wisdom than one's own tradition has thus far attained" and therefore they must recognize "the ability of a tradition in faithfulness to its past to be enriched and transformed in its interaction with the other traditions." If they don't affirm this ability, they can't really dialogue (Cobb 1990, 86-87). Even William Placher, after insisting that we can't impose rules or set agendas for the dialogue, recognizes that unless the participants admit that they might be wrong and the other person right and that therefore there might be something important to learn from others, the conversation will go nowhere (Placher 1989, 147-48).

When one stands back from these various versions on the attitudes or conduct necessary for the task of conversing with the other, they sound quite similar to what Habermas would call the necessary components for "an ideal speech situation"—those attitudes or conditions that we all implicitly endorse every time we genuinely try to talk with someone else: that all have the possibility to speak their mind, that all be open to what is said to them, that all seek to convince by way of persuasion not violence. Agreement on such guidelines before the dialogue takes off may not constitute common ground for conversation, but without endorsing such guidelines, whatever common ground there might be will never be found.

GLOBAL RESPONSIBILITY: RAW MATERIAL FOR THE COMMON GROUND OF DIALOGUE

We have seen that there are many people who have been buffeted by the diverse and relativizing winds of postmodernity but who have resisted those winds and insisted on, or trusted in, the need and possibility of real dialogue. They have proposed their various ways of grounding that insistence and trust. A "fusion of horizons" can take place; we can rely on an "analogical imagination"; a "shaky common ground" between cultures can be discovered or created; we can learn to speak foreign cultural and religious languages; there is a universal Spirit or universal history that makes all this possible. Such people, chastened by postmodernity yet nonetheless committed to conversation, should, I suggest, find an important and perhaps decisive ally among those who, like myself, are proposing a pluralistic globally responsible model for interreligious dialogue.

A global responsibility for *soteria*—for the well-being of the threatened Earth and all its threatened tenants—can provide the framework, content, motivation, fiber, and directives for a dialogue among religions that would be able to navigate a course between the Scylla of one universal absolute truth and the Charybdis of many totally diverse truths. If people today are looking for something that will ground their trust in the possibility of authentic dialogue and that will direct their efforts to make this possibility a reality, I think they can find it here: a global responsibility for human and ecological well-being.

Because such a concern for *soteria* naturally and automatically creates *solidarity*, it will provide motivation and commitment for the task of interreligious conversation. As we saw above, both William Placher and John Cobb recognize that one of the basic prerequisites for any kind of interreligious exchange is that all religious persons admit the need for and value of dialogue. While Placher and Cobb find such a need to converse clearly and centrally present in Christian tradition, they hold that "other traditions will have their own set of reasons for engaging in such conversation" (Placher 1989, 117). But can they be so sure? Do *all* religions contain within their beliefs and worldview a recognition of the need to take up a conversation with other traditions? Do all Christians? Indications are to the contrary.[5]

Here is where global responsibility for human and ecological suffering can help. It can provide, from a common source outside the traditions, the motivation to stir up a globally recognized need for dialogue. Persons from all religious traditions *can* (I am not saying that at the moment they *do*) see, feel, and respond to the crises facing our Earth; such recognition *can* lead to the conclusion that the religions must respond to these crises. A sense of solidarity is an invitation to interaction and conversation.

Global solidarity and responsibility can also aid participants in interreligious discourse in resolving one of the most delicate questions they face: where to begin. Or, as Heidegger would put it, how to enter the hermeneutical circle. If every act of understanding is a hermeneutical circle of question and answer, preunderstanding and new data, your horizon and our horizon, then on which side of the circle do we take up our conversation. How can we start without privileging our side over yours? Here again, I think a soteriocentric or globally responsible approach to dialogue can help. Our starting point is not inherent in the unique perspective of any one tradition; that is, the dialogue does not begin by looking *within* the traditions, but rather by looking *beyond* them to the fires of human and planetary suffering that burn all around us.

It is the voices of the millions who for the most part stand outside the official precincts of religion and who have not attended the international interreligious conferences who are calling religious persons together and beckoning them to act and speak together in order to heal the wounds of the world. It is these suffering victims who, as I will suggest below, have the "first" or the "privileged" voice in the dialogue and who thus prevent any pre-established religious position from having a privileged place. It is the victims of this world who start the hermeneutical circle turning.

They also keep it turning by providing it with a defined and regulative content (not in a way that excludes other content but that provides an approach to whatever other content will and must be part of the conversation.) *Soteria* or global responsibility for eco-human well-being can provide clear and engaging substance to Gadamer's rather abstract notions of "effective history" that enables differing horizons to fuse; the history that the hermeneutical task is effecting is a history of our struggles to preserve and foster and defend life—and thus to enable history itself to continue. It is precisely here, in our shared grappling with concrete, practical questions of poverty, injustice, and ecological policy that our horizons can be effectively and profitably fused. And as I will try to show in chapter 8, if our religious horizons can fuse on these practical issues, they can more likely fuse on other more theoretical or credal issues.

In Tracy's method of using an analogical imagination in the dialogue, the shared commitment to eco-human liberation and well-being can provide, as it were, the raw material for the analogical imagination. Here, in the mutual effort to respond to victims and overcome the injustice that is torturing them, we can more readily and practically discover how the other's very different notion of peace or well-being can become a possibility for us. Our shared concern for the suffering of victims sensitizes us to a variety of different ways of responding to their victimization; we are open to many other ways, for our driving concern is not to defend our way but to remove their suffering. Thus, for example, in a soteriocentric dialogue our analogical imagination can be stretched and enriched as we witness how the utterly *different* Buddhist notion of emptiness can become a *possible* way of having compassion with and responding to the victimized planet. Responding to and stimulated by the realities of suffering, the analogical imagination can be more fruitful than we ever imagined!

A soteriocentric global responsibility can also give more clarity and power to Panikkar's image of the *Pneuma* or Spirit in whom we have to have "cosmic confidence" if we are to believe that our ineradicable differences are the stuff out of which we can and must build communication rather than separation. We can see signals of this Spirit and feel the power of its presence in the way our global crises are calling us to a global responsibility. Our confidence that this Spirit is real and universal is not blind or empirically unverifiable. Rather, we can hear this Spirit speak with a voice that transcends our cultural differences and calls us to join hands as we both affirm our own particularities and open ourselves to those of others in an effort to remove the human and ecological suffering that confronts all of us. The universality of suffering has given a universal voice to the Spirit. Because we can hear the urgings of the Spirit in the cries of the victims, we can say, "I know in whom I trust" (2 Tim 1:12).

But to announce a universal Spirit who makes dialogue possible is not to announce a universal foundation that all the participants can sight and affirm. The Spirit is not the bringer of absolute, universal truths, which can then be made concrete as the unchanging foundation for our shared search for truth. In proposing the metaphor of a universal Spirit calling us through the victims of the world, I am not proposing a single truth that we can all finally come to or a universal foundation on which we can all build a new world order. Rather, I am suggesting a *process*, a way of being and acting together by which a community of communication can be initiated and maintained, but never completed. It is a process in which we respond to problems or concerns we can all identify as universal; these will then provide us with the inspiration and the data out of which we can act and talk together and so form a greater community.

The truth that we will discover will not be a propositional statement that we will all affirm; rather, it will be a way of being together in which we find that we can indeed move between each other's worlds in a effort to enhance the well-being of all the world. In David Krieger's words and images, "'true' in this sense is less something that we know than something that we do. Truth is thus to be ascribed less to a proposition, no matter how great the consensus supporting it, than to a form of life, a global form of life, which we may characterize as 'cos-motheandric' solidarity" (Krieger 1990, 231). This solidarity links cosmos, humanity, and divinity in a mutuality and interconnectedness in which we are all responsible for each other's well-being. Such a solidarity can be affirmed only on the basis of some kind of a belief or trust in a universal Spirit—or in something that establishes our identity, yet connects us in unity, and calls us to care for each other. The Spirit then is not a foundation but an interrelatedness that fosters unity through particularity, in shared compassion.

THE ESSENTIAL PLACE OF LIBERATIVE PRACTICE IN INTERFAITH DIALOGUE

To call for a soteriocentric interreligious dialogue that will have global responsibility for its context, starting point, and goal is to propose a form of dialogue in which *praxis* plays an integral role. As chapter 8 will lay out more clearly, I am urging a dialogue in which persons from different religious views will not be able to speak together religiously or theologically unless they are also (even, first of all) acting together practically for the well-being of this world. Certainly such an emphasis on praxis does not exclude other essential ingredients in our efforts to speak to and understand each other—such as study, prayer, ritual sharing. But it *is* saying that if these other ingredients are not mixed with the praxis of global responsibility, then they will be ineffective or not as effective as they can be.

THE REBIRTH OF PRACTICAL PHILOSOPHY

To propose praxis as an essential, even primary, component for dialogue is, I believe, nothing new or strange. It reflects an epistemology—a model for the way we know—that in the West is both ancient and newly refurbished. Aristotle recognized it, and contemporary philosophers are reappropriating it. Truth, especially truth that matters deeply to us, is always practical; it is tied together with our struggles to live our lives, to figure out how we want to live and why. Our search for, our recognition of, and our verification of truth therefore are stimulated and guided by these practical concerns. According to Aristotle, our most sensitive antenna for knowing the truth is not a keen intelligence but *phronesis*—the practical wisdom or prudence to know something is "true" because of the "good" effects it will produce in the living of life; such practical wisdom, evidently, is rooted and nurtured by a moral life. If the "true" is the "good," then the true will be what the good person does. Truth then is perceived and perceivable by the practical wisdom of the good person.[6]

This recognition of practical wisdom or practical thinking is a common thread, often in different colors or textures, running through the efforts of contemporary philosophers who struggle with the question of how we come to know the true and the good. Thus, there has been in recent times a "rebirth" of practical philosophy.

> It is a consequence of taking to their logical conclusion the theories of Hans-Georg Gadamer, Paul Ricoeur, and Jürgen Habermas; the pragmatism of William James and John Dewey; and the neo-pragmatism of Richard Bernstein and Richard Rorty. . . . These thinkers, in spite of their differences, share one fundamental idea, that is, that practical thinking is the center of human thinking and that theoretical and technical thinking are abstraction from practical thinking (Browning 1991, 8).[7]

The key role played by practical thinking or concern for praxis in Gadamer's hermeneutics is often overlooked. Following Aristotle's lead, Gadamer recognizes that "application," or the concern for the practical, real-life significance of truth, is not something that is possible only after we have come to a clear idea of what is true. Rather, it is there from the beginning. "Application is neither a subsequent nor a merely occasional part of the phenomenon of understanding, but co-determines it as a whole from the beginning" (Gadamer 1982, 289). In other words, the process of understanding is guided from the beginning by the questions of what we are doing or what we should be doing; every such "doing" or "praxis" is "theory-laden"—it has or needs some kind of theory or philosophical explanation. The search for truth is the dance between these two realities—*praxis* and the *theory* that it demands or clarifies. In fact, the tight definition of praxis always includes theory: we act, which requires us to think about our action, which leads to further action, which demands further reflection. The two go together, but it is the action which holds a certain primacy. Thus, "application to practice is not an act that follows understanding. It guides the interpretive process from the beginning, often in subtle, overlooked ways" (Browning 1991, 39).

Praxis is coming to be recognized as playing a pivotal role in dealing with the postmodern dilemma often described as the "Cartesian anxiety." This anxiety results from, first, feeling the need to base our lives on truth and, second, the postmodern recognition that all truth is relative and therefore questionable. We find ourselves caught in a vicious hermeneutical circle; the interpretation never ends, for every time we affirm something as true we are reminded by the postmodern albatross on our shoulder that our affirmation is only a limited cultural construct or that there are other constructs that we should also check out, or that our view is possibly manipulative of others. And so the circle continues to turn.

Practical wisdom can help us, not to abandon the circle, but to stop it long enough to make real affirmations. Practical thinking tells us what we already sense—that truth is related to acting, that acting leads us to truth. More simply and practically, there are decisions to be made, there are projects to be carried out, there are realities in our life and in our world that must be addressed and changed. These practical demands will enable us to sense or feel the truths or "theory" necessary to ground and guide these actions. Praxis, therefore, both demands that we make judgments of truth and then provides light and awareness for making those judgments. The truth that praxis enables us to affirm will not be an absolute, definitive truth that will get us off the hermeneutical circle; no, we will recognize that it is relative, singular, dangerous. And yet, we will also know that we can affirm it and act on it—with an affirmation and action that are as firm as they are also open to eventual criticism and clarification.[8]

I do not think we are oversimplifying these insights from practical philosophy when we boil them down to what may sound like a cliché: we know truth by doing it. The presupposition for this bald statement is one that most people, I trust, would want to affirm: truth, by its very nature, is transformative. This is especially the case with religious truth. Truth is not meant to remain only in our heads, nor is it the product solely of our heads. Truth must be lived, which means that our hands, along with our heads, have something to do with the realization and discovery of what is true. Thus, the statement of Gustavo Gutiérrez might not be as extreme as it at first sounds: "Knowledge is bound up with transformation. We come to know history . . . in the process of transforming it and ourselves. As Vico put it long ago, we really know only what we ourselves do" (quoted in Gutiérrez 1979, 18-19). Or in Dermot Lane's paraphrasing: "Knowledge and truth are given to us in the experience of changing the world. . . . Knowledge and truth are presented as bound up with action and performance" (Lane 1984, 2-3).[9]

Therefore, when theologians or philosophers of religion extol the mystical nature of truth—that is, that we know truth in the very self-authenticating *manifestation* of it to us in particular experiences or in our encounter with classical texts—they should not forget that truth is also known in the *transformation* of ourselves and the world. If there is manifestation without transformation, we have cause to be suspicious of our truth. Indeed, what practical philosophers and liberation theologians are suggesting is that it is primarily in *practical transformation* that *mystical manifestation* can most reliably be identified.[10]

If praxis or practical thinking is integral to our search for, discovery of, and evaluation of truth, then what we have been exploring in this chapter comes down to the recognition that there is a common praxis or a common content for practical thinking available to all religious people, on the basis of which they can carry on their search for truth together. The common content for this shared praxis is, as we have urged, the needless suffering that is devastating humanity and the planet. If religious persons can together confront the crises facing humankind, if they can take these practical issues as the starting point for their reflection and action, if they can engage in a shared project of transforming structures of injustice and ecological exploitation, then they will have new opportunities not only for interpreting their own traditions intra-textually (as the postliberals would hold), but also "cross-textually," in a way in which they can communicate and interpret their texts and traditions for each other. I am suggesting that the hermeneutical role that praxis is playing in contemporary Christian theology might also be the role it can play in interreligious dialogue. In the following statement by Dermot Lane, instead of "theological reflection" read "interreligious dialogue": "This prereflective commitment to the praxis of liberation is something that precedes theological reflection, becomes the object of theological reflection, and judges theological reflection" (Lane 1991, 34-35).

Admittedly, in appealing to practical philosophy and to liberation theology and to the place of *phronesis* or practical wisdom in knowing the truth, I am appealing to Western and Christian tradition and experience. I do that knowingly, but I also do it expectantly, in the hope that what is suggested here will be acceptable to other traditions and will ring true with their experience and texts. My personal and academic suspicions are that for all religions and all religious persons, truth is practical and transformative. We know the truth of Buddha, Jesus, Muhammad in the living of it, and in the living of it our lives and world are changed.

THE WORLD AS IT IS DOES NOT ALLOW DIALOGUE

I would like to suggest a further, even more practical reason why liberative or transformative praxis must play a pivotal role in interreligious dialogue: the world as it is does not allow for authentic dialogue between persons of differing cultures and religions; unless this world is transformed, we cannot truly speak with each other. The reasoning behind these sweeping statements has to do with what we have already referred to as the "ideal speech situation" necessary for any conversation. For any genuine exchange between different persons to take place, all persons or groups have to have full and free access to the table of dialogue; all must be heard and be taken seriously. In the words of Vatican II, for dialogue to work, it must be *"par cum pari"*— equal with equal (*Decree on Ecumenism*, no. 9). Gregory Baum states it more practically: "The conversation involving two or more participants is only fruitful if there exists a certain equality of power among them" (Baum 1986, 92).

But that's the problem. Given the inequalities in our world today and the way those inequalities are created and sustained by the structures of economic, political, and military power, there is no common table of discourse in our world where all have ready access, where each voice counts as much as the others, where each participant feels free and unthreatened.

> Dialogue demands equality. Honest conversation is not possible between partners that have an unequal access to power. For the power modifies his speech so that his superior position remains protected; and the powerless is too vulnerable to be perfectly honest. Inequality of economic, political and cultural power is the great barrier that keeps humanity divided (Baum 1994, 13).

I dare say that those who cannot see this may themselves be captured and blinded by the same structures that bind both oppressed and oppressors; such people are in need of being "liberated" with help from the oppressed.

What is needed, therefore, at least as a propaedeutic to dialogue, is a shared effort to create ideal speech situations in the world or in our own neighborhoods. And that means praxis—acting together. Naturally, this is not simply a process of first this, then that—first liberation, then conversation. And yet, a conscious, active awareness of the inequalities in our society and of the way some people are not taken as seriously as others must be part of our dialogical mentality; otherwise, our conversations will be seriously lamed. Therefore, a concern for liberation and justice must be an animating current in all dialogue; the dialogue itself must be a means of changing structures of suppression or exclusion and so of allowing everyone to have a voice.

When we approach the other in dialogue, it is not sufficient to affirm and open ourselves to *difference*. Besides affirming that difference, we must also affirm his or her *freedom and dignity*. And if such freedom and dignity are lacking, then we must act to make them possible. To delight in difference but to be unconcerned about dignity is to be only half-human in reaching out to the other.

> The valuation of difference, which leads to sustained encounter and knowledge of the other, then, entails a praxis of resistance against anything that disempowers the other. . . . Liberating praxis therefore is not just a practice of "the good" in face of intolerable evil; it is also a necessary condition for affirming something "true" about the other's cultural difference (Mark Taylor 1991, 159-60).

Present in the desire to communicate and the effort to create universal communication is a political élan supporting the struggle for emancipation. Liberation is the precondition of dialogue and mutual understanding (Baum 1994, 13).

How can I respect and affirm someone else's otherness if that person is not allowed to be what he or she wills to be? Thus, another condition for the possibility of genuine discourse with an other whose identity is dominated by structures of socioeconomic or racial or gender oppressions is first to resist actively and act to overcome the domination. "Celebrating difference" and "resisting domination," therefore, become integral elements in the same act of discourse; dialogue demands a commitment both to difference and to emancipation. "This brings the struggle for liberation and justice and the struggle for knowledge amid relativity much closer to one another than we often think" (Mark Taylor 1991, 164; see also 157-59).

THE PRIVILEGED VOICE OF VICTIMS IN INTERFAITH DIALOGUE

Closely connected with the centrality of liberative praxis in the kind of dialogue I am proposing is the central role that the *victims themselves* must play in this dialogue. Again, I am taking another focal element of liberation theology and proposing it as something that persons of other traditions can recognize as essential and helpful in the task of interpreting our traditions to each other. Within the dialogue, the victims and those who are suffering injustice—which includes those who speak for the suffering Earth and animals—have a "hermeneutical privilege." This privilege is valuable and necessary for two reasons: in order to have authentic dialogue, and in order to prevent dialogue from being coopted by ideology.

IN ORDER TO HAVE AUTHENTIC DIALOGUE
If interfaith dialogue is going to be more than an academic exchange of information about our differing traditions, it will have to adopt some kind of correlational tactic, analogous to the method of correlation proposed for Christian theology; partners in the dialogue will have to speak not only about their respective religious traditions but also about how those traditions are being understood and need to be re-understood in our contemporary world. Our dialogue, in other words, will have to correlate our traditions with our experience of ourselves and the world.

But our postmodern world presents us with a triangle of realities and demands; if we neglect any one of the three, we are not authentically living in or responding to the world. It is the triangle—or as Mark

Kline Taylor calls it, the trilemma—of having to be faithful to our own *identity* and tradition, of having to be genuinely open to the *plurality* of other traditions, and of having to *resist the domination* that afflicts our world (Mark Taylor 1990, chap. 2). All too often our efforts to affirm our tradition or to connect it with the plurality of other traditions have been carried out without an awareness of the injustice and domination causing so much human and ecological suffering in this world. Much too blithely we have spoken about "common human experience" or the "human condition" or "humankind" without an awareness that the condition or experience of most humans in our world is one of domination and suffering.

Therefore, in the mix of identity-plurality-resistance that should make up the content and dynamic of interreligious encounter, we must award a primacy to our resistance against domination and to our concern for suffering, both human and ecological. This is a primacy based not on any kind of ontological priority of suffering over plurality or identity but, rather, a primacy grounded in *predominance*—that is, the simple but horrible fact that there is so much suffering in the world and that it so surrounds and threatens all of us. Therefore, we must accord a privilege or primacy to the voices of these who are suffering; otherwise, our dialogue is not representative of or responsive to the world as it is. Rebecca Chopp has stated this with clarity and passion:

> To be poor is the representative human experience; only by standing with the poor and by focusing our interpretative lens through the poor may we, too, adequately experience and interpret history (Chopp 1986, 48).

> Only by standing with those who suffer—the poor and the oppressed, the living and the dead—shall we see the reality of human existence (Chopp 1986, 151, see also 122).

When we of the "established" classes or "developed" nations or "mainline" religions begin to listen to and take seriously the reality and the witness of the countless victims of domination, something both frightening and marvelous can happen to us. Similar to the awakening of a Zen experience, we find ourselves viewing the world differently. Our usual way of seeing ourselves and our nation and the community of nations is "interrupted," maybe "subverted," perhaps even "ruptured." We become "enlightened" to the reality of domination and injustice and how this pervades so much of who we are as citizens, consumers, and religious beings (Tracy 1987a, 71-72). As it is communicated to us through the bodies and voices of victims, "suffering . . . ruptures our categories, our experiences, our history; suffering demands a new paradigm of interpreting existence and Christian [also religious] witness. . . . This question, the question of suffering, functions . . . to demand new interpretations and understandings, new ways of conceiving and answering questions, new ways of ordering questions and concerns" (Chopp 1986, 120). This presence of the victims and their suffering in the interfaith dialogue will both rupture and reroute the conversation.

But I also venture to suggest that the reality of suffering communicated in the presence of victims can provide the interfaith dialogue with as "common" a ground as can be found in our pluralistic, multiperspectival, relative world. This is due not only to the *universality* of suffering—the fact that it is found everywhere in similar forms and with similar causes—but also because of its *immediacy* to our experience. Yes, as we have recognized, all experience is interpreted. But if there is any experience where the gap between the experience and the interpretation is as short or quick as it can be, it is suffering. While interpretations about the cause or the remedy of suffering will abound, the sense of suffering as a reality that calls us to some kind of resistance is, I dare say, almost given in the very experience of suffering itself.

I want to express this claim as cautiously as possible, but I do not want to equivocate. Suffering has a universality and immediacy that makes it the most suitable, and necessary, site for establishing common ground for interreligious encounter. Francis Schüssler Fiorenza is also cautious but clear in advancing the same claim: "Suffering brings us to the bedrock of human existence and cuts through the hermeneutical circle" (Fiorenza 1991, 135). It cuts through the circle by bringing the endless movement of interpretations to a temporary stop and enabling us to make truth claims that call us to action. Our interpretations of suffering are close enough to its reality to warrant our common action and resistance.

> Suffering is, so to speak, at the seam between interpretation and reality. Although it is not without interpretation and one's horizon deeply affects one's suffering, our bodily existence is affected in such a way that gives suffering a "mediated immediacy." Language about the "hermeneutical privilege of the oppressed" is justified to the extent that it points to this immediacy (Fiorenza 1991, 135).

And this immediacy is available to all cultures and all religions. The filter of interpretation, in other words, has a harder time coming up with divergent perspectives on the reality of suffering; suffering is too immediate to be suffocated under the pillow of a hundred interpretations. Fiorenza can therefore go on to claim a "negative universality" for suffering:

It moves from a negative experience, a contrast experience, to a more universal challenge. Suffering often produces a claim with a negative universality, which positive social and political programs do not have. The presence of suffering challenges structures and programs so that often, although there is disagreement over how to ameliorate suffering, agreement exists about the evil of suffering (Fiorenza 1991, 136).

We might say that suffering can serve as a "negative common ground" for interfaith dialogue; on this negative common ground the dialogue, nourished by the contributions of the victims of suffering, can elaborate more positive common ground of shared ethical commitments and actions.[11]

Because the reality of suffering must be part of the content of interfaith dialogue, the presence of sufferers or victims in the dialogue is necessary. This necessity can also be argued from the very nature of the hermeneutical task as understood by Western "masters of interpretation" such as Gadamer and Habermas. If there are no absolute foundations for truth, if truth is not given to us on an untarnished and untarnishable silver platter that is beyond all particular interpretations, if all we have are our differing, culturally limited perspectives on truth— then the path to truth can be only that of a broad conversation among our various perspectives. The conversation must be as inclusive, as broad as possible. We need, as the specialists tell us, a "wide reflective equilibrium" between as many viewpoints as possible. In the words of Charles S. Pierce, this requires a trusting to

the multitude and variety of arguments rather than to the conclusiveness of any one. Its reasoning should not form a chain which is no stronger than its weakest link . . . but a cable whose fibers may be ever so slender, provided they are sufficiently numerous and intimately connected (quoted in Mark Taylor 1990, 63).

The recognition that our conversation, if it is going to be reasonable and effective, has to be *inclusive* leads us to the equally important but unsettling recognition that it has been *exclusive*. I trust that for most of us it is an undeniable, though often neglected reality that a vast assemblage of human beings has either been excluded or not able to participate in the conversations and deliberations taking place in our academies, halls of governments, and churches. These people have been called the "wretched of the Earth," the "underbelly of history." They are the people who, for a variety of reasons, have not counted or who simply have not been thought about, or if they have been thought about, either have been excluded or not taken seriously. Theirs have

been the "defeated knowledges." If they have been the victims of economic injustice, they have also suffered from "cognitive injustice."

> Just as society has its victims, so discourse has those who are
> excluded from discourse. The "other" is not simply the other of
> signification but also represents those whose voices are not present
> within the tradition, are not present within the discourse inter-
> preting the tradition, and have no voice in interpreting their iden-
> tity and self-determination (Fiorenza 1991, 136).

If our conversations-toward-truth must include the genuinely other
in order to be successful, then we have to be clear on where we find
these others; the other is not only the culturally and religiously different, but also the social-politically excluded. In fact, I am suggesting
that these others-through-exclusion have a primacy of inclusion, that
they have a special voice in the conversation, that their experiences
and witness have a "hermeneutical privilege" in searching for the true
and the good.

This primacy is based, first of all, on the simple and unsettling fact
that they have been excluded for so long; now "cognitive justice" must
be done. The conversation is radically maimed, and our rationality is
crucially deprived, if the voices of the voiceless are not brought into
the conversation and given a first hearing. Only so can our conversation be sufficiently broad to be serious.

> Recognizing the voices of those absent from the conversation—
> often voiceless because of death, persistent hunger, or systematic
> distortion of their social and political life—is *the crucial way* by
> which the fullest breadth of conversation can occur, a breadth
> needed for the truth of reasoning to occur and be sustained (Mark
> Taylor 1990, 64, emphasis mine).

The voices of the excluded victims—including those who can speak
for the victimized Earth—have a privileged place in the discourse, therefore, not only because they are so different but because their difference
is challenging and, as stated earlier, can rupture and reroute our awareness. "It becomes necessary to make the community of discourse as
inclusive as possible. One cannot simply appeal to experiential evidence as the warrant for truth; one has to bring the interpretation of
conflicting paradigms and traditions into dialogue and conversation
with the neglected and often repressed voices of others" (Fiorenza 1991,
137). Paradoxically, in order to get "the whole picture" into our pur-
view, we have to look at one of the most insignificant or unnoticed
parts of that picture. While all particulars are necessary to make up
the whole, there are certain particulars that serve as keys for unlock-

ing the pattern of the whole. As the Indian theologian S. Arokiasamy puts it: "The moral commitment to the dignity of every human person (*sarvodaya*) is mediated by the critical option for the last and the least (*antyodaya*)" (Arokiasamy 1987, 547).

The privileged place of the excluded, oppressed and suffering can also be argued, as suggested above, from the massiveness of this suffering and from the fact that it represents the experience of one-fourth of the human race. Such vast numbers need to be represented, somehow, in interreligious discourse. But it is not just the massiveness of this experience that privileges it. Also the content or the *quality* of the experience of unjust suffering and exclusion is such that it enables the victims to know things that the established can never know by themselves. This has to do with the victims' greater experience of negativity. Though negativity is certainly part of the life of every mortal, the oppressed experience it both in a quantity and quality that make their experience different from that of the economically well-off and the politically powerful. Victims, therefore, have "an insight born of radical negativity not experienced by the more elite, centrist groups" (Mark Taylor 1990, 65). More concretely, the oppressed can offer insights into social and political realities that those in the center simply cannot have. Victims have "learned more about the culture of the powerful than the powerful know about those they subjugate" (Mark Taylor 1990, 65). Such insights about the negativity of human existence and about our established culture are not just "interesting"; they are urgently essential if our conversations are going to have anything to do with addressing the ills of the world.

But just what is meant in assigning a hermeneutical privilege or a priority to the voices of the voiceless? Certainly, I am not suggesting that theirs are the only voices to be heard. A central concern for overcoming oppression and suffering does not deny, indeed it demands, that our conversations and efforts be and remain *plural*. The voices of the affluent, of the middle class, of mystics and artists must be heard together with the voices of the oppressed. Also, the priority and privilege given to victims does not mean that their views or claims are simply and always normative. Victims can also have distorted interpretations of their reality and dangerous plans to remedy it. There are no absolutely privileged seats, no final gavels, around the table of dialogue.

Attempting to describe the privileged place of victims, I suggest that it means that no conversation can be considered complete unless the voices of the suffering have been heard. Also, these voices must be heard, not only "first" (as David Tracy admits), but also "constantly" (Mark Taylor 1990, 66) and seriously. To take them seriously, to be able to listen to them, we will have to recognize that it will often be difficult to hear and to understand them and that we will have to overcome initial reactions of mistrust and avoidance. Speaking from his privileged place in academia, Tracy acknowledges this:

> All the victims of our discourses and our history have begun to discover their own discourses in ways that our discourse finds difficult to hear, much less listen to. Their voices can seem strident and uncivil—in a word, other. And they are. We have all begun to sense the terror of that otherness. But only by beginning to listen to those other voices may we also begin to hear the otherness within our own discourse and within ourselves. What we might then begin to hear above our own chatter, are possibilities we have never dared to dream (Tracy 1987a, 79).

Mark Kline Taylor offers a balanced though demanding statement of the privileged place victims play in enabling our dialogues to be truthful and transformative; his words, I believe, can be understood and affirmed by followers of all religious traditions:

> This intensification of inclusiveness is not just the patently human and humane thing to do . . . it is also the widening of the conversation so that truth might be experienced. Truth need not be uncritically viewed as the sole possession of the oppressed; but the latter do have hermeneutical privilege as the ones who are necessary for intensifying the dialogical conditions within which truth may be disclosed. . . . For pluralists dwelling liminally in dialogical community, recognizing the privilege of the oppressed voices is no mere option. It is necessary to their experience of truth. And if an inclusive, dialogical approach to truth is ultimately all we have, then the privilege of the oppressed is essential indeed (Mark Taylor 1986, 48-49).

IN ORDER TO PREVENT THE COOPTATION OF DIALOGUE "UNDER THE MCDONALD'S ARCH"

In our examination of the critics of pluralism in chapter 3, I think the most unsettling warnings came from those who used a political analysis of language and of discourse to show how proponents of pluralistic, all-inclusive, open-ended dialogue can be, and have been, coopted by the economic-political powers that be. The cutting content of their admonitions is quite straightforward: our interpretations, our language, do not simply *limit* our own grasp of truth, they can also *oppress* the ability of others to assert and live their own truths. Language is not only limiting; it is also self-serving of one group and oppressive of others. David Tracy has taken these admonitions seriously:

Every discourse bears within itself the anonymous and repressed actuality of highly particular arrangements of power and knowledge. Every discourse, by operating under certain assumptions, necessarily excludes other assumptions. Above all, our discourses exclude those others who might disrupt the established hierarchies or challenge the prevailing hegemony of power (Tracy 1987a, 79).

We might easily miss the deeper, all-pervasive content of what is here being recognized about language and interpretation. What we did not face in the immediate past (modernity) and what has become frighteningly clear today (one of the postmodern insights) is that such exclusion of others, such power-serving and self-serving acts, are not just an occasional "misuse" of language that can be removed much as we clear a frog out of our voice. Rather, we are speaking about "systemic distortions," pervasive tendencies within all use of language—a disease in our vocal cords![12] We cannot interpret and we cannot speak without hearing—and often responding to—the siren call of ideology, the inclination to use our "truth" for our own power or dominance:

Ideologies are unconscious but systemically functioning attitudes, values, and beliefs produced by and in the material conditions of all uses of language, all analyses of truth, and all claims to knowledge. . . . Ideologies are carried in and by the very language we use to know any reality at all" (Tracy 1987a, 77).[13]

As the critics in chapter 3 uncomfortably pointed out, these systemic distortions of language can become systemic distortions of dialogue.

Practitioners of interreligious dialogue who are aware of the worm of ideology in all their language and in all their dialogues try to respond by announcing the necessity of "hermeneutical suspicion." Our first step is always to cast a suspicious eye on our knowledge and programs and calls to dialogue—to face and ferret out where it is that our truth claims are power claims. Here, precisely here, is where the voices of the oppressed must play a privileged role in the dialogue. Without their voices, we cannot carry out a hermeneutical suspicion of our own tradition or of our own contribution to the dialogue. Alone, by ourselves, we are self-serving. Aloysius Pieris, who practices dialogue in the midst of Asia's suffering and oppression, speaks clearly and to the point: "The people who can truly purify a religion of communalist ideology are not the theologians or the religious hierarchs, but only the conscienticized victims of that ideology" (Pieris 1989, 308-9).[14] Only with the help of the oppressed can the oppressors face their own oppression.

John O'Brien can therefore conclude his careful examination of the role the option for the poor should play in theological method by asserting that the hermeneutical privilege of the poor must be given a "relative normative status." And the reason for this is not that the poor and the suffering can claim any kind of a moral superiority or a normative grasp of reality; rather, their privilege is a "therapeutic" one—necessary to diagnose and remedy our ideological distortions. What O'Brien states about "theological method" can, I suggest, be affirmed about "dialogical method" by members of all religions:

> Thus, the hermeneutical privilege of the option for the poor in theological method is not an ethical privilege, nor even an analytical one in terms of theory or praxis considered in themselves. Its privilege lies in the fact that it is the *irreplaceable* perspective from which theology can critically correct its methodological self-awareness. In essence, it does this by exercising a therapeutic role, whereby it creates conditions for theologians to come to an awareness of the practical roots of their models of discourse (O'Brien 1992, 159, see 150-61).

We can prevent—or at least defend ourselves against—the cooptation of dialogue by making sure that in *all* of our interfaith encounters the poor and suffering and those caring for the suffering Earth will be *present* and will have a *privileged place* in our conversations. In other words, we will recognize and insist not simply that "each voice contributes equally" but that some of us have a more urgent and a more helpful word to speak—namely, those who in the past have not spoken and who in the present are victims. If dialogue must always be *"par cum pari"* (equal with equal), there are also those who are *"primi inter pares"* (first among equals). In assigning a privileged role to the poor, we will have to move out from "under the McDonald's arch."

But if the suffering and the victimized are truly to exercise a hermeneutical privilege in our dialogues, it will not be sufficient for those with the power to simply *listen* to them; we will also have to *act* with and for them. Understanding what the suffering are saying, grasping the structures of oppression that keep them in bondage and that afflict our planet, is not simply a matter of "theory." It can come only from praxis. Here we link up with what was said above about the essential, prior role of practical reasoning in all understanding. As we shall examine further in chapter 8, our present-day world demands that those who engage in dialogue engage in some kind of liberative praxis. Without such praxis, we will not be able to "hear" the voices of the privileged victims, and our dialogue will be distorted or coopted.

What is demanded . . . is an alternative practice, that is, gestures and acts of solidarity with movements that wrestle against those unjust structures. Such a practice would modify the consciousness of the participants and affect the reading of their own religious tradition. . . . a new practice [is] an indispensable dimension of the quest for theological [dialogical] truth (Baum 1991, 13).

•

Throughout the last two chapters my approach to what we are calling a liberative or practical interfaith dialogue has been basically ethical. I have invoked "global responsibility" and made exhortative appeals to the moral imperative of responding to the sufferings of humanity and the Earth. And indeed, I feel deeply that such ethical responsibilities weigh on all engaged in dialogue; to eschew these responsibilities is, I fear, to corrupt dialogue.

But I hope that the ethical, earnest tones of what we have been exploring do not obscure the exciting promise of a globally responsible, liberative, interreligious dialogue. What we do out of moral responsibility can be enjoyable and invigorating and surprising. From what this chapter contains, and especially from what I will be taking up in the following chapters, I hope it will be clear that the moral *obligation* of making global responsibility an essential part of dialogue can become a hermeneutical *opportunity* that will add dynamism and new light to our efforts to understand each other's religious traditions. The suffering poor and the suffering Earth can provide the religions with "hermeneutical links" and with new eyes and ears with which to see and understand each other. By affording a centrality to liberative praxis and by recognizing a privileged voice for the oppressed, we religious persons have the opportunity, I believe, of understanding ourselves as never before. My expectations are that just as Christian theology has been revitalized and redirected by the decision to interpret the gospel through the eyes and struggles of the oppressed, so interfaith dialogue will be renewed and revisioned through a shared praxis of global responsibility that will ground and direct the dialogue.

But before we begin our explorations of how such a liberative dialogue can work, I want to take up a question that is unavoidable in the light of this chapter: Is global responsibility, or a liberative dialogue, something that all religions would want to or could endorse? Is it an "ethical imperative" that *all* can feel? Or is it, once again, another example of Christians pushing their own agenda? In the words of some of the critics we heard from earlier: "About *whose justice*—or *whose liberation*—are we talking?"

6

WHOSE JUSTICE? WHOSE LIBERATION?

Directing the Many Salvations to the One World

Is global responsibility and a dialogue that gives priority to liberating people and planet from unnecessary suffering something that all religious traditions can affirm? Or is such a soteriocentric approach to dialogue once again another camouflaged maneuver to control the discourse with a Christian or a Western agenda? When we dramatically invoke such terms as *global responsibility* or *liberation* or *"soteria"* as the context or goal or priority for the dialogue, can we be sure that these notions will be understood in basically the same way by all the participants in the conversation? So we have to ask, whose justice, or whose *soteria*, are we talking about anyway? At this point, many contemporaries imbued with a postmodern consciousness will chime in with some very pertinent questions: isn't this whole proposal for a globally responsible or liberation-centered dialogue just another attempt (at best naive, at worst calculating) to fashion the golden calf of an absolute norm or foundation before which believers of all traditions must now bow? Doesn't justice or liberation now become the absolute, final norm for all truth—all the more idolatrous and pernicious when it is *my* understanding of justice or liberation that functions as the final norm?

These are the questions we shall try to take seriously in this chapter. Because they are such important and complex questions, answers can be neither neat nor final; the responses I offer are more dialogical explorations than philosophical or theological arguments. In the first part of this chapter, I will try to show that the very nature of religion and religious experience, as we view it in its many-splendored forms, indicates that all (or at least most) religious traditions have the capability, if not the established record, of affirming global responsibility as ground and goal for interreligious encounters. As I will argue in part 2, this capability is all the more enhanced today when our Earth, in both its sufferings and its newly discovered mysteries, is becoming a locus for shared religious experience and vision.

GLOBAL RESPONSIBILITY—CAN ALL RELIGIONS ENDORSE IT?

The core proposal of this book is that all religions take on global responsibility as a central ingredient in their efforts to understand themselves and other religious communities. I've been urging the *necessity* of a soteriocentric or globally responsible model for dialogue. But is the necessity a *possibility?* That's what we're investigating in this chapter, for if what I am claiming as necessary is not possible, then the project is either a pipe dream or a manipulative maneuver. Thus I hope to show that from a religious phenomenology—that is, from what religion looks like and feels like in its authoritative scriptures and witnesses—it appears that all religious traditions, in various ways and degrees, do contain the capacity, if not the need, to promote the *soteria* or well-being of humanity and the Earth.

Before I start finding it everywhere, I'd better add some further clarity to just what is meant by *soteria* or eco-human well-being. The first thing to recognize is that the term, in itself, is not very clear. I'm proposing it not because it has a well-defined content that can be recognized immediately by persons from all cultures or religions; rather, I'm using the notion of *soteria* or eco-human well-being as a heuristic device, a notion that tells us enough to enable us to discover even more. *Soteria* therefore can serve the interreligious dialogue as a beacon that points us in a particular direction and then provides enough light to discover what there is to find as we move forward, together, in that direction. The direction is clearly indicated; what we will find, as each of us pulls out his or her particular flashlight to illumine the path, remains to be seen.

What I intend by *soteria* is similar to what Hans Küng has in mind when he proposes the *humanum* as the ground and criterion for religious conversations. For Küng, the *humanum* can provide the raw materials of a global ethics; he intends

> a universally ethical, truly ecumenical basic criterion which is based on the *humanum*, that which is truly human, and specifically on human dignity and the basic values which are subordinate to it. . . . So that would be morally good which allows human life to succeed and prosper in the long term in its individual and social dimensions: what enables the best possible development of men and women at all levels (including the levels of drives and feelings) and in all their dimensions (including their relationship to society and nature) (Küng 1991, 90).

Though Küng may be a little too optimistic about reaching consensus as to just what really would promote "the best possible development of men and women," still he points the global conversation in the right direction. To his *humanum*, however, I would like to add the *cosmicum*, that is, the ecological. If we focus only on the human, we can too easily slip into the anthropocentrism that has condoned the misuse and the murder of nonhuman life and life-support systems. Küng himself recognizes that humanity's well-being is inextricably tied to the Earth's well-being; a global ethics, then, must be rooted in a concern for the human *and* the ecological.

But if we are speaking within the arena of religious discourse, if we are asking what religions can contribute to the formulation of a global ethics, then I would urge that the symbol of *soteria* or salvation be used to image and indicate that which can serve as the common concern and criteria for an interreligious dialogue. I propose the symbol of *soteria* because the religious contribution to meeting the needs and crises of our world is different from that of the humanist or secularist insofar as it draws on something that cannot simply be reduced to or identified with humanity or the material order. In their incredibly various ways, the religions recognize and proclaim that if we are going to be able to promote the greater life of the *humanum* and the *cosmicum*, we will have to acknowledge or wake up to the *divinum* that animates or transcends the human and the cosmic. The religions aim to bring about some kind of an enlightenment, transformation, or linkage by which humans and the world discover a vision and a power that they did not experience beforehand. In Panikkar's language, religions remind us that reality is *theanthropocosmic*—a unity in distinction between the divine, the human, and the cosmic. To realize and promote this reality is to enhance the well-being of all—and that is salvation or *soteria*.[1] *Soteria,* therefore, is the well-being of humans and planet that results from feeling and living the immanent-transcendent Mystery (Panikkar 1993).

However one may understand the divine or the transcendent component of *soteria*, when I urge that multiple religious traditions can endorse a global responsibility for the *soteria* of the world, I am making both a positive and negative assertion. Positively, I believe that representatives of all the religions can find within their own traditions a desire to promote human and ecological well-being and visions of how that might be done; this is where we witness a grand diversity among the religions. The negative side of my assertion provides the motivation to embrace this diversity and the hope that it will lead to unity: some followers of all religious traditions, precisely because of what their religious experience and teachings tell them, will feel called or impelled to speak a resolute "no" to the sufferings, human and ecological, that torment our world. This is where, I believe, we witness unison among the religions—in their determination to resist, to re-move, to re-form the causes of such widespread suffering.

That this must be done is (or can be) the common call of all reli-gious traditions; how it can be done calls forth the diversity of the traditions. This commonly recognized necessity is the ground of hope that the diversity is indeed complementary rather than contradictory— a source of cooperation rather than of division.

ALL RELIGIONS *CAN* TAKE ON A GLOBAL RESPONSIBILITY

From both an observational or down-to-Earth view of the world of religions and from the witness of academics who blend observation with theoretical analysis, religion in all its exuberant forms has to do with changing this world for the better. Yes, religion has to do with God or the Ultimate, and with life after death, and with altering or expanding our consciousness—but it also has to do with confronting, specifying, and then repairing what is wrong in the way human beings live their lives together in this world. Whether we call it evil or igno-rance or incompleteness, there's something wrong or incomplete or mistaken with the state of the world as it is, and religion wants to do something about it. In some way, every religion wants to make better or heal or avoid what isn't right or working in society and the world. In other words, some form of what we might call *soteria* or salvation is envisioned and sought after. Gordon Kaufman, a Westerner, puts it this way: "Every religious tradition promises salvation in some form or other, i.e., promises true human fulfillment, or at least rescue from the pit into which we humans have fallen. Every religious tradition thus implicitly invokes a human or humane criterion to justify its ex-istence and its claims" (Kaufman 1981, 197-99).[2]

Speaking from an Asian perspective, and from a broad knowledge of Asian religions, Aloysius Pieris is even more explicit. He believes that all religions take their origins from some kind of a primordial liberative experience. The symbol of a "liberating Spirit," Pieris feels, is appropriate. Differing religions can be seen as various languages which give polyphonic voice to this liberating Spirit: "Each faith is a language of liberation, that is to say, a specific way in which the Spirit speaks and executes its redemptive intention in a given cosmic-human context" (Pieris 1989, 297). Pieris recognizes that this Spirit as symbol is open to a broad interpretation: "The 'Spirit' could be understood as the human or the divine Spirit. In non-theistic religions such as Bud-dhism, Jainism, or Taoism, it stands for the *given* human potentiality to speak, to seek, and find total human liberation" (Pieris 1989, 297). He also points out what is so evident in the religious world today— that what is primordial can become lost and therefore have to be re-trieved: "Religion is *primordially* a liberation movement, if seen in the context of its origin, though it does tend *subsequently* to be domesticated by various ideologies; that is to say, religion ever remains *potentially* liberative, even if *actually* subservient to non-liberative structures" (Pieris 1989, 296).

The multireligious participants in a Conference of World Religions that met in Colombo, Sri Lanka, in August of 1987 also recognized a "primordial liberative experience" within their various Asian traditions: "All religions have a Primordial Liberative Experience, a memory of that experience which is perpetuated in rituals, rites, and traditions, and a process of interpreting the Primordial Experience which makes the religion relevant to the challenges of contemporary society." Examples of this Experience they found in the Exodus narrative, Jesus' proclamation of the Kingdom of God, the Meccan experience, Buddha's leaving the palace for a life of homelessness ("Opting for the Poor" 1988, 76). At a similar meeting in the same year in New Delhi, sponsored by EATWOT and drawing together spokespersons from multiple traditions, there was another common recognition that the energy of liberation can be mined from all the given traditions of Asia. This energy springs from a common source that the conference called "wholeness." It is an ideal that cannot be confined only to the future, or to another world, or to the interiority of human consciousness but must, in some way, also touch and transform this world. "All religions . . . aspire after a 'wholeness' (*shalom, sarvam*) in which the limitation of everyday life will be overcome, its tensions resolved, its brokenness mended. It is this search for wholeness that makes a religion liberative. For the ultimate goal towards which it strives breaks in upon our experienced world, inviting us to judge and transcend it" (EATWOT 1988, 154).

Religion, therefore, calls on what is more than human (at least the human as we now experience it) in order to transform or liberate the human. In the words of V. Harvey, "When we call something religious we ordinarily mean a perspective expressing a dominating interest in certain universal and elemental features of human existence as those features *bear on the human desire for liberation and authentic existence*" (quoted in Tracy 1990a, 54, emphasis mine). To transform the human context will mean, generally, to oppose or resist the forces that stand in the way of change or newness. Thus David Tracy, ever cautious about general statements regarding religions, can recognize:

Above all, the religions are exercises in resistance. Whether seen as Utopian visions or believed in as revelations of Ultimate Reality, the religions reveal various possibilities for human freedom. . . . When not domesticated as sacred canopies for the status quo nor wasted by their own self-contradictory grasps at power, the religions live by resisting. The chief resistance of religions is to more of the same (Tracy 1987a, 84).

Therefore, according to Raimon Panikkar, to even raise the question whether religion has anything to do with changing this world is to fall victim to a dualism that runs contrary to the ideals of most, if not all, religions. It is a dualism between God and the world, or religion and politics, that stems, not from the content of religious experience, but from external efforts (especially in the West) to spiritualize or privatize religion and thus dilute its political power (Panikkar 1983, 52). Gandhi, then, was right when he announced: "I can say without the slightest hesitation and yet in all humility that those who say that religion has nothing to do with politics do not know what religion means" (Gandhi 1957, 504). Or maybe they know very well what it means but seek to deny or stifle the power of religion.

THE ETHICAL WELLSPRING OF RELIGION

The claim we have been making that religious experience bears an integral link with eco-human wholeness is really a reflection of the broader claim that religion and morality are essentially bonded. Theologians rightly warn against a reduction of religion to morality; such a reduction portrays religion or faith as nothing but pretty stories to dress up and justify the way one chooses to act or to construct society. Such a reduction is a gross simplification, but the danger of reduction should not blur the reality of relationship. In fact, I would tend to agree with those who hold that to sever the bonds between ethics and religion is to pull the plug on authentic religion. In a sense, ethics is the lifeblood, or better, the wellspring, of religious experience and religious life.

In simpler terms, there is a vital link between behaving and believing—with a genetic priority (which doesn't mean an ontological priority) going to behaving. In the effort and struggle to figure out, and then live out, how we can best "behave" in this world, we find ourselves in contact with what can be called the Sacred. In trying to determine how we can live in a way that will be *peace-filled* for ourselves and for our society, in seeking to ground the moral feelings that we have about what makes for a *wholesome* life and society, and especially in trying to be faithful to living such a life when it becomes tangled in cross-purposes and seems to hurt our momentary self-interests—in all this we can find ourselves, or feel ourselves—part of or touched by a larger Mystery or Process. In order to *behave* in ways consistent with such classical statements as the Ten Commandments or the Eightfold Path, we find ourselves *believing* or having to believe in that which grounds and animates and makes possible such a way of behaving. I'm not talking about a logical or intellectual process; the link between behaving and believing, or between morality and religion is experiential—yes, mystical. What I am suggesting cannot be proven, but I think it can be discovered by looking carefully at one's own moral experience (which presupposes that one is trying to live a moral life).

What we are considering here is but the theological or religious application of what we discussed in the previous chapter under the rubric of "the rebirth of practical philosophy": "Truth, especially truth that really matters to us, is always practical; it is tied together with our struggles to live our lives, to figure out how we want to live and why. Our search for, our recognition of, and our verification for truth therefore is stimulated and guided by these practical concerns" (see page 82 above). If this is so about the general way we search for and come to affirm what is true about life, it is also and especially so about the way we come to know the truth about the Sacred or the Great Mystery. Religious experience, one can say, is born in and nourished by moral experience. In the effort of trying to realize "right action" and "right speech" and "right profession," the Sacred is touched by or revealed to us. We know the Way by following the Way, by feeling the resonance or sympathetic vibration between our life's way and the Way. This is why the great religious figures of history have insisted on "following" (Jesus) or "practicing" (Buddha) or "letting-go" (Lao Tzu) or "obeying" (Moses and Muhammad) in order to *know* the truth of their messages.

From the perspective of how this world came to be and how it is sustained, we will give *worship* or ritual a priority in religious life, for in liturgy we recognize the priority of the Divine over the finite. But from the perspective of how we come to know the Divine, we will give the priority to ethics, for it is in the struggle for "right living" that we come to know and feel what we are to worship and confess. Again, orthopraxis (right acting) has a practical priority over orthodoxy (right confessing). Daniel Maguire makes this point with a clarity that borders on overstatement: "Morality is primary; religion, God-talk and theology derive from and explain this foundational moral reverence. That which does not enhance human and terrestrial good is in no sense sacred. Religion can take root only in genuine moral awareness. The foundational moral experience is the foundation of religious experience" (Maguire 1993, 39). Again, this is not to reduce God-talk to morality; rather it is to insist that all God-talk has an ethical birthplace.

Therefore there can be a danger, both for philosophers and participants in religious dialogue, to take up God-talk or religious language too quickly. To try to understand our differing God-talks, we should first "walk the talk" together; we should first try to walk together in the "moral commons" which is the birthplace for the differing ways of talking of the Sacred. "Scholars who seek out the 'common essence' of religions regularly miss the moral commons on which religions meet.

This comes from introducing God-talk too early, or from seeing *derivative* explanations of the experience of the Sacred as *foundational*. Moral-talk is logically and epistemologically prior to God-talk" (Maguire 1993, 40).

If moral-talk plays a foundational or genetic role in all God-talk, if religious people have to "walk the talk" before they can really talk (to themselves or to others), if it is in our concerns for right living in this world that we come to sense or know the Mystery of this world, then I do not think that global responsibility will be considered foreign matter or an imposed topic in the encounter of religions. Global responsibility is a contemporary term for right living. If to be religious means to live (or, try to live) a moral life, then to be religious means to live a globally responsible life. To be globally irresponsible is tantamount to being irreligious. I trust that significant numbers from all the world's religious communities can affirm this.

THE MYSTICAL-PROPHETIC DIPOLARITY OF ALL RELIGIONS

Naturally, in claiming that all religions are world-oriented and bear an energy that can change the Earth, I am not saying that this is all they contain or that this is their only concern. Besides this world-transforming energy, there is another category of power that is just as important. Scholars have spoken of both the *prophetic* and the *mystical* powers of religion. But they have often used these categories to divide religions vertically, one from the other. Thus they have distinguished the Abrahamic religions of the West from the Indic religions of the East. According to this division, Judaism, Christianity, and Islam are prophetic religions involved in the world; Hinduism and Buddhism are mystical religions calling their followers to disengage from the world and explore their own inner depths (Küng 1986a, 174-77). What I am suggesting, however, and here I am following the lead of scholars who know Asian religions much more deeply that I do,[3] is that these differences between the prophetic and the mystical do not run vertically between religions but horizontally within them.

In each religious tradition we can find both mystical and prophetic experiences and ideals. And the line between them is not so much a wall that separates but a bond that unites and mutually nourishes. So we must admit and encourage the mystical-prophetic dipolarity that vibrates and flows back and forth within our own and all religious traditions. This dipolar energy of religion animates a twofold project, each aspect essential, each calling to and dependent on the other: to transform both the within and the without, to alter inner consciousness and social consciousness, to bring about peace of the heart and peace in the world, stirring the individual to an earnest spiritual praxis and also to a bold political praxis.

The dynamic and call of this mystical-prophetic dipolarity is what tells Christians that they can love God only when they are loving their neighbor, or Buddhists that wisdom is not possible without compassion, or Hindus that the yoga of knowledge or devotion must be combined with the yoga of action in the world. Neither the mystical nor the prophetic is more fundamental, more important; each calls to and has its existence in the other.

Certainly the dipolarity or the balance will be maintained differently within different religions, or within different denominations of the same religion, or at different stages within an individual's personal journey. Frequently—all too frequently—the balance is not maintained. Then we have mystics whose spirituality becomes self-indulgent, insensitive, or irresponsible; or we have prophets whose actions become self-serving, intolerant, or violent. When the mutual feedback system between the mystical and the prophetic within a religion breaks down, the religion becomes either an opium to avoid the world or an indult to exploit it.

Aloysius Pieris, on the basis of his studies of both Asian and Western spiritualities, sees this dipolarity as a mix between *gnosis* and *agape*—wisdom and love. While it is true that Buddhism has given a focal position to *gnosis* or "liberative knowledge" and Christianity has done the same with *agape* or "redemptive love," both ingredients have been—and must be—present in both traditions:

> What must be borne in mind is that both gnosis and agape are *necessary* precisely because each in itself is *inadequate* as a medium, not only for experiencing but also for expressing our intimate moments with the Ultimate Source of Liberation. They are, in other words, complementary idioms that need each other to mediate the self-transcending experience called "salvation." Any valid spirituality, Buddhist or Christian, as the history of religions attests, does retain both poles of religious experience— namely, the gnostic and the agapeic (Pieris 1988b, 111).

Recognizing this same polarity or unity in difference, David Tracy calls for a mystical-prophetic approach to the study of religion and to interreligious dialogue. He sees religious experience as a pendulum swinging back and forth between manifestation and proclamation: between, on the one hand, the overpowering and empowering mystical experience in which we bump against the limits of our existence and then find ourselves beyond those limits, and, on the other hand, the restive and explosive prophetic experience in which we confront the hopelessness of the human situation and then find ourselves called to resist and transform it. "The new hermeneutical practice become living theology [he could add, interreligious dialogue] is best described as 'mystical-pro-phetic.' The hyphen is what compels my interest" (Tracy 1990b, 904)[4]

So today, "in all the major religious traditions, there is a search for new ways to unite those mystical and prophetic trajectories" (Tracy 1990a, 100). In an age in which we are horrifyingly aware of human and ecological sufferings, and of the devastating dangers seeded within this suffering, every religion is being challenged to rediscover the pro-phetic power of its tradition and to unite it to the mystical. The pro-phetic power is there, perhaps beneath a mystical overgrowth, per-haps hidden in narratives and symbols which spoke to a different age and which are in need of revisioning for this age. If this power is not tapped or refurbished, the religious tradition will lose its ability to speak to and engage the many persons today who feel the prophetic challenge of our suffering world.

This challenge to resurrect the prophetic and reunite it with the mystical is especially clear and pressing in a country like India. There is a growing awareness among those engaged in the Hindu-Christian dialogue that the conversations of the past, which explored the mysti-cal traditions of Brahmanic Hinduism and of monastic Christianity, are insufficient for the India of today. These traditions are in urgent need of being balanced and enriched by an equally intense dialogue about the prophetic impulse of popular, Bhakti traditions and Chris-tian liberation theology (Wilfred 1992). From his vantage point on the Indian subcontinent, T. K. John states this challenge for all religions:

> In and through dialogue among religions a transition from the traditional narrow focus upon religious values and experience to a vision of a new world order and of possible collaboration among religions to bring this about seems to be emerging as the voca-tion of religions. In other words, the worth of a religion is ex-pected to be in terms of its potential to make a substantial contri-bution to the collective effort of people to bring about a new way of living (John 1989, 46-47).

Today, the mystical energies of religions throughout the world are inspiring—as inspire they must—prophetic calls to bring about a truly "new way of living" in this world. And so they are making a globally responsible dialogue among religions possible and promising.

A Shared Diagnosis and Remedy for the Human Predicament

But we can go a step further. As we survey the vast terrain of reli-gious history and experience, we can identify, I suggest, not only an undercurrent of concern for transforming this world, not only a dipolar flow between mystical and prophetic experience, but also an analogously similar *diagnosis* of what is wrong with our world and a *prescription* for what must be done to fix it. The operative word in that last sentence is "analogously." I am not suggesting that all the religions of the world are really proposing identical or essentially similar soteriologies—programs for how the world and we humans are to be "saved." Rather, my experience in interreligious dialogue and social action (an experience shared by many others I suspect) has been that when one plunges into the vast diversity of religious analyses of what's wrong with the human predicament and how it might be set aright, when one wrestles with the very real and powerful *differences* in these analyses and programs, one finds that the differences one is wrestling with turn out, for the most part, to be friends rather than foes. As David Tracy would describe it, after a Christian is thoroughly perplexed, frightened, and frustrated by the difference, say, between the Buddhist insistence that only the present moment is real and the Christian affirmation of a eschatological future, it can happen that this difference reveals itself not as an utter contradiction but as a genuinely (albeit unsettling) *new possibility.*[5]

More specifically, it seems that the analogous similarities between the differing religious views of humanity's fundamental problems take shape around the issues of the *nature of the self* and how the self can be understood or experienced differently. According to the myths, doctrines, and ethical admonitions of most religions, humankind's woes flow from a pool of disunity and dis-ease fed by a false notion of the self; to remedy the situation we must dry up or replace the contents of that pool. The problem, in other words, has to do with the way we understand and live out our sense of who we are. Either we understand ourselves incorrectly, or our selves, in their present state, are corrupted or incomplete. In either case something has to happen to the self, either notionally or really. We have to either understand or experience our selves differently; or our selves have to be infused with new or healing energies. Whether the fix is cognitional from within or ontological from without, it has to lead to a different way of acting in and of relating to the world around us.

So the problem recognized analogously by different religions has to do with separation or selfishness; and the remedy has to do with relationship and mutuality. In many different ways, most (all?) religions seek to convert the energies of one's self from a centripetal to a centrifugal movement and so to broaden the focus of concern from not only me or us (egocentricity) to Other or others (altruism). We have to find ourselves outside of ourselves; to realize who we are, we have to experience ourselves as part of something that is greater than what we understand ourselves to be right now. John Hick, using Western terminology, seeks to summarize all this by describing the analogously common goal of most religions as a shift from self-centeredness to Reality-centeredness (Hick 1989, 299-309).[6]

Admittedly, as feminist critics point out, such ideals of a selfless self have been fashioned by patriarchal religions; that is, by men whose primary "sin" has been an inflated self that abuses other selves, and not by women whose primary "sin" has been a deflated self that allows itself to be abused by others.[7] Thus, what I am proposing here as a diagnosis common to all religions requires a feminist hermeneutics of suspicion that will assure that the selfless self does not become the enslaved or subordinated self (Saiving 1979; Plaskow 1980, 51-94). Still, I think feminists would agree that the "saved self" or new self is one that is sustained in the web of mutuality rather than in the cell of egocentricity (Keller, 1986).[8]

So it appears to many purveyors of religious history that every religion, at least in its vision if not in its practice, seeks to place its followers in contact with a Reality or to provide them with an exercise whereby they can break the bonds of ego-clinging in order to embrace and be part of and so be transformed by that which is other. In so doing, the religions seek to promote "that limitlessly better quality of human existence which comes about in the transition from self-centeredness to Reality-centeredness" (Hick 1983, 467, 464-65).

Sallie King appeals to this transformed self in her response to the postmodern argument that because all experience is socially constructed, it is impossible to know if there is a common mystical core within all religions (Katz 1978). She grants that it is impossible to get at this core by simply comparing what the different traditions *say* about it; a comparative analysis of "Nirvana" or "God" or "Tao" or "Dharma" gives us no assurance that they all have a common reference point. But if we look at how persons *feel* and especially at how they *act* after they have undergone some form of mystical experience, we can talk about the likelihood of something in common, even though we can never define it. All mystical experience, it would seem, brings about a new sense of self, or what King calls a new "existential grounding" for the self. There is a "radical transformation of the experiential self sense, a radical axiological and existential grounding" (King 1988, 275). The self finds itself rooted and animated in something that is broader than the ego-self, something that connects it with other selves and with the world.[9]

Here a "reality check" is necessary. To hold up the transformation of the hidebound self into the other-oriented self as a diagnosis and remedy common to most religions is to hover in the realm of religious ideals—what the religions generally preach. It is not their historical track record—what they often do. Such discrepancies, persistent throughout religious history, must be admitted. There is within every religious tradition what Paul Tillich has called "the demonic"—the possibility, indeed the propensity, to be turned in the direction opposite the other-oriented vision of its founder or original witness. Within the heart of every religious body there dwells not only Dr. Jekyll but Mr. Hyde, not only "the culture of utopian peaceableness," but also the "culture of violence and war" (Boulding 1986, 502). In our postmodern consciousness, we realize, perhaps more clearly than ever, that the religions' vision of self-less love and liberation has been turned into the ideological weapons of dominance and conflict. And so I make this claim for a common diagnosis with a sense of realism and sorrow, and with a conviction of the need constantly to call religions to live up to their ideals.

ARE THERE UNWORLDLY OR ANTI-WORLDLY RELIGIONS?

Some might object that even though there may be such a common self-transforming message within all the religious traditions of the world, this does not necessarily mean that all religions would endorse a globally responsible dialogue. Those who urge such a dialogue are talking about liberation and transformation in and of *this* world. Are there not religions that envision a transformation of the self without any kind of transformation of society or the world? Isn't the transformation that some religions speak of either purely internal, within the individual, or eschatological, to be realized in a world after death? Along the same lines, don't we find that many religions, far from calling for transformation of the social structures, have provided adamantine support for keeping things the way they are?

One can only answer "yes" to these questions. It is also undeniable that in the symbolism and doctrine of many religious traditions, certainly including that of Christianity, there is an apparent flight from the world and from responsibility for it. This flight is directed either to an eschatological vision of our true home in the next life or to a retreat into a spiritual-mystical center insulated from the sufferings of this vale of tears. I think there are two basic and very different reasons for such otherworldliness: religions run from the world because they are being used as a means to keep the world as it is, *or* because they are serving as a diversionary device to subvert the world. In the first case, the flight from the world is real; in the second, it is a camouflage for eventual engagement in the world.

The first manner of fleeing from the world is all too evident in the history of every religious tradition. Otherworldly theologies are often the product of what we have already spoken of as the ideological abuse of religion—when the power packed in religious narrative and symbolism is appropriated by the dominant classes in order to maintain their own control and economic advantage. Rosemary Radford Ruether has called this the "sacred canopy" form of religion (giving a further political twist to Peter Berger's original use of the term) (Berger 1969):

> "Sacred canopy theology" assumes that the dominant social or-
> der is founded by God [or grounded in the Dharma]. Its social

relationships are given by God as the order of creation. The king-ruler was seen as the divinely appointed representative of God on earth. To obey the king-ruler was to obey God. The social hierarchy of man and woman, ruling class over subject classes, the election of a privileged nation to rule other nations as God's people—all this is seen as "natural," divinely given, and expression of God's will (Ruether 1990, 73).[10]

Today, thanks to our so-called postmodern awareness, with its origins in the emancipatory battle cries of the Enlightenment and Marxist critique, we are more alert than ever to how much all religions—without exception—can be, and have been, comfortably ensconced under the sacred canopy. Often this coopting or diffusing of the liberative-prophetic content of religious experience takes place through a manipulation of the mystical element—more precisely, by breaking the balance between the mystical and the prophetic. The mystical experience becomes a safe haven and a comfortable escape from the cruelties of poverty or warfare; thus, religion assuages the pain but it does not heal the wound. An example of this is pointed out by historians of the Hindu traditions when they describe how the powerful blending of the mystical and prophetic in the Bhagavad Gita was soon diluted by the controlling classes; thus the populist, caste-critical message of Lord Krishna for all his devotees became privatized into a personal, individualized devotion (Fernandes 1992).

Christians, too, amid all their justified pride about the prophetic critique and the preferential option for the poor that is inherent in the message of Jesus (and in his Jewish background), have to remind themselves that it certainly wasn't always so. All too often, and for all too long, the prophetic point of Jesus' message was blunted or packed away amid the comforts of the sacred canopy. For medieval Christians, for example, the world was viewed as a place of suffering and bondage which could not really be changed; the bondage was not accidental or reversible. Rather, it was a warning to humans not to try to change too much by their own efforts. The role of the church was to remind people of this and, working with princes and authorities, to make the human sojourn here on Earth as tolerable as possible. "Prior to the Enlightenment and the French Revolution, the last thing that the church thought was that the central vocation of the Christian was to overturn the existing social order" (Burrows 1992, 131-32). The sacred canopy stretches wide. Yet, insofar as it distorts the liberating message to be found in each tradition, it can be dismantled. And that, as this book is arguing, is what can happen, must happen, and is happening among many of the world's religions today.

I have described the other reason for the world-fleeing phenomenon among some religious traditions as tactical—as a holding or a diversionary device. Marjorie Hewitt Suchocki offers an insightful and helpful perspective on why and how such devices are employed. She holds that the otherworldly views that we do find among religious communities may not have been part of the earliest stages of religious history. Rather, they arose, as it were, as coping mechanisms when a religious community found itself in what seemed to be a hopeless situation—when, for instance, the socioeconomic structures, often defended by political-military powers, or the devastating forces of nature made it seem impossible to realize the religion's vision of salvation in this world. The focus was then shifted to a better life "beyond"; such otherworldly adaptations often became frozen into belief systems.

Suchocki suggests that the qualities of the "other worldly realm" or of the "mystical-monastic community" are what the particular tradition originally intended for *this* world, and it is these visions that can form the basis or starting point for a multifaith dialogue that directs its concerns toward global responsibility.

> It is possible that each religion's deepest valuation of what physical existence should be lies, not in its coping with the exigencies of history, but in its projection of the ideal. By looking at each religion's vision of the ultimately perfect mode of existence for its saints or holy ones, whether that vision be otherworldly or not, we might find some echo of unanimity on the value of freedom from suffering.
>
> Using justice as a norm means that the primary visions within each religion of what societal life should be in a "perfect" world is a source of judgment that can be used internally within each religion to judge its present societal forms of justice (Suchocki 1987, 159, see 156-60).

Suchocki's case is bolstered by the sociologists and historians of religions who have revealed how the apparently otherworldly images of popular religion are often packed with hidden, transformative power for this world. James Cone argues that this was true of black slaves in the United States; he reminds us that "black eschatology" is not "merely compensatory" and that "language about God and heaven does not always lead to passivity" (Cone 1975, 159).

> Liberation as a future event is not simply *other*worldly but is the divine future that breaks into their social existence, bestowing wholeness in the present situation of pain and suffering, and enabling black people to know that the existing state of oppression contradicts their real humanity as defined by God's future. . . . The statement about heaven becomes revolutionary judgment against the system of oppression. The future becomes a present

reality in the slave's consciousness, enabling him to struggle against the white system of injustice (Cone 1975, 159-60).

What looks like religious opium can well be revolutionary dynamite. However we understand the de facto, undeniable otherworldliness of many religious communities—as either exploitative corruption or tactical maneuvers—the conclusion of this brief analysis is that such efforts either to escape from or conform to what is happening in the world is not inherent in what a religion is, or can be, all about. Otherworldly spiritualities can be—I am saying, should be—combined with or transformed into this-worldly engagements with the eco-human crises facing our generation. All religions have at least the potential for global responsibility.

THE EARTH: COMMON GROUND
FOR ENCOUNTERING THE SACRED

So far, our proposal has been that differing religions can and must share a global responsibility for eco-human well-being and justice. Even though many contemporary scholars are extremely uneasy with such a universal proposal (and would want to cut it up into socially constructed pieces), I think that global responsibility enables religious persons to take an even bolder step. In this section I would like to explain why I, along with others (whom I shall be referring to), am convinced that the kind of global responsibility we have been talking about can be not only a shared commitment but also a *shared context for religious experience*, feeding and reforming our different religious traditions. Global responsibility is not only an *ethical task* that all religious persons can take up together; it can also be a source of *shared experiences* by which believers from different communities can better understand and communicate each other's religious stories and language.

Let me try to clarify what I mean, without watering it down. The challenges that face us in our suffering brothers and sisters and in our suffering planet are calls to all religious persons to be not only *prophets* transforming the system but also to be *mystics* plumbing the depths of the Divine or the Real. To feel global responsibility, to give oneself to the task of struggling for *soteria* in this tormented world, to join hands with victims and to experience victimization in the struggle for justice, to feel claimed by the sacredness of the Earth and called to protect the Earth—such human experiences and activities constitute a universally available locus, an arena open to all, where persons of different religious backgrounds can feel the presence and empowerment of that for which religious language seems appropriate.

Yes, the language will be different. Yes, there will be many other ways in which the Transcendent can touch us or explode within our consciousness. Still, I think we can all recognize that to respond to the sufferings of our fellow sentient beings is an undertaking in which we ourselves are taken under and claimed by something that is more than what we are or that goes beyond our everyday awareness. Working for eco-human justice becomes a common context in which we find ourselves using our different religious stories and symbols. So our experiences of injustice are different, as is our language, but at the same time, these differing words are flowing from a common experiential process. There is, I dare say, something "common" within the diversity. We are "communing" with that which sustains or might be the goal of our various traditions. Working together for justice becomes, or can become, a *communicatio in sacris*—a communication in the Sacred—available to us beyond our churches and temples.

And because *different* kinds of religious experiences arise out of the *same* commitment to global responsibility, we can be even more confident that many (if not most) of our religious differences will turn out to be not contradictory but analogous and complementary. Here David Tracy's analogous imagination can have an even greater and more promising pay-off. If our differing religious imaginations are stimulated and sustained by the same commitment to and struggle for eco-human justice, then when we confront the genuinely other in stories and practices, it can well turn out to be, as Tracy hopes, not a total stranger but a friend inviting us to new possibilities of imaging and living the Divine. In struggling for justice and ecological responsibility we are communing in the Sacred. But just how does this work?

EXTRA MUNDUM NULLA SALUS—OUTSIDE THE WORLD NO SALVATION

Edward Schillebeeckx helps us understand how global responsibility can be a "communication in the Sacred" when he takes the long-standing ecclesiocentric dictum *extra ecclesiam nulla salus* (outside the church there is no salvation) and turns it on its head to read *extra mundum nulla salus:* outside the world there is no salvation (Schillebeeckx 1990, 5-15). Here Schillebeeckx is speaking not just to his fellow Christians but is announcing a reality that he feels can be recognized and affirmed by all religious persons. It is precisely in the confrontation and struggle with a world littered with limitations and inadequacies (to put it philosophically), or with suffering and injustice (to put it existentially), that we can, and do, encounter the Divine. Again, his language is Christian, but the experience he is describing can, I believe, be caught and illuminated by a variety of religious symbols and narratives.

Schillebeeckx describes a basically identical worldly process in which many people, from a variety of religions and cultures, find themselves today. They encounter situations of "negative experience of contrast" before which they find themselves pronouncing, first, a spontaneous and forceful "no" to what the situation is, and then a resolute "yes" to how it might be transformed. In this explosive "no" and then in this determined "yes," we find the first stirrings of religious experience—what Schillebeeckx calls "pre-religious experiences"—there are "important human experiences, namely negative experiences of contrast: they form a basic human experience which as such I regard as pre-religious experience and thus a basic experience accessible to all human beings, namely that of a 'no' to the world as it is" (Schillebeeckx 1990, 5). The "no" doesn't just stand there. Spontaneously, it can give birth to a "yes" by which persons are claimed and called to resist and reform what is before them:

> The fundamental human "no" to evil therefore discloses an unfulfilled and thus "open yes" which is as intractable as the human "no," indeed even stronger, because the "open yes" is the basis of that opposition and makes it possible. . . . Both believers and agnostics come together in this experience. That is also a rational basis for solidarity between all peoples [we can add, all religions] and for common commitment to a better world with a human face (Schillebeeckx 1990, 6).[11]

This "natural" or "given" human response of resistance leading to hope and action is the raw material, as it were, out of which religious experience or faith can take form. This is what Schillebeeckx means by "no salvation outside the world"; it is in the confrontation with and struggle to improve the world that the reality of the Transcendent/ Immanent makes itself felt. For Schillebeeckx, the praxis of involvement in the world has a primacy in religious experience and in what Christians call revelation:

> Revelation presupposes a process meaningful to men and women, an event that already has relevance for them and liberates them, without direct reference to God, *etsi Deus non daretur* [as if God didn't exist]. What is decisive is the good action which brings liberation, without which religious nomenclature becomes this, a meaningless facade and redundant superstructure. . . . Only in a secular history in which men and women are liberated for true humanity can God reveal his own being.
>   Salvation from God comes about first of all in the worldly reality of history, and not primarily in the consciousness of believers who are aware of it (Schillebeeckx 1990, 7, 12).

Jon Sobrino, again using Christian language which I suggest can be meaningful and translatable for other religious traditions, makes the same claim when he holds that the reality of God-experience is first found in an "honesty with and fidelity to reality"; he means a commitment to acknowledging and resolving the realities of suffering and injustice.

> Honesty with and fidelity to reality is more than a prerequisite for a spiritual experience of God. It is its very material as well. Apart from, and independent of, this honesty and fidelity, we neither grasp revelation nor respond to it. . . . Apart from honesty with the real . . . one can no longer have an experience of God, either from the side of the object (God, who no longer is revealed in reality) or from the side of the subject (the beclouded heart of the human being who does violence to reality) (Sobrino 1987, 21-22).

These are strong statements, perhaps too strong. The emphasis on this-worldly, prophetic involvement seems to exclude other forms of religious experience. Remove their exclusive tones, however, and they still make a positive assertion that can, I trust, be taken seriously by persons of different religious traditions: By first "feeling" the presence and power of Something More in our efforts to overcome the "negative experiences of contrast," we know what we are talking about when we use our religious language. Here the experience is illuminating the language and the language is forming the experience; there is a nondual reciprocity between the two. Religious language such as "truth" or "love" or "justice"—or "Dharma" or "Tao" or "*karuna*"—takes on new or added meaning and power in both identifying and expanding what we have already felt in our struggles to pronounce our "no" and remain faithful to our "yes."

In feeling called or claimed by the suffering that torments persons and planet, we find ourselves enabled both to understand this call and to understand the religious language that identifies the source or ground of this call as Something or Someone real. Sobrino states this in Christian terms: "In my view, the very existence of a crucified people brings out, and in its most radical form, a seeking for ultimate reality and for the reality of the divine" (Sobrino 1987, 140). When we are acting for justice, when we are acting for the sustainability of the environment, we are acting not only with other humans but with a Reality or Process or Truth that sustains our activities. Schillebeeckx puts it in theistic terms:

> The one who believes in God sees faith in the superiority of justice and goodness to all injustice as an experience of the meta-human (for people clearly cannot produce it in their history), an experience of the absolute presence of God's pure positivity in the historical mixture of meaning and meaninglessness which is

called the "human" phenomenon and its history (Schillebeeckx 1990, 97).

The struggle to overcome the reality of suffering and injustice not only provides us with the experiential "receptors" with which we can use and understand religious language; it also brings about within us an existential process which, as I suggested earlier in this chapter, can be found, in various garbs, within most religious traditions. In the usually complex and painful effort to speak a "no" to suffering and carry out a "yes" to transforming this world, our individual selves are deconstructed. We find the center of gravity in our lives shifting from our individuated self to other selves and, even, to a broader Reality. We are *de-centered* and so refocused. Sobrino describes this process as he has seen it take place among many of his companions (some of them martyrs) in El Salvador : "This de-centering of oneself, this transfer of one's ultimate concern from oneself to the life of the poor, redounding as it does to the attainment of one's own life as well, is the subjective experience of the holy. It may be that, at the level of formulation, one cannot go much further. Words may seem insufficient" (Sobrino 1987, 110). This experience of losing-gaining oneself, of becoming a no-self/true-self, is a commonly described quality of religious experience in most traditions. Sobrino says it can happen outside the monastery or temple and in the impoverished villages or ravaged rain forests, amid all cultures and religions.

To sift and summarize the essential ingredients in the religious experience that is available cross-culturally in the struggle to overcome suffering and promote the well-being of persons and planet, I think something like the following process describes what takes place; this process can happen within any person, in any religious culture:

- In the face of what we deem to be unnecessary human or ecological suffering, we find ourselves *resisting*. This is what Schillebeeckx describes as the "no" that erupts out of us in the face of "negative experiences of contrast."
- We feel ourselves *obliged* to act. Resistance cannot be only internal, moral. It requires involvement, action. Here the "yes" starts to take shape.
- The sense of obligation carries with it a sense of being *empowered* to act. Confronting the enormity, especially the impossibility, of the task, we find ourselves beyond our own resources.
- As the action begins to take place, we sense a kind of *enlightenment* regarding a vision of how things can be different. The enlightenment is not necessarily the fruit of a direct mystical experience but, rather, takes shape under the force of resistance against the horror and pain that actually does exist. Insight comes out of opposition; in saying no, we visualize the contents of a "yes."

- As we carry out the action and follow through on the enlightenment, we fail, we suffer, we witness our companions imprisoned or
disappeared. And still, we find ourselves *emboldened to hope*. The
empowerment persists in hope even when our actions are powerless. We experience some form of an other-power in our self-power.

Some such religious, or pre-religious, experiences can be common
to devotees of all paths. My suggestion, therefore, is that just as persons from various spiritualities have sought for a multifaith
communicatio in sacris—a sharing of religious experience—in ashrams,
monasteries, and participation in each other's meditational or prayer
practices, so today they can also share their religious experiences and
language in the concrete praxis of a global spirituality and the struggle
for eco-human justice that such responsibility demands. We can commune in the sacred as we commune in the sufferings of our world.
Thus, a group of sixteen representatives of various religious paths in
India could conclude their dialogue with this joint statement:

When we stand for justice and freedom and for people's right to
life with dignity, we stand for those realities and values, in terms
of which *all faiths image the Mystery of the Divine*. . . . The downtrodden people with their history of hope and struggle is the *locus,* the place, of authentic encounter with God. In confronting
injustice and working for a new India, a new world, where people
are equal and free, and where resources are for all, there exists a
profound spirituality even if it is not recognised, made explicit.[12]

7

THE ONE EARTH AND OUR MANY STORIES

Eco-human Well-being as a Criterion for Religious Truth

In the previous chapter we tried to take an accurate, honest look at what is involved in being religious and in being globally responsible. We saw that for many people, being religious includes being concerned about and responsible for this world, while for just as many people, taking on responsibility for and commitment to this world propels them to the reality of—or at least the question of—matters religious. To know the Sacred is to care for the Earth; to care for the Earth is to be touched by the Sacred.

In this chapter we first will explore another way—broader and perhaps more challenging and promising—in which the Earth can speak of the Sacred and thus provide a common ground for interreligious dialogue. Then, in the second part of the chapter, we will take up the knotty issue of how the Earth can function as a basis not just for understanding each other's religious beliefs but also for evaluating them; here we examine a claim that many postmodern people say is impossible—that justice or eco-human well-being can serve as a universal criterion for truth without becoming a new foundational or absolute norm for truth, that justice can be an ever-reliable counselor who helps us but who never takes us off the hook of having to make our own decisions.

THE EARTH: A COMMON STORY FOR SHARING PARTICULAR STORIES

A number of contemporary scientists, philosophers, and theologians are suggesting that the Earth is providing us not only with a context for experiencing the Divine/Truth in a vast variety of ways (as we suggested in part 2 of the previous chapter), but also with a *common story* by which we can better understand our different religious experiences, link them, and give them some unified shape. All these thinkers—perhaps we should call them visionaries—are seeking to understand religious phenomena in relation to scientific and ecological phenomena.[1] I'm referring to theologians with dirty hands and earthy heads such as Thomas Berry, Sallie McFague, Charlene Spretnak, Jay McDaniel, Rosemary Radford Ruether, and to scientist-philosophers such as Brian Swimme, Fritjof Capra, Charles Birch (see references). If I can bring their various concerns and claims into a focus, it would be something like this: Given what we *know* about how the universe came about and how it functions, and given what we *have done* to our earthly corner of the universe, today the Earth itself, providing our place within and scenic view of the universe, offers all humans (that means all cultures and all religions) a *common cosmological story.*

This story, as people are trying to tell it today, has two facets: a) As a *religious story,* it tells us who we are and how we might find the Truth that religions seek; it provides us, in other words, with a cosmological myth in which we can understand our individual myths. b) As an *ethical story,* it provides us with general but still usable norms for adjudicating the truth claims that we as human, especially as religious, beings find ourselves making. Briefly, let me try to describe the content and functions of this common cosmological story:

A COMMON RELIGIOUS STORY

"For the first time in our history, we have empirical evidence for a common creation story." So declared a group of fifty representatives from a variety of religious traditions in what they called "An Earth Charter," prepared by the International Coordinating Committee on Religion and the Earth for the Earth Summit in Rio de Janeiro, June 1992.[2] They were announcing on the international level what some theologians have been saying among themselves and their communities: science, in what it tells us about how the universe originated and how it works, is providing all religions with a *common creation myth.* What Thomas Berry and Brian Swimme call the universe story can function as a transcultural religious story (Berry/Swimme 1992).

In drawing on the findings of science, these theologians are not seeking to resolve the religion *vs.* science debate; they are not concluding that finally science has proven the existence of God or established the validity of a religious worldview. Rather, these theologians are suggesting that if religious persons will listen to—or "eavesdrop" (McFague 1991)—on what is generally agreed upon among contemporary scientists (biologists, astrophysicists, cosmologists), they will find a creation story that enlightens, confirms, and excitingly expands their own religious stories of what the world is and how we are to live within it; more significantly, the universe story will provide a common hermeneutical framework to link a variety of religious stories. Physicist Brian Swimme puts it this way:

> Though scientific knowledge has put lethal weapons in our hands, it has also provided the Earth with the first common story of our origins and development. The scientific enterprise has eventuated in a creation myth that offers humanity deeper realization of our bondedness, our profound communion not only within our species, but throughout the living and non-living universe.
>
> Precisely because this story of the universe comes to us through our investigations beginning with our eyes and ears and body, we can speak of a transcultural creation story. Members of every continent are involved in discovering and articulating this story. Members of every religious tradition are involved in its telling (Swimme 1988, 86).

A fundamental tenet of this scientific creation story resonates with an ingredient in most religious creation or origin stories: since all that exists originates from a common source and process, there is a connectedness, a common stuff, permeating all creatures, living and non-living. Everything that exists shares a common "cosmological lineage" (Spretnak 1991, 20). McFague describes the "primordial flaring forth" which is the parent of us all:

> In broad strokes, the story emerging from the various sciences claims that some fifteen billion years ago the universe began from a big bang, exploding matter, which was infinitely hot and infinitely concentrated outward to create some hundred billion galaxies, including our galaxy, the Milky Way, itself containing billions of stars and housing our sun and its planet. . . . All things living and all things not living are the products of the same primal explosion and evolutionary history and hence are interrelated in an internal way right from the beginning. We are cousins to the stars, to the rocks and oceans, to all living creatures (McFague 1991, 31).

Besides revealing the common origin and heritage of all creatures, the scientific story also displays how all such creatures function; that is, how they have unfolded and continue to unfold. The entire universe is thoroughly *interrelated and organic*; what one is and what one makes of oneself takes place through dependence on others, through relationships and connectedness. "No tribal myth, no matter how wild, ever imagined a more profound relationship connecting all things in an internal way right from the beginning of time. All thinking must begin with this cosmic genetic relatedness" (Swimme 1988, 87). Such interrelatedness makes for a dynamic universe—constantly moving, changing, in process. And this means that the universe is radically open—creative of ever new novelty, things never seen or imagined before, yet things that have their origin from relatedness to what went before. Such is the picture of our world and our universe offered by this new cosmological myth.

It is a myth that can be taken on, I believe, by most of the world's religious traditions; while it does not contradict the basic content of religious myths of origin, it can clarify, vivify, and perhaps transform them. As with all myth, this cosmological story will both give expression to religious convictions and experiences that are already present and at the same time it will give birth to deeper persuasions and a deeper sense of the creative Source. Perhaps with Berry and Swimme we can even use a term that theologians have bandied about for centuries: *universal revelation*. The Earth itself, as it is seen by science, can become (I am not saying must become) a source of new insights and feelings for the relation between the Transcendent and the finite. "Our new sense of the universe is itself a type of revelatory experience. Presently we are moving beyond any religious expression so far known to the human into a meta-religious age, that seems to be a new comprehensive context for all religions" (Berry/Swimme 1992, 255).

Given our new awareness of the universe and our sense of ecological kinship with it, we can perhaps speak of the universe as a larger religious community in which the particular and diverse religious communities of history can now recognize each other and come to see how their individual stories are part of the universe story. "Religion begins to appreciate that the primary sacred community is the universe itself. In a more immediate perspective, the sacred community is the Earth community. The human community becomes sacred through its participation in the larger planetary community" (Berry/Swimme 1992, 257). Within this newly discovered Earth community, religions can understand themselves and other religions in new ways.

Such words are visionary; they do not represent what is presently recognized or going on in the world of religions. But given the truth of what we know about the universe, given our momentous responsibilities for it, is it not a vision worthy of our trust and commitment? Is it not a vision that will help remedy the insularity and antagonism that has darkened and twisted so much of our religious histories?

> This common story is available to be remythologized by any and every religious tradition and hence is a place of meeting for the religions, whose conflicts in the past and present have often been the cause of immense suffering and bloodshed as belief is pitted against belief. What this common story suggests is that our primary loyalty should be not to nation or religion but to the Earth

and its Creator (albeit that Creator may be understood in different ways) (McFague 1991, 34).

A COMMON ETHICAL STORY

What we know about the Earth and the universe today provides
religions not only with the possibility of a shared religious story but
also, and I think more importantly, with the necessity of a common
ethical task and the shared guidelines to carry out that task. Again, it
is especially on the ethical level that the universe story can exercise a
practical unifying force among the religions; at the same time, the task
with which our common creation story challenges us can provide a
compelling response to the relativizing corrosion of a postmodern attitude which insists that any attempt at common ethical programs or
criteria is destined to drown in the sea of diversity.

The chapter in the universe story that is presently being lived out
and written might fittingly be titled, in the words of Harvard biologist
Edward O. Wilson, "Is Humanity Suicidal?" (Wilson 1993). We are
indeed "flirting with the extinction of our species" as we witness and
cause the extinction of thousands of other species. The task of preventing this suicide and the broader geocide is the most compelling
and unsettling ethical imperative facing humankind today. "In spite of
continuing political tensions among nations, the most dangerous threat
to the world's well-being is not war but the closing down of the Earth's
most basic systems, which support us and all other forms of life"
(McFague 1991, 20). Not to respond to this threat and this ethical
imperative is to renounce or diminish our humanity.

Because this is true for peoples in all cultures, of all religions (in
different degrees, of course, for the impoverished *campesino* in El Salvador and the multinational executive in New York), our common
universe story, with its ecological awareness and demands, provides us
with the motivation and the means to break the roadblock that many
people try to place before any kind of a universal ethical venture based
on universal ethical criteria. To the postmodern insistence that every
value or every moral project is but an individual social construction
valid only for its own backyard, to the refusal of many today to endorse any kind of universal or "meta" discourse that would rally the
multicultural troops in a united campaign, we can hold up our common universe story that tells us we are all interrelated in our origins, in
our functioning, *and* in our responsibility for saving our species and
endangered planet.

With Charlene Spretnak, I think we can speak of "the 'metadiscourse'
of the universe," which can link our individual discourses, or of the
"grand cosmologic," which can inform the logic of all cultures. Before
we are located in our separate, diverse cultural-religious houses, we
are located, more deeply and decisively and responsibly, in the cosmic

neighborhood, in the one world in which we all share and which connects us all with each other and which, today, pleads with us for its own salvation (Spretnak 1991, 81, 105).

There is, therefore, a "place" where we all stand together, where we share common experiences, concerns, and responsibilities: our Earth, beautiful in its mysterious connectedness and evolution but also menaced in the devastation that the human species has wrought upon it. This Earth provides the religions not only with a religious community in which they can share myths of origin, but also with an ethical community in which they can identify and defend common criteria of truth. In their basic content, such criteria will probably be something like those being worked out by international ecological groups, especially nongovernmental—criteria that seek to balance the promotion of life for individuals and for eco-systems. I'm not claiming that such universal ethical criteria are ready-made or that they can be neatly articulated in a kind of ecological decalogue. But I am stating that the universe story, or the new creation myth, which religions can today communally affirm, will provide them with the materials and perspectives with which to successfully though never finally work out global ecological norms.[3]

As was urged in chapter 5, the religions of the world have a special, perhaps determinative, role in responding to the ethical-ecological demands of our common creation myth. Many people engaged in the environmental struggle are coming to realize the truth contained in the reminder of Native American and other primal spiritualities that to save our Earth from impending ecological devastation more is needed than practical programs and new political-economic policies; as essential as such practical, concrete measures surely are, they will turn out to be ineffective or unpersuasive for both individuals and nations unless they are nurtured and animated by a sense of the sacredness of the Earth.

If we regard the Earth and all its creatures as merely finite, as disposable tools to achieve our own good, we will not dispel our ecological nightmares; what we need, in Christian terms, is a truly sacramental awareness of the Earth that will enable us to feel the Earth as the presence or manifestation or life of the Sacred; the plants and the animals, therefore, have a dignity and value of their own as "children of God" and members, with us, of the divine family. Whether it is expressed in theistic terms (as I just did) or in secular language, some such sense of the sacred or mysterious value of the Earth is prerequisite for an effective ecological program (Nasr 1992, 105-6). If the struggle for social justice demands a bedrock of spirituality, this is, perhaps, even more true of the struggle for ecological justice and the integrity of creation.

And I would hold that most, if not all, of the world's spiritualities can respond meaningfully to that task. Not always in their actual behavior through history but generally in the original vision and teachings of their founders, the "wisdom traditions" that have successfully made it through the obstacle course of human history all teach some form of respect for life, of interconnectedness, and of the need to overcome self-aggrandizement and to treat others as we would want them to treat us. As initial efforts have already indicated, spokespersons for the world's religious communities are forming a common front in revealing and opposing the self-centeredness, the consumerism, the disregard for life that feed the monster of ecological devastation now consuming the globe. Here especially the religions can unite: "The core teachings and practices of the wisdom traditions . . . are thoroughly subversive to the monstrous reduction of the fullness of being that the Earth community currently faces through the dynamics of an increasingly manipulative, globalized, consumption-oriented political economy based on rapacious growth and the supposedly pragmatic destruction of being-in-relation" (Spretnak 1991, 9).

So when our efforts for a globally responsible interreligious dialogue are challenged with the fitting question of "whose justice?," we can give one clear and equally challenging response: the Earth's justice. Yes, the critics are right—every understanding of justice is socially mediated and motivated. But here is one form of justice that we must all not only be concerned about but in some way agree on: all nations and religions must devote themselves to the common task of saving and sustaining the integrity and life-giving powers of the planet. If the job isn't done jointly, it won't be done! It's as simple and yet as profound as that. The hope expressed by Thomas Berry is as idealistic as it is imperative, and it seems to me that we have no choice but to endorse it: "Concern for the well-being of the planet is the one concern that hopefully will bring the nations [and the religions] of the world into an inter-nation [and interreligious] community" (Berry 1988, 218).

ECO-HUMAN WELL-BEING (*SOTERIA*): A UNIVERSAL CRITERION FOR TRUTH

Having proposed that all religions show the capability of genuine concern for human well-being in this world, having described how the state of the present world (especially the drama of the universe story) is calling forth this capability, I must recognize the stubborn truth that there is no clear, identifiable unity among the religious communities on how we are to respond to the needs of this suffering planet. The specter of diversity once again rears its defiant head and announces the counter-claim: "The sufferings of people and planet indeed may present the religions with a common problem. But just because you have a common problem (maybe even a common diagnosis of the problem), you don't have the assurance of a common answer." Thus, the question of "whose justice?" can never be simply or totally dismissed. The diversity of religious experience and traditions will not allow it.

David Tracy states the problem more academically and more pointedly:

> There are family resemblances among the religions. But as far as I can see, there is no single essence, no one content of enlightenment or revelation, no one way of emancipation or liberation to be found in all that plurality. . . . There are different interpretations of what way we should follow to move from a fatal self-centeredness to a liberating Reality-centeredness. . . . The responses of the religions, their various narratives, doctrines, symbols, and their often conflicting accounts of the way to authentic liberation are at least as different as they are similar. They are clearly not the same (Tracy 1987a, 90, 92).

ECO-HUMAN JUSTICE: A CROSS-CULTURAL CRITERION

How can we fashion consensus out of such stubborn diversity? How can we mediate between two differing views about what will ensure authentic liberation? In a particular context, for instance, a Buddhist calls for the total selflessness of nonviolence, while a Christian urges the self-giving of armed resistance. How might a shared commitment to global responsibility and eco-human justice help adjudicate the truth between them? Can what I am calling *soteria* really function as a common lens by which persons from differing religions can not only listen to and learn from each other but also criticize each other, correct each other, and so come, together, to articulate and live truth claims that they feel are universal?

Tracy himself tries to show how religious diversity does not necessarily means religious divergence. Genuine conversation, he believes, can take place between different, even contrasting, religious perspectives; religious communities *can* resolve their differences. Tracy outlines three general criteria for religious truth which he thinks could be acceptable to persons of different religious traditions and which therefore can enable them to reach joint judgments:

a) "The truth of a religion is, like the truth of its nearest cousin, art, primordially the truth of manifestation" (Tracy 1990a, 43). In religion, we know something to be so because it *manifests* or reveals itself to us; we know it because, like the beauty of art, we feel it. More practically, it *makes a claim* on us; it grasps or lays hold of us. So, if the stories or rituals of your religion can tug at and claim my heart, if I feel their truth manifested before me at least as a "suggestive possibility" (Tracy 1990a, 40), I can share your truth, and so we can come to mutual agreement.

b) But what touches the heart must also speak to the head; even though there is no cross-cultural consensus on what *reasonability* means or requires, Tracy believes that all religions will recognize the need for some kind of "cognitive criteria of coherence with what we otherwise know or, more likely, believe to be the case" (Tracy 1990b, 901). However we work out the connections, religious truth known primarily through the heart must be brought into a productive conversation with the intellectual truths we know through common sense, good thinking, and our scientific understanding of the world.

c) Finally, there must also be "ethical-political criteria on the personal and social consequences of our beliefs" (Tracy 1990b, 901). How do our religious experience and beliefs make for a better world, both our own and that of society? Tracy offers two reasons why all religions could agree on the validity and necessity of such criteria: "First, the religions themselves—especially but not solely in their prophetic strands—demand this. Secondly, our very nature as human beings demands ethical assessment" (Tracy 1990a, 46).

Certainly, all three of Tracy's criteria—the mystical, the reasonable, the ethical— must enter into the mix that is interreligious dialogue; all three must contribute to the process of making shared assessments of truth. But if we ask which of these criteria can best help us break through the postmodern roadblock of "incommensurability," if we explore which of them offers what religions have most in common, then I suggest that the most reliable and applicable criterion is that of ethical-political concern for human and ecological suffering. Here we find common and usable materials to make the first crossings between our differing cultural religious perspectives.

The religious or mystical experience of what Tracy calls manifestation and the determination of the cognitive criteria that make for reasonability are much more subjectively or culturally conditioned than are the ethical demands arising from starvation or destruction of the rain forests (though all ethical responses are culturally colored). Ethical and liberative criteria, insofar as they are directed toward problems or issues that are truly common to us all, are better able to serve as the starting point or foundation on which we can move on to discuss the manifestation and the rational coherence of our individual truth claims. And if, as I suggested in the previous chapter, such common ethical struggles can lead us to *shared manifestations of a Power or Sacred Mystery* that animates our global responsibility, then we have an even more reliable common criterion for truth.

So of the three cross-cultural criteria for working toward shared assessments of truth among the incorrigible diversity of world religions—personal experience, cognitive coherence, and ethical fruits—it is the last criterion that is "most cross-cultural." Questions concerning the ethical fruits of a particular belief or practice—that is, whether it does remove suffering and promote well being—provide common ground on which persons of differing traditions can stand and effectively discuss their differences and work toward consensus. The critical data regarding the ethical effects of one's claims are much more "at hand" than are appeals to one's religious experience or to what makes rational sense. One's own religious experience and one's way of being reasonable are buried deeper below the sediment of culture and society; certainly we can dig them out and share them; but I am urging that there is other ground, more accessible and more urgent, where we can begin our sharing.

If followers of various religious traditions can agree in the beginning that whatever else their experience of truth or of the Divine or of Enlightenment may bring about, it must always promote greater eco-human well-being and help remove the sufferings of our world, then they have a shared reference point from which to affirm or criticize each other's claims. Such ethical concerns do not provide immediate solutions to interreligious disagreements, but they do constitute a walkable path toward such solutions.[4]

So I would agree with Francis Schüssler Fiorenza when he proposes "solidarity with the suffering" as the source of criteria that will enable persons from diverse cultures and religions to come to shared conclusions about truth and value and action. Such ethical solidarity affirms the diversity of viewpoints and thus warns against the danger of an "objectivism" of only one absolute perspective, but it also demands that out of the diversity we make judgments and take action that will relieve the suffering. Thus it avoids the dangers of postmodern relativism (Fiorenza 1991, 133-34).

Precisely because human and ecological suffering is both *universal* and *immediate* it can serve all religious persons as a common context and criterion for assessing religious truth claims. In its universality, human and ecological suffering confronts and affects us all; in its immediacy it has a raw reality and challenge that is somehow beyond our differing interpretations of it. As mentioned in chapter 4, this is why "suffering brings us to the bedrock of human existence and cuts through the hermeneutical circle" (Fiorenza 1991, 135). The stark image of a child starving because of poverty or of a lake polluted because of chemical dumping has an immediacy that breaks through our differing cultural interpretations of it. It stares us in the face and questions us before we can fully understand or interpret it. It is this questioning face of the suffering that enables religions to face and question each other and come to joint assessments of truth. Thus, a concern for ethical-political criteria in the face of suffering can work cross-culturally.

But in order to work, it is not enough that the participants in interreligious dialogue simply "bear in mind" the reality of the suffering, of the victims of human or ecological injustice; it is not enough that they announce to each other and the world that they are "globally responsible." If ethical-political criteria resulting from "solidarity with the suffering" are really to bear fruit in the dialogue, if the "hermeneutical privilege of the oppressed" is really to function as a source of dialogical decision-making, then the suffering oppressed themselves and those who can speak for the oppressed species and the Earth will have to be not simply the *object* of the dialogue but active *participants* in it. If their voices are to be heard, they will have to be present as they have not generally been present within the arena of interreligious dialogue. The suffering, the victims, will have to have an active part in determining the agenda for the dialogue, the procedure, and format, yes, the place and the language, too! Just how all this can be arranged is not easy to say, for certainly this has not been the style or the practice of dialogical conferences as they have been planned and practiced over the past decades. But the excluded will now have to be included. If religious spokespersons are serious about basing their discussions on ethical-political criteria and on global responsibility, then they will have to prove this seriousness by inviting to the dialogue those most affected by present ethical and political realities.

But what is required is more than simply inviting the suffering and oppressed to the table of dialogue. If their voices are not only to be heard but understood, if the reality of their suffering and ethical concerns are to be felt and not just registered, then somehow all the participants in the dialogue need to be actively involved in the praxis of working against eco-human injustice and promoting more life-giving policies in the structures of governments and economics. One can hear the message of the suffering only if one is struggling, and therefore suffering, with them. Dialogical conversation must include, in some way, dialogical praxis for liberation and well-being. Just what this means and how it can be carried out will be the concern of the next chapter.

With the voices of suffering beings actively present in our interreligious discourse, participants will be able to apply ethical-political criteria all the more realistically and effectively. The marginalized and oppressed, however their voices and experience can be authentically heard within the interreligious dialogue, can serve as "arbiters" or a "court of appeal" when there are differing views among the religious spokespersons as to just what are the ethical fruits of a particular religious claim. Such decisions, in other words, are not to be made only, or primarily, by the "religious experts." The persons directly affected will give witness about just how their lives have been changed and enhanced, or limited and threatened, by a particular religious conviction or behavior. They will make known, for instance, how images of God as transcendent or immanent affect their attitudes to this world, how beliefs in karma or afterlife have contributed to their well-being now, how nonviolent or armed forms of resistance can improve their situation. Not that their views or experiences will be the final verdict in any discussion. Still, I am convinced that their voices will generally be an effective, if not decisive, help in the difficult task of honoring the diversity of religious views and yet formulating out of that diversity decisions and programs that will promote global responsibility.

Mark Kline Taylor uses the image of a web to describe an intercultural, interreligious dialogue in which the victims of the world form the outer strands that will help constitute the web's fruitful interrelatedness and its ethical strength and limits:

> Interpretation involves making connections in conversation, the continual intersecting of different persons, groups, perspectives, and practices. All of these, however, go on within the limiting function set by the web's outermost strands. These are like the limiting function that oppressed groups can play in a truly wideranging, diverse conversation. Those who are excluded from conversation—by having their voices silenced, their bodies taken away, their everyday practice shackled—count as the most radically different ones within a conversational process that values differences (Mark Taylor 1990, 66).

ECO-HUMAN JUSTICE: A RELATIVE-ABSOLUTE CRITERION

Using a shared, interreligious concern for eco-human well-being as our criterion for truth, we will also be better equipped to detect or create what for many postmoderns is the always elusive path between "objectivism and relativism" (Bernstein 1983)—between arming oneself with "one and only" claims and abandoning oneself to the winds of "anything goes." A commitment to eco-human well-being can provide us, I am suggesting, with a universal norm or criterion of truth that is, paradoxically, both absolute and relative. Our particular perceptions of eco-human justice can serve us as norms that both bind and free at the same time: we are bound to follow and defend what we see as "true," but freed to hear and accept what still remains to be seen. We feel called upon to assert and to assume absolute, resistant, committed positions, and yet we realize at the same time that such positions are limited, relative, open to change and correction. We are giving ourselves absolutely to something we have grasped only relatively. Just how this works is not easy to spell out in words and concepts; that's why we call it a paradox.

Langdon Gilkey helps us grasp and practice this paradox. Calling his fellow theologians to recognize that the paradox of truth as a relative absolute is "the clue to the center of theological understanding" and interreligious dialogue (Gilkey 1987, 47), Gilkey explains that "absolute" requires "relative" in the same way that "Infinite" requires "finite." Just as the Infinite meets us in the finite and is thus "finitized," so also truth exerts its absolute claims on us through relative, particular forms. Thus, the Absolute, in order to be absolute for us, must be relativized and particularized. In the finite relative, we encounter and are claimed by the infinite Absolute. There is no other way, so it seems, to experience Divine truth except in this relativizing fashion; yet, the relativizing effect is never total, for we feel that the Absolute, though speaking through relative forms, remains just what it is—absolute. As Gilkey puts it: "The dialectic works both ways: relativizing the manifestation on the one hand, and so all incarnations of the absolute, and yet manifesting as well *through* the relative an absoluteness that transcends it—otherwise neither liberating praxis nor creative reflection would be possible" (Gilkey 1987, 49).

The last clause in that previous sentence is important and illuminating: the *absolute* quality of truth is spelled out especially on the practical, ethical level of liberating *praxis*; the *relative* is felt on the *reflective* level. In what truth calls us to do, in the liberating praxis it generates, it can be absolute; yet when we reflect on how we have known this truth and the limitations of our knowing it, we feel the relative aspect of truth. This same dynamic between absolute and relative expresses itself also in the different ways the very same truth touches our heart and our head. When truth enters our heart, it seems to take full possession; it becomes "the good," and the good lays claim on our heart and feelings, calling forth commitment. If the good and true are focused on really important matters, then that commitment is total, our dedication to it is absolute. But insofar as this same truth is housed in our head, we find ourselves admitting that it is bigger than our brains, that there are other truths; so we are also claimed by the relativity of truth. The dialectical tick-tock of absoluteness and relativity is sensed in any affirmation of and commitment to truth.[5]

While Gilkey lays out the relative-absolute nature of *all* truth, I want to suggest that this paradoxical quality of truth is especially evident—and livable—when we are dealing with truth that promotes eco-human well-being. When I make a claim that something is true not primarily because it makes logical or coherent sense, and not mainly because it corresponds to my tradition, but because it is necessary for promoting human justice and ecological sustainability, then I am experiencing two things: a) I feel that insofar as this truth is essential for the well-being or salvation of the planet or other beings, I must stand up for it, defend it, maybe be ready to die for it; my truth is an absolute for me. b) But I also feel that I can and must be open to any other version or edition of truth that will enable us to attain these same goals of well-being, or to understand them even more adequately; I realize and am challenged by the relativity of the truth I am proposing and living.

So it is especially on this practical level—in a globally responsible dialogue in which eco-human well-being and justice serve as the standard of truth—that religious persons can experience their truth claims to be both absolute and relative. In holding up eco-human justice as the basis and criterion for dialogue, religious persons are laying a foundation on which each can take strong, yes absolute, stands, and at the same time, each can be open and eager to find anything else that might show what justice means and how it can be realized. While making absolute claims about justice which require them to *resist* the claims of others, they will at the same time *embrace* those others and be ready to learn from them. "One vision of justice can temper, criticize, and deepen another, and through dialogue each vision might grow richer in understanding and implementation. . . . In the process of dialogue, justice is not only affirmed, but also created" (Suchocki 1987, 160). We know that eco-human well-being is a project that will ever stand uncompleted—a project that will always be beyond both our comprehension and our actualization. So while we know what we have to do and struggle for, we also know that there can be no one vision or plan by which to attain the fullness of justice and eco-human well-being.[6]

Christians should have no trouble with such a relative-absolute criterion for truth, for Jesus gave them just such a criterion in his proclamation of the Reign of God; it was an eschatological reality, both "already" and "not yet" present in this world. As *already* present in its demands for love and justice, it arms its followers with absolute commitments and determination; as *not yet* fully realized, it reminds Christians that there is no final version of this Reign, no one way of making it real, for there is always more to come. The Reign of God, then, is both absolute and relative.

Such reflections on eco-human well-being as a relative-absolute criterion of truth can be insightful, maybe even inspiring. To put such insights into practice, however, can be messy, unsettling, and painful, for they require that we match our intense commitment to our own notions of justice and salvation with an equally intense openness to the views of others. On the practical, ethical levels where people's lives are at stake, where ecosystems are being devastated, this isn't easy. It requires that we be genuinely open to brand new ideas, to utterly different ways of realizing, or even conceiving, the human good. We have to be ready to be surprised, stretched, maybe humiliated.

Personally, I can attest to such stretching in my own limited efforts to carry out a liberative dialogue with persons of Asian or Native American traditions. I have been bewildered, then enlightened, by a Hindu and Buddhist perspective that is less concerned with social transformation than with karma (selfless action) and *yajna* (sacrificial action) by which the cosmic order is constituted. Rather than committing themselves to political action for democracy or a government born of human decisions and organization, Buddhist and Hindus may prefer to devote their efforts toward what might be termed a "dharmocracy" or government stemming from cosmic order. To take such differences seriously demands that I recognize that peace or liberation cannot be reduced to my Western, Christian notions of justice, human rights, equality, autonomy.

In the original traditions of many cultures—African, Asian, Native American—there appear to be no precise words for *human rights* "because their relationships are conceived in terms of 'duty-of-infinite-gratitude' towards one's ancestors, one's community, the cosmos, etc. This is the case, for example, with the notions of *Dharma* among the Hindus, of Thanksgiving among the Mohawks, of Community among the Africans" (Vachon 1985, 34-36). Especially in conversations with Native Americans on how to practice eco-justice, I have found my notions of relationship to the land and to animals and my feelings of how I fit into the natural order thoroughly challenged; they tell me that we are all a circle rather than a hierarchical chain of being. Not sure just what that means, I have found my image of democracy being stretched into that of a biocracy. Native Americans' "notion of democracy is radically different from that of the anthropocentric West at its best, since, for them, 'the People' does not mean human only but also every living creature. It is a cosmocentric notion" (Vachon 1985, 37). In such conversations and shared activities with others, I have found that my commitment to eco-human well-being remains absolute, but at the same time it is relativized.

LIBERATIVE DIALOGUE: A PROPOSAL, NOT A PROGRAM

In holding up global responsibility or concern for eco-human liberation and well-being as the context and criterion for interreligious dialogue, I hope it is clear that I am offering to my religious brothers and sisters a broad proposal, not a neatly defined program. Really, I am offering an approach to the dialogue, not a fixed set of rules or definitions. I feel deeply that the ingredients for a soteriocentric or globally responsible dialogue outlined in these last three chapters can be acceptable to followers of other religious paths, but I'm not sure. I think that this kind of dialogue will bear abundant fruit, but I'm not clear just how it works or what these particular fruits will be.

The heart of the globally responsible dialogue that I am proposing bears a broad but striking resemblance to the centerpiece of the method my teacher, Bernard Lonergan, proposed for theology. He thought it was a method that theologians not only of different Christian perspectives but of different religious persuasions could accept. The keystone of the six "functional specialties" that make up Lonergan's method of theology is what he terms "foundations"; basically, it calls on theologians to carry out their efforts to mediate the meaning of religion to their cultures on the foundation of a *personal conversion.* Such conversion he understood in a mystical sense as a "falling in love unrestrictedly." It was the fulfillment of an "intellectual conversion," by which one pursues the truth honestly, and of a "moral conversion" by which one lives the truth as best one can. In the falling in love unrestrictedly of religious conversion, one is empowered in a new way to pursue and live the truth, even if one does not know clearly or self-consciously what one is in love with. Such a conversion would give one the deeper sensitivity or the critical antennae to properly understand and judge all the data involved in interpreting the tradition (Lonergan 1972, 101-24; 267-93).

In a similar way, I am proposing that if all the participants in interreligious dialogue are converted, the dialogue will work. But the conversion I mean here is not the religious conversion of falling in love unrestrictedly (though that is certainly not excluded) but the "worldly" conversion of devoting oneself unrestrictedly to the well-being of our suffering relatives and planet. If all participants in dialogue are genuinely converted to eco-human well-being, if this is the pre-religious priority in their lives, then I am quite certain that something like the globally responsible dialogue that I have outlined will work.[7]

Just how it will work cannot be known before the dialogue itself. Like every serious dialogue, *solvitur ambulando* (loosely: "we will know the path by walking it" (Tracy 1987a, 47). What our global responsibility and our commitment to eco-human justice mean and require in particular situations can be determined only within those situations—on the basis of unreserved listening to each other, directed by our conversion to the suffering neighbor or planet, inspired by the witness of the victims themselves. As we walk and talk and act together, we will make our decisions. Why the decisions are correct, why we must sometimes agree with or learn from our fellow participants in dialogue and sometimes oppose them—this will be much more a matter of feeling, of ethical intuition rather than of hard-and-fast rules. We are talking here of *phronesis*—the ability of the good person to know the good, of the ethically converted to know the ethical.[8]

And as persons of different religious communities walk this path of a globally responsible dialogue, they will discover not only what the suffering world demands of them but also what they have to offer. In chapter 6 I tried to show that all religions have the ability to respond to the ethical demands of our threatened world, that they all have a liberative content in their scriptures and traditions. But this ability or this content may lie hidden; it may be in the form of seeds needing nurture in order to grow. A conversion to the well-being of others and the Earth may be, in other words, the occasion for religions to rediscover themselves and to see, as perhaps they have never seen before, the this-worldly liberative power in their stories and rituals. In concluding comments on a book that tries to assemble the liberative message of various religions (Cohn-Sherbok 1992), William Burrows admits the ability of various (all?) religions to respond to the demands of eco-human justice—and to see themselves differently in that response:

> What is indubitable is that our authors [in the book *World Religions and Human Liberation*] show that the liberation praxis motif is capable of being subsumed into various traditions as they ponder responses to the contradictions, injustices, and outrages of the present. . . . That traditions as varied as those represented in this book can envisage the future as one of resisting oppression in liberationist modes, I suggest, says more about the openness of great traditions to radical reinterpretation and reorientation than it does about liberation as a central motif in their classical constitution. To that extent, liberation can fairly be called a commensurable concept. But it may have to become so *as these traditions address the future more than as retrievals of their past* (Burrows 1992, 135).[9]

If this process is carried out—if different religious communities respond to the challenge of interpreting themselves and listening to and learning from others on the common ground of global responsibility—then these communities will also *create* a response to the postmodern or postliberal concerns we heard about in chapter 3. It will be a response that both affirms and yet goes beyond what our postmodern awareness tells us about the cultural construction and limitations of all truth and ethical positions. Yes, the ultimate foundation for any ethical stance is the community in which it was created and for which it makes sense. But today, given the anguished needs of our species and our Earth, all of us are offered both the necessity and the possibility of belonging to both our particular ethical communities and to the global ethical community. Our truth claims and our ethical decisions must be—and *can* be—formed not only in our individual community but also in our global community. Certainly, this global community of dialogical, ethical discourse is not yet present, but it can be formed, and it is forming (Cady 1987).

It will be a "community of communities," a paradoxical but actual community in which we belong both to our own religion and culture and yet genuinely participate in the global community struggling for eco-human justice and well-being. It will be a community in which we are both particularists and universalists, making strong claims on the basis of our particular religious convictions but knowing that such claims might be relativized in the wider conversation with other strong claims and with the even stronger demand to remove human and eco-logical suffering. As I have said before, if there are those who say such an ethical community of communities is a pipe dream, then I respond respectfully but firmly that we have no choice today but to dream such dreams.

And there are promising indications that such dreams are taking shape. The number of multireligious conferences which are taking as their starting point or context social or ecological problems is grow-ing. Also, there is an ever-mounting body of literature which gives challenging substance to the way different religious communities are developing their own responses to the threats and sufferings of human or planetary devastation and injustice. In Christian terms, differing religious communities throughout the world are developing their own versions of an "eco-human theology of liberation"; in it they are car-rying out both a hermeneutics of suspicion (recognizing and confess-ing how their traditions may have served as tools of dominance or exploitation) and a hermeneutics of retrieval (rediscovering and recre-ating the liberative-ecological content of their foundational stories or values).[10] The process of such a liberative retrieval of religious tradi-tion is common to multiple communities; the fruits of the process are as varied as the different communities. But varied fruits of a common process make for the stuff of dialogue. Again, our hope for an ethical-dialogical community of communities is strengthened.

The last two chapters will offer suggestions on how such a globally responsible multifaith dialogue can be carried out and what we might learn from particular examples in which it already has been put into practice.

8

HOW DOES IT WORK?

Practical Suggestions for a Globally Responsible Dialogue

The empirical data for this chapter is not yet at hand. That makes it a difficult chapter to write. The vision held up in this book so far—a genuinely correlational dialogue among different religious believers who will take global responsibility for eco-human well-being as the context and criteria of their encounters—is just that, a vision. Although over the past decades interfaith meetings and dialogue centers have sprouted like mushrooms after a spring rain, few of them have been nurtured in the soil of concentrated concern for and shared commitment to removing eco-human suffering and promoting eco-human justice. Thus, even though I want this chapter to provide specific information on the practical *doing* of globally responsible, correlational dialogue, all I can offer, for the most part, is advice and guidelines on what I *think* will work, not on what has been amply tested and proven effective.

So this chapter will offer specific steps for the process of such a dialogue, advice on its context, and suggestions on how to resolve certain difficulties that inevitably will arise. And yet, it is not going to be all general advice. Over the past decade, there have been various attempts at this kind of a liberative or globally responsible meeting of religions. Scattered and fledgling though they be, these pioneering efforts can serve as sources of encouragement and guidance as to what does or does not work. Most of the examples that I will describe briefly and comment on will be drawn from southeast Asia—India and Sri Lanka; given both the rich religious diversity and the devastating human-ecological sufferings that mark these lands, they are ideal laboratories for experimenting with new, globally engaged forms of interreligious interaction.

HOW THE WHEEL OF LIBERATIVE DIALOGUE TURNS

The practical procedure for dialogue that I outline will most likely sound alarm bells for many critics of pluralistic models for interreligious encounter; "cultural imperialism," "imposing one's own method on others," "totalizing tactics" might be some of the accusations leveled at what I am calling a globally responsible method for dialogue. In chapters 4 to 7 I tried to show how seriously I want to take those warnings. After exploring in chapters 4 and 5 why a concern for eco-human suffering *should* be the context and starting point for interreligious conversations, I tried to make a case in chapters 6 and 7 for such an approach as something that followers (some, not necessarily all) of most religions *could* accept as appropriate to, and not imposed upon, their own religious self-understanding and practice.

And that is how I want to present these practical steps for dialogue—as a proposal, an urgent proposal, that I think will make sense across religious boundaries. Certainly, it will be adjusted, adapted, and expanded as it is discussed from different religious perspectives. But I think that it can, in its basic intent and content, be accepted as a way of "doing dialogue." Once these practical guidelines, however, are accepted, they will exercise a certain priority over other ways of carrying on interfaith dialogue, a priority that will not exclude other methods but will certainly infuse and order them.

DIALOGUE: A SECOND STEP

In proposing these practical guidelines for interreligious dialogue, I am admittedly taking the essentials of one particular method and suggesting that it has a universal validity and applicability. Not surprisingly, that method is drawn from my own cultural and religious background. Stating explicitly what has been implied in this book so far, I am urging that the essential ingredients of the methodology of liberation theology can be profitably and appropriately adjusted and applied as a methodology of interfaith dialogue. My suspicion is that this "liberative method," though elaborated within a Christian context, is not at all limited to that context. As the Zen Buddhists like to say about their own spiritual practices, this liberation method is not restricted to one religion but has universal relevance.

The kernel or distinctive ingredient to such a liberative (or globally responsible) method of dialogue is contained in the liberation theologians' crisp announcement: "Theology is always a second step" (Boff 1987, 23; Gutiérrez 1973, 11). Applied to the interfaith context, *dialogue* (as usually understood) is always a second step. The theoretical underpinning for such a bold declaration is contained in what we examined in chapter 4, "The Rebirth of Practical Philosophy." More immediately and more persuasively, liberation theologians, in their concrete situations of exploitation and poverty, have found that to use their actual struggles for justice as the lens with which to "reread" or "rehear" their scriptures and traditions has enabled them to see and hear things that were previously hidden to them. Praxis not only guides but reveals understanding; active, committed involvement with struggles for eco-human justice does something to one's powers of perception.

Without such praxis, we are to a certain but significant degree blind; with it, scales that we were not even aware of fall from our eyes. Thus, for liberationists this "pre-theological" or "prereflective commitment to the praxis of liberation is something that precedes theological reflection, becomes the object of theological reflection, and judges theological reflection. . . . This praxis of liberation both as a point of departure and as an ongoing reality becomes foundational for the whole of liberation theology" (Lane 1991, 34-35; see also Boff 1987, 23). Read "dialogue" instead of "theology," and we have the core of a globally responsible method for dialogue. Without limiting this priority of praxis to a simplistic chronological interpretation, this method urges that all our efforts at dialoguing or understanding each other be preceded or accompanied or pervaded by some form of shared practical efforts to remove eco-human suffering. This is the springboard for a liberative or soteriocentric method of dialogue: participants in the dialogue do not begin with conversations about doctrines or rituals, not even with prayer or meditation (though, as we shall see, such academic or mystical undertakings are integral components of *all* multifaith dialogue). Rather, the encounter begins on the level of some form of liberative, engaged praxis. Together the participants determine what are, in their particular social or national context, the examples of human or ecological suffering that they feel called to address. And together they attempt to do something about these pressing realities of poverty or hunger or exploitation or environmental devastation.

From this effort, even though it will be complex and perhaps unsuccessful, even though the effort will admit of different analyses and remedies, there will result a context, or an atmosphere, or a new sensitivity, on the basis of which the participants in the dialogue will be able to understand themselves and each other in new ways. As Samuel Rayan, from his own experience of such multireligious efforts at human betterment in India, describes it: "In the process of a liberating, whole-making collaboration with God and neighbor, the different spiritualities will progressively discover one another, discover themselves with their weaknesses and strengths, and encounter more intimately the Mystery they bear, symbolize, and convey" (Rayan 1990, 130, 139).

Also from his Asian vantage point, Michael Amaladoss describes what he has found to be the main characteristics and requirements of a liberative dialogue. First of all, persons of different religious communities will feel themselves unified by an energy that is not explicitly religious; they find themselves gathered together by a call that comes to all of them from beyond their immediate religious communities—the call of the suffering and marginalized. They are called to *do something*. And as they begin this doing, the sense of togetherness grows. "The principle of unity is precisely the praxis of liberation" (Amaladoss 1992a, 166). Then, as their praxis progresses, especially as it encounters the obstacles of human or governmental resistance, the differing religious communities will recognize their common role carried out in different fashions; that is, to provide the "common grounding that would inspire collectively the community called to liberation," for "in any society that is committed to liberation, the role of religion is one of providing inspiration, prophecy, challenge, hope in terms of the ultimate. In a multi-religious society the various religious play this role together" (Amaladoss 1992a, 166).

For Amaladoss, the venue of such globally responsible dialogue will have to move out and beyond what are the general meeting places for professional religious dialoguers. The *locus* of dialogue—the physical, socioeconomic setting—and the social class of the participants now assume crucial importance for both the process and the hoped-for success of the dialogue. "This means that interreligious dialogue must descend from the level of experts to that of the ordinary people—the poor—who are struggling together for liberation and fulfillment. It would be shown more in symbols and gestures and common activity rather than in abstract discussions. It will be a dialogue of life and struggle" (Amaladoss 1992a, 166, 172). To begin with praxis, the dialogue has to locate itself where the praxis is taking place.

Finally, but not conclusively, Amaladoss describes that toward which such a practical dialogue flows: when religious people share in a common struggle *as* religious people, they will, eventually and necessarily, have to speak about religion. They will have to share what it is that animates and guides them in their determination to heal the suffering of others and of the Earth. From his own experience in India, Amaladoss has discovered that religious persons who share a common struggle for justice will want not only to "share . . . perspectives of faith," but they will also "seek a convergence at the level of faith. This will be particularly possible and even advisable when we are speaking together not as faith meeting faith in their individuality, but faiths committing themselves together to promote justice" (Amaladoss 1992a, 171). The sharing or converging of differing faith perspectives will, of course, not only bring about deeper religious cordiality, but it will also call the participants to continue the struggle with greater resolve and bondedness.

COMPASSION-CONVERSION-COLLABORATION-COMPREHENSION

Such a practical or liberative method of dialogue accomplishes a smoother and more effective turning of the "hermeneutical circle"—that process by which we move out from our limited horizons to understand or interpret a text, a person, or a culture that has not been within the horizon of our comprehension. (Such texts, of course, can be those of our own culture and religion.) The movements of this circle—or the spokes of this wheel—have been variously described, usually in pairs: praxis and theory, experience and reflection, identity and otherness. In the liberative or globally responsible method I am proposing, the hermeneutical wheel turns on four spokes, or four movements, that constantly support and call for each other. In all of them, the "interpreters" or searchers for truth are called out of themselves; they are never alone; the act of understanding is always an act that involves an other. Thus, all of the words describing these four spokes begin with Anglicized forms of the Latin prefix or preposition *cum* ("with"): com-passion, con-version, col-laboration, com-prehension. In understanding how each of them involves and affects the participants of dialogue, we will better grasp what such a liberative model requires and promises.

Compassion: This is the "condition of the possibility" for the kind of liberative dialogue I am talking about. This is the first movement toward such an encounter among persons of differing religious communities. Unless they all, from their varied perspectives and for their varied reasons, *feel compassion* for those who are suffering or for the Earth, the kind of dialogue I am talking about will not take place. I am not saying that all persons feel such compassionate responses to suffering or victimization; to make such a claim would be to ignore what Christians call the reality of sin or what Buddhists see as ignorance. But there are many people who *do* feel compassion; they find it arising out of their humanity and out of their religious experience and convictions.

Such persons will find themselves linked in a twofold direction: with those who are the victims and also with others who find themselves responding with similar compassion. Here we have the first seeds of what Michael Amaladoss called "the principle of unity" among the participants in dialogue (Amaladoss 1992a, 166). The compassion I feel wants to join with the compassion you feel; compassion makes us brother and sister to each other. The reality of victims and of suffering calls us to community and to dialogue.

Conversion: To feel with and for others who are suffering is to be claimed by them. They not only touch our sensibilities, they call forth our response. Truly to feel compassion is to be *converted*; our life is turned around, changed. Compassion makes demands. We can no longer live the way we did before we felt this compassion. And once again, to experience such a turning around and the calling that it contains is to be turned toward and called with other people who have had the same kind of experience. We want to join others who have also experienced such conversion. There is no talk yet of what to do or of any common plans and projects. There is just the common conversion, the common calling to do something about suffering or injustice that brings us together.

But it *is* a shared conversion. In chapter 7 I suggested that such an experience of feeling called or claimed is a religious conversion. From my religious perspective, such an experience of being so deeply touched and turned by the plight of another human or sentient being both looks and feels like what I would call the action of the Spirit (or the reality of the interconnected Dharma). But whether we term this kind of conversion a religious experience or not, the practical effects are the same: we find ourselves responding to a reality that we want to change or ameliorate, and in doing this, we look for others who are also seeking similar responses.

Thus, in the first meetings of a liberative dialogue, persons of different faith communities will talk about how they have felt compassion for and how they feel changed by experiences of eco-human injustice or suffering—or how they themselves have been victims. This makes for a genuine coming together—a meeting of minds and hearts. We tell each other how and why we feel called upon to do something about the malnutrition in the village, the lack of medicine or schools, the expropriation of land, the devastation of the forests. In a liberative dialogue, we first feel together, cry together, and hope together. Such shared conversion experiences can be just as effective—maybe more effective—than the shared religious experiences we can have through meditation or ritual. There is an existential, human bondedness already alive and active before we actually speak to each other as religious persons.

Collaboration: Compassion for the suffering and conversion to their cause naturally and necessarily leads to action. Having been called by the same concerns about suffering due to injustice, members of different religious communities will also feel themselves called to act together in doing something about the reality of suffering. Here we arrive at the heart of the liberative praxis that will tighten the existential, human ties among persons of very different religious backgrounds. First, this praxis will require that after having agreed on what problems they want to address, participants in dialogue seek to identify and understand the origin or causes of such problems. This will call for some kind of shared socioeconomic analysis. Admittedly, this is where the diversity of religious perspectives will come into play; there will most likely be no one analysis of the cause of the suffering and oppression and therefore no one program or plan for its solution. Such diversity of analyses and such a storehouse of remedies is precisely the richness that the diversity of religions brings to the task of saving our planet.

That this diversity of analyses and proposed solutions will lead to collaboration rather than division is something that must be worked at especially during this first "practical" stage of the dialogue. Hope that such efforts will bear the fruits of solidarity and collaborative efforts is based on two other integral ingredients to a liberative dialogue:

a) All efforts to listen to each other's analyses and proposals will be rooted in and nurtured by compassion for the suffering; thus, the dominant concern that guides the discussions is not the desire to promote one's own agenda or religious convictions but to remove the suffering and remedy the situation. Our conversion to the well-being of this Earth and its victims will enable us both to speak our minds boldly but also to step back in order to listen and try new ideas and tactics.

b) More effectively, our multireligious efforts to build collaboration out of our differing analyses and plans will be guided and kept in check by one of the central elements of a liberative method of dialogue: what we have called in chapter 5 "the hermeneutical privilege" or the "epistemological priority" of the victims and the struggling poor. It is they to whom we must listen first, they who will "arbitrate" between the differing contributions made by the differing religious communities. A liberative praxis means identifying with and learning from those who are the primary victims of injustice. It is especially the victims who will be the interpreters or the "hermeneutical bridges" that will enable persons of diverse religious experience and beliefs to listen to and understand each other.

And so, on the basis of a richly diverse yet unified analysis of the causes of suffering, always acting *with* and not just *for* the marginalized, this interreligious community of praxis will *act together* for justice, for peace, for ecological sustainability—in whatever concrete ways it has agreed upon in its particular situation. This acting together will gather the different religious communities all the more into a common community of shared courage, frustration, anger, anguish; it will bring them together in a shared experience of fear, of danger, perhaps of imprisonment and even martyrdom. It will also bond them in shared success and joy in bringing about change and in transforming structures of oppression and suffering into communities of justice, cooperation, and unity. Such shared experiences, rising out of a shared liberative, transformative praxis, will enable persons of differing religions to be and feel themselves together as co-workers and as friends in a deeply human way. To work and suffer together, to fail and succeed together, transcends culture and language and religion.

Comprehension: Such practical-personal togetherness opens the doors to *religious* togetherness. Having suffered (compassion) with the suffering and come together in response (conversion) to their plight, having labored with and for them, religious persons can begin—will feel called to begin—the task of comprehending or understanding each other. Under the natural movement of praxis, the hermeneutical circle now moves to reflection, discussion, study, prayer, and meditation. But all these efforts to share and understand on the religious level will take place in the same arena that compassion and conversion and collaboration were felt and lived out: *together.* Such pursuits will *not* be confined to where they traditionally have been carried out—back home, in one's own temple or church or mosque. Rather, religious persons who have acted together will now speak and witness religiously together. Buddhists and Christians and Muslims—having acted and suffered together, having been called together in a new way by the victims of this Earth—will now reflect and talk together about their religious convictions and motivations. Now they will attempt to "rehear" or "re-view" their scriptures and beliefs and stories and explain not only to themselves but to others what it is that animates and guides and sustains their compassion, their conversion, and their collaboration for eco-human well-being.

As Edward Schillebeeckx sees it, this is a new form of ecumenism. "A common concern in solidarity for the poor and oppressed reunites men and women in the *'ecumene of suffering humanity'* and this action in solidarity can then bring us back to theory; in other words, through orthopraxis we can again confess and express in new words an authentic and living orthodoxy" (Schillebeeckx 1990, 83). This will be an orthodoxy that is made intelligible and shared with members of other traditions—a shared orthopraxis, as it were, leading to a communication between orthodoxies. In other words, what I am envisioning here is an interreligious renewal analogous to the Christian ecclesial renewal experienced by many Christian communities that have followed a pastoral program inspired by liberation theology. When religious persons reflect on their religious heritage on the basis of a praxis of commitment to the poor and oppressed, they find themselves "bringing forth new treasures" from old treasures; they see and hear and understand their own *and* each other's scriptures and beliefs with new eyes and new heart.

For example, having heard and actually seen how the Four Noble Truths or the nirvanic experience of *pratitya-samutpada* are enabling and directing Buddhist partners in the transformation of village life in Sri Lanka, Christians can come to appreciate and appropriate such beliefs/experiences in genuinely new and fruitful ways. And Buddhists will be able to grasp better the Christian belief in the Reign of God or in the resurrection of Jesus having witnessed how such visions of the future and such a sense of the living Christ have inspired Christians in their efforts to transform society and never give up hope. In the United States, it has been the shared commitment of Christians with Native Americans to save the Earth from technological and consumerist devastation that has enabled Christians as never before to grasp and learn from the world-affirming Native American spirituality.

We have already begun to catch glimpses of the fruits of comprehension and mutual religious enrichment that can grow from the tree of shared interreligious liberative praxis. For me, the following claim of John Gort is not at all exaggerated or naive: "Joint interreligious praxis among and on behalf of the poor will yield not only the enhancement of a greater measure of justice but also an increase of communication and understanding. It is in the crucible of praxis and solidarity that religious beliefs, perceptions, experiences are tested and given deeper and broader meaning and context" (Gort 1991, 73).[1]

BASE HUMAN COMMUNITIES

Implied in what I have been urging so far is that such liberative, globally responsible dialogue can take place only in a *community*. This kind of interreligious encounter cannot take form if carried out by people who come together for a weekend at a dialogue center or university. A dialogue that begins with, or essentially includes, some form of liberative praxis must be realized in a community of people who are coming together to act and analyze. Thus, there have been many, especially in Asia, who are urging that interreligious dialogue be carried out especially (not exclusively) in *base human communities*.[2]

The model here is that of the base Christian communities that have sprung up throughout Latin America and have proven to be transformative of both church and society. In a multireligious context, the model must be expanded and adjusted. The formative nucleus remains the same: the resolve to make critical, transformative links between religious values and the suffering due to eco-human injustice. Basic communities of this type gather in order first to recognize and analyze their situations of exploitation or marginalization and then to ask how these realities can be brought into a critical, life-giving conversation with the religious convictions represented in the group.

In the age-old multireligious reality of Asia, and in the brewing multireligious context of Europe and North America, there is the growing sense that what has been done so productively in Christian communities can be done also in multifaith communities. When the "many poor" realize that they also represent the "many religions," such base human communities begin to grow. They are grounded in the common *human* problems facing the followers of all the religions of a particular location. Speaking from his multireligious and suffering context of Sri Lanka, Michael Rodrigo announced in 1986 that the growing "dialogue of life and development with justice" is bringing BCC's (Base Christian Communities) to become "BHC's" (Base Human Communities) (Rodrigo 1988).[3]

In their practical functioning, BHCs are no different from BCCs: they begin with discussion of where they and their communities are hurting; they listen to each other's stories of discrimination, lack of medical care or education, abuse by government or local powers. They will talk also about their efforts to work together, about what has or has not been effective, about how they have hoped and suffered together. And *then* will come the distinctive differences. Felix Wilfred, from his experience with such communities in India, describes the multireligious sharing and communication that contribute to the identity and strength of these groups:

> The religious experience of the followers of various religions will go to reinforcing the bond of unity and lead to concrete projects for transforming society. Common readings from the Koran, Gita, Bible, Dharmapada, Buddha, etc. will form a regular feature of these communities. . . . [They operate] for the cause of workers, peasants, especially of the unorganized sector, for the defense of the dignity and rights of women, tribals, etc. The spirit and tradition of each religion on these questions could be brought to bear for joint action and furnish deeper motivations. . . . One should not think of these communities as merely experimental or exceptional; they should become widespread and common in Asia (Wilfred 1986, 50, 53).

Base human communities are being proposed not only as a positive, pluralistic means of responding to cries for justice and well-being, but also as a way of preventing the abuse of religion. Michael Amaladoss, who has witnessed the exploitation of religion for self-serving political goals that in India is called "communalism," warns against the danger of any one religion alone mounting a program for social or ecological betterment. "It seems advisable that we do not have political groupings based on a particular religious identity in a multireligious country. Politics and religion is a dangerous mixture that we can do without in India" (Amaladoss 1992a, 169). But if the mixture is politics (or socioeconomic programs) and multiple religions, the danger that any one religion may be taken up as a political smoke-screen or a weapon to promote the interests of a particular party is greatly diminished. There are the checks and balances, as well as the close personal bonds that come out of joint praxis, and these will serve as diagnosis and medicine for inclinations to use religion to promote hatred rather than cooperation. The best remedy for the exploitative abuse of any one religion is to call its members to a community of discourse and collaboration with other religious believers.

Yet, in forming such base human communities, history cannot be forced into a closet. There is the reality—the raw, horrible, bloody reality—of the way religions in a particular context or country have moved people to cut each other's throats rather than join each other's hearts and hands. In most parts of the world—whether the Hindu-Muslim strife in India, or the Jewish-Christian animosity in Europe, or the Native American-Christian horrors in North and South America, or Catholic-Protestant warfare in Northern Ireland—it is impossible to call forth base human communities and a globally responsible and cooperative dialogue among religions without first recognizing the realities of such historical and present-day interreligious violence and exploitation. "Recognizing" means reviewing, admitting, talking about, maybe even reconstructing ("re-membering") history.

Such a realistic recognition of history is important, or even prerequisite, for the formation of base human communities for at least two reasons: it enables real, perhaps suppressed, feelings of anger or shame to be expressed; and it sets the stage for repentance and the asking of forgiveness. In order to establish the trust necessary for persons of differing religious histories and experience to act together, they first must be honest about how they feel toward each other in the light of past history or present realities. And then they must ask forgiveness of each other and resolve, together, to overcome or burn off the negative karma that unavoidably results from such histories. Only so can they begin to collaborate in the formation of positive karma. Or, in the language of Christian liturgy, some kind of entrance rite of confession and repentance must precede the actual efforts to act together for eco-human well-being.

In the language of Christian liberation theology or of hermeneutical theory, such an entrance rite would embody and be directed by a *hermeneutic of suspicion*. In fact, liberationists would say that this is the energizing warm-up for, or the first turn of, the hermeneutical circle between the *praxis* of liberation and the *reflection* on religious scriptures and traditions. Juan Luis Segundo, for instance, warns that before Christians can reread or re-hear the Bible and tradition with the eyes and ears of the oppressed, they must first prepare themselves to acknowledge how these sacred texts have been used as instruments of ideological suppression and manipulation of one group or class by another (Segundo 1975, 7-9).

Similarly, in multireligious communities of action and reflection on each other's religious heritage, the participants must first be suspicious of how their traditions may have been abused. They need to prepare themselves for what the dialogue will spell out in greater detail—how they have used their religion or sold out their original vision to "adjust" to the status quo, to curry favor with the mighty, to hold the reins of dominance over others. There is no ideologically pure religion; all religious communities have sinned. But that such ideological abuse inevitably creeps into all religious consciousness and practice is not the greatest of evils; it is far more dangerous to be unaware or to deny that this is the plight of all religions, including our own. Thus, the first turn in the wheel of a globally responsible interreligious dialogue, or the first preparatory step in forming base human communities of many religious believers, is to be suspicious of the evil that may have been done or is being done in the name of our religion. In other terms, we must first examine our religious conscience—or allow others to help us examine it—confess our sins, ask forgiveness, and then move forward together to act and reflect interreligiously.

And if this be done—if in base human communities persons of differing religious paths come together to ask forgiveness for how their religions have separated them and then seek to forge ways in which their religions enable them to first act together and then understand each other more deeply—then perhaps the experience that Aloysius Pieris has had in his base human communities of Buddhists and Christians in Sri Lanka will be multiplied throughout the world: "Here co-pilgrims expound their respective scriptures, retelling the story of Jesus and Gautama in a core-to-core dialogue that makes their hearts burn (Luke 24:32)" (Pieris 1987, 175).

To Oppose without Excluding

But hearts will not always burn in unison and collaboration. That would be to paint a much too rosy picture of liberative or globally responsive dialogue. Precisely because the stakes are so high in the common concern for eco-human justice—life or death for persons and planet—participants in such a dialogue are going to be much more involved and passionate than if, say, they were discussing their different views on the nature of angels or afterlife. As already recognized, in a liberative dialogue, although the problem that everyone recognizes is one, the solution is not. There will be a splash of differing diagnoses and remedies for the one problem. And while we are hoping that for the most part this diversity will spawn complementarity, this will not always be the case. Differences will sometimes make for contradictions, and that means disagreements. And because the subject matter of the disagreements are life-and-death issues, differences will also lead to opposition and resistance. More painfully, I may find your religion's analysis and solution for our common problem to be not only incomplete or incoherent or ineffective but *intolerable*. My voiced "no" will call me to some form of practical opposition.

This is where a globally responsible dialogue or a base human community can not only fall apart but explode. In a very practical way, we are facing the theoretical question we raised in chapter 6: "Whose justice are we talking about? Whose justice will take precedence?" If I not only find your justice incorrect but intolerable, then your justice has become for me an injustice. Miroslav Volf, who has witnessed the clash of religious justices in his former Yugoslavia, states the danger disturbingly: "When competing accounts of justice clash, one person's justice becomes another person's barbarity. And when one person's justice is another person's barbarity, society sinks into bloody chaos. Is there a way out? Only if we can end the struggle of justice against justice" (Volf 1994, 4).

Volf offers some helpful, though difficult, advice on how we can find a way out of the clash of justice against justice. He proposes that if our liberative dialogues on eco-human justice are seen only in terms of oppression *vs.* liberation, we all too easily can end up at each other's throats. We must also see our difficult dialogues in the framework of exclusion *vs.* embrace. The torrent of suffering enveloping so much of our globe today originates fundamentally, according to Volf, not from oppression but from exclusion. We cut ourselves off from each other; we pin our well-being only on our own selves; we think that we can simply "be" and forget that we can only "be with." Thus, true and lasting well-being can come not simply through liberation and the providing of civil and economic rights (as essential as these goals may be), but rather well-being will depend on a true embrace of the other, on making room for others precisely in their otherness and difference from or even opposition to us (Volf 1992).

Volf spells out what this means for a liberative dialogue in base human communities: "We cannot expect to agree on justice if we are not ready to distance ourselves from ourselves and make space within ourselves for the other. There can be no justice without the will to embrace the other, just as there can be no genuine embrace without justice" (Volf 1994, 9). This means that even when we are in disagreement over our notions of justice, even when I find that your notion of justice is intolerable and that I must resist it, even then I will resist in a way in which *I do not simply exclude you.* I still try to maintain our connectedness; I still am open to carrying on a further conversation, even in the act of resisting. This is not easy. It is really at the heart of Gandhi's and Martin Luther King's nonviolent movement of resistance. They struggled resolutely against what they felt were intolerably oppressive systems, and yet they did so in a way in which they never excluded their opponents as an enemy. Those with whom they differed were still others with whom they hoped to nurture a dialogue.

To embrace and practice this paradox of resisting and embracing at the same time will require, further, that all participants in a globally responsible dialogue try to follow what Volf calls "enlarged thinking." Drawing on perspectives from Hannah Arendt (1961) and Seyla Benhabib (1992), Volf urges an attitude that I see as part of the very lifeblood of a globally responsible dialogue among religious persons: even when we are convinced to our core that our program of eco-human justice is correct, even when we are convinced that we must resist the program of the other, we must do so out of the realization that such convictions are only part of the picture, that there is always room for further vision, even for unexpected moderation and correction. We must always be ready to expand our thinking, yes, even our moral convictions. So even when we oppose the other, we must at the same time embrace the other; in resisting, we must also listen; in standing firm, we must be ready, also, to change.

> We can enrich and correct our convictions about justice by engaging in the exercise of "enlarged thinking" in encounter with those who do not belong to our tradition—by letting the voices and perspectives of others, especially those with whom we might be in conflict, resonate within ourselves, by allowing them to help us see them, as well as ourselves, from their perspective, by readjusting our perspectives as we take into account their perspectives. As we open ourselves for each other's perspectives, we can hope that competing justices will become converging justices (Volf 1994, 8).

To be as deeply committed to our programs for eco-human justice as we are genuinely open to modify and redirect those programs in the light of what we can learn from others—this is to work with eco-human justice as a *relative absolute criterion,* as was described in the previous chapter. Because we feel an *absolute* commitment to what we see as the requirements for eco-human well-being, we are ready to *oppose* all that would endanger this vision, but because we know that our visions are always *relative* and limited, we will never simply *exclude* what we are opposing. Again, we are walking the razor edge of paradox: to oppose and yet also to embrace.

NONVIOLENCE AND THE PRIVILEGED VOICE OF VICTIMS

This ideal of adhering to eco-human justice as a *relative-absolute* norm, this determination to embrace whatever we have to oppose, is difficult and elusive. To help make it more of a practical possibility, I offer two further suggestions or guidelines for how such a paradoxical policy can be affirmed and practiced in the dialogue.

a) What was said in chapter 5 about the hermeneutical privilege of the victims has a very concrete, practical role to play in helping us determine when we are to resist and when we are to embrace. Here is where the victims of eco-human injustice, or those who are suffering most, must carry out their privileged, mediating role in a liberative dialogue. It is they who will help us know whether our programs for promoting well-being or removing justice are "true"—how well these programs or beliefs actually work. It is the victims who will help open us to seeing the liberative, transformative content and power of beliefs or practices which we have never considered or which seem from our isolated perspective to be oppressive. If all religious participants in the dialogue are primarily listening to those who are most in need of liberation and transformation, and if these victims are thoroughly part of both the liberative praxis and the religious reflection that make up a globally responsible dialogue, then the religious communities will be better able to listen to each other. Any attempts to take absolute positions or to oppose the programs or claims of others will have to have, as it were, the seal of approval from the victims and the oppressed. Where that approval is lacking, where the oppressed are raising further questions or caveats, there is the signal that our supposed absolute stance must be reconsidered through more authentic listening to the others. The balance or rhythm of absolute-relative norms, or of full commitment and full openness, will be guided by the experiences and voices of the victims.

b) Also, and just as important, if eco-human well-being is to serve as a relative-absolute norm within an interreligious dialogue, it can do so only if the dialogue is always *nonviolent*. Nonviolence is a practical means—indeed, it is the expression—of living out our relative-absolute commitment to global responsibility. "The ability to stand for the truth as one sees it in the realm of experience and action in such a way, however, that one's own view is always open to correction and thus to place one's own existence at stake—is possible only as nonviolent praxis" (Krieger 1990, 239). Gandhi's commitment to *satyagraha* was a commitment to a liberative truth (*swaraj*—the freedom of India) that was both absolute and relative. Fully, absolutely, committed to the truth of human equality and the need for Indian independence, Gandhi nevertheless did not violently force his views on the British; rather, he respected them, embraced them, tried to affirm them and learn from them. He was as absolutely resistant as he was absolutely open to cooperate where he could.

So in our liberative dialogues, we are fully committed to the truth as we see it. We witness eagerly and we resist resolutely, but we never do violence, whether physical or psychological or cultural. That means we treat the other person as a valued partner from whom we can learn, even when that other is an opponent. Nonviolence is a paradox of both strength and weakness, of resisting and bending, of a relationship with truth and with others that is both absolute and relative.

GLOBALLY RESPONSIBLE DIALOGUE
AND OTHER FORMS OF DIALOGUE

Another practical issue in the exercise of liberative or globally responsible dialogue has to do with how it relates, if it does at all, to
other forms of interreligious encounter. On the contemporary wave of
interest in religious pluralism and interreligious dialogue, there rides
an exciting variety of approaches to interfaith exchange:
- those that concentrate on the reading of *texts* (e.g. Clooney 1993);
- those that compare *doctrines* or *themes* (e.g. Neville 1991; Joseph
  Raj 1989; W. C. Smith 1993);
- those that compare religious *founders* (e.g. Lefebure 1993; Ishanand
  1988; Cragg 1984);
- those that want simply to tell *stories* and to enter imaginatively into
  each other's narratives or symbols (e.g. Biallas 1991; Carmody and
  Carmody 1988; Dunne 1972);
- those that focus on appreciating and sharing each other's religious
  experience through prayer, meditation, ritual (e.g. Mitchell 1991;
  Bede Griffiths 1976; Abhishiktananda 1984).

To answer how a liberative or globally responsible dialogue relates
to these other forms, one might use the categories employed in the
beginning of this book to describe theologies of religions: exclusivism,
inclusivism, pluralism. In stressing the urgency of a liberative cooperation of religions, are we *excluding* other forms of dialogue as passé or
irrelevant? Or are we suggesting that these other forms of encounter
are valuable in themselves but have their meaning only insofar as they
are *included* in and support a liberative dialogue? Or is a globally
responsible dialogue, urgent though it may be, simply *one among many*
ways for religions to touch each other, without any right to maintain
that it, or any other form of dialogue, is better or more urgent than the
others? As we admitted earlier, although these three categories are most
helpful in pressing one to define one's values and methods, they often
prove too neat or tight to be applied definitively.

In any case, I would describe as *pluralistic* the way most people
look upon the different types of dialogue; they would hold (if asked)
that there are a variety of approaches to multifaith encounter, and all
of them have their place, according to the disposition or context of the
interlocutors. To hold that one approach is to be preferred over others
is to lose sight of the variety of ways of being religious and of being
human.

Recent Vatican pronouncements have summarized these forms of
dialogue. In the 1984 statement of the Pontifical Council for Interreligious Dialogue,[4] "The Attitude of the Church toward the Followers of
Other Religions," and in the 1991 document "Dialogue and Procla-

mation," the Council first described a general dialogical disposition that should infuse the entire life and attitudes of a religious person. It then went on to distinguish three types of dialogue that such a disposition should promote:

1. "The dialogue of *action,* in which Christians and others collaborate for the integral development and liberation of people" ("Dialogue and Proclamation," no. 42).

2. "The dialogue of *theological exchange*" or of "*understanding*" in which "the partners come to mutual understanding and appreciation of each other's spiritual values and cultural categories and promote communion and fellowship among people" ("Attitude of the Church," no. 34).

3. "The dialogue of *religious experience,* where persons, rooted in their own religious traditions, share their spiritual riches, for instance with regard to prayer and contemplation, faith and ways of searching for God or the Absolute" ("Dialogue and Proclamation," no. 42).

Pointing out that "the different forms [of dialogue] are interconnected" ("Dialogue and Proclamation," no. 43), the Council does not want to "establish among them any order of priority" (ibid. no. 42). Nor does it say that they *have to be* interconnected. In other words, each form of dialogue is just as good as the others. Although one form can nurture another—for example, shared religious experience "can give more life to theological discussions" (ibid. no. 43)—such interplay is not necessary. This is what I would call a soundly pluralistic view of the various types of dialogue: they are equally valid and can support each other.

I find the same pluralistic viewpoint among many theologians. John Cobb, for instance, would hold to this position insofar as he insists that there should be no predetermined agenda for the dialogue, no required, mutually recognized starting point. The dialogue must be completely open-ended, without any prerequisites (Cobb 1990). In other words, the dialogue may assume any form its participants wish. The postliberal theologians described in chapter 3 would also be in this pluralistic camp, for they stress that to give preference to any type or topic of dialogue would be to privilege that area and so impose a particular preference on all the others. Thus, at the most, they would allow only ad hoc or provisional preferences: sometimes we will study texts, sometimes we will trade experiences, sometimes we will concern ourselves with practical issues of hunger or ecology—whatever we happen to agree on at the moment.

Such an undefined, open-ended, catch-as-catch-can pluralism of types of dialogue is *not* what I am recommending in this book. Although I resolutely affirm the value of all three types of dialogue, and while I recognize that in a given situation one form of dialogue may be more appropriate than another, I would still want to achieve a clearer and more demanding connectedness between the various forms of dialogue. And yes, I do want to *set priorities* among the ways religious persons can come together. But this is not a priority of value, which holds one form of dialogue to be better or more authentic than the others; rather, I am speaking of a priority of urgency and a priority of practicality. This book has so far suggested that given the state of our world today, the dialogue of action or of global responsibility has a certain urgency over other forms, and it promises to infuse the other forms with a greater effectiveness. And let me say again, such a priority for the dialogue of liberative action is a preference that I do not wish to impose on or demand of others; it is a choice which I feel can and will be made by numerous followers within all the world religious communities.

The priority of urgency that I believe can be recognized and affirmed by multiple religious communities is based on the moral awareness that I described in chapter 2; that is, the amount of suffering, human and ecological, that we are aware of interculturally today, plus the degree of danger that faces all peoples and species on this Earth, is such that persons in all religions are agreeing that their religious identities must be lived out in response to these moral challenges and responsibilities. This means that their efforts to interact with each other must also include this common concern for eco-human well-being. This does give the "dialogue of action" a definite, though certainly not exclusive, priority. It does not require that every time we come together for dialogue we have to concern ourselves with matters of eco-human suffering or injustice. But it does demand that if other forms of dialogue, such as that of understanding or shared experience, do not in some way, at some time, make connections with the plight of the suffering, if they don't lead to or call for a dialogue of action, then there is something seriously lacking in these forms of dialogue. I know this is a hard saying, and one that sounds judgmental or even imperialistic, but I am only asking whether interreligious sharing that refuses to concern itself in any way with the reality of eco-human needs can be authentic dialogue.

I also have argued that persons of varying religious backgrounds can today recognize that the dialogue of action has a priority of practicality which is based on an hermeneutical awareness available across religious boundaries. If we go about our dialogue more or less along the lines suggested so far in this chapter—that is, if some form of globally responsible praxis is the "first step" in our coming together—then we are setting up the hermeneutical context in which we will be better able to understand each other and share each other's religious experiences and symbols/stories. Dialogue, in other words, will work better if it is based on and guided by a prior (or at least concomitant) commitment to shared efforts to achieve eco-human well-being. So, if our dialogues of study or of shared experiences are not situated in a dialogue of action, they are missing something that would improve their effectiveness. Thus, shared praxis has a practical priority.

The priority that I am attributing to the dialogue of action does not, I believe, remove or reduce the real plurality of the various forms of dialogue. Though one form has a moral and practical priority, they are all necessary and interconnected. And so, just as I have insisted that the dialogues of study or of religious experience are inadequate if cut off from the dialogue of action, I must also affirm the reverse: a dialogue of liberative action that is not sustained and guided by a dialogue of study and spirituality will eventually fade away or go astray. To be prior does not mean to be better; to be more urgent does not mean to be more important.

And so the different religious members of a base human community, after or while they are working and organizing and struggling together, will also have to "do their homework." They will have to learn about each other; that means study each other's sacred texts, listen to each other's explanations of beliefs or practices, yes, learn each other's languages. I say "will have to." But what is necessary will, I expect, prove to be natural. People who work together and share commitments and laugh and cry as they struggle together for a common goal will want to learn more about each other. They will want to listen to each other, and they *will be able* to listen to each other much more successfully than if they had not worked together. Shared praxis will naturally, necessarily, lead to shared study and reflection. If it doesn't, something is wrong with the praxis.

With the same necessity and spontaneity, I suggest, religious persons who act together for eco-human justice will also want to pray/meditate and celebrate together. The dialogue of action will have to, will want to, flow into a dialogue of shared religious experiences. This movement from action to contemplation/celebration will arise from the nature and self-definition of interreligious base human communities. They are communities not simply of people who come together for the same kind of eco-human well-being and transformation, but they define themselves as *religious* people who do so. From their differing perspectives, they are people who recognize that such acting for justice must be grounded—grounded in something that inspires, sustains, and directs the praxis: in grace or in wisdom or in enlightenment, in the Spirit, in the Tao, in emptiness. All of these terms signify very different ways of being grounded, but all of them point to the need of some kind of grounding. And so the eco-human co-activists will become, also, religious co-searchers. They will seek to share their experiences, and there will be, in ancient Christian terms, a *communicatio in sacris*—a communication in the Sacred that will be called for by their collaboration with and for the oppressed.

The base human communities will become instances and examples of the dipolarity between "mysticism and prophecy" (or between "wisdom and compassion" or "gnosis and agape" or "action and contemplation") that many scholars say can be found, in different blendings, in most religious traditions. As South American liberation theologians have realized from the beginning of their movement, the more one immerses oneself in the sweat, tears, frustration, and elation of the struggle for eco-human justice, the more one feels the need for a Center that will sustain the struggle and prevent it from slipping into violence or self-promotion (Gutiérrez 1984; Sobrino 1987). "The mystical centre needs the prophetic centre if it is not to become airborne. . . . But equally the prophetic centre needs the mystical centre if it is not to become arrogant, narrow, and unlovely" (Robinson 1979, 64-65).

But in the kind of interreligious interaction I am proposing for the base human communities, we must beware of describing the dipolarity between mysticism and prophecy or between the dialogue of action and the dialogue of religious experience too neatly or clearly. As I tried to say in chapter 7, the kind of liberative praxis that I am speaking about can already, in itself, be a religious or mystical experience. To act for justice is to act from the Center; it is to be in harmony with that which is. So if there is a nonduality or a unity of opposites between the Christian experience of love of neighbor and love of God, or between the Buddhist sense of nirvana and *samsara* (or *prajna* and *karuna*), or the Gita's understanding of *bhakti marga* and *jnana marga*—then, already in action, there is contemplation. And therefore shared liberative praxis will not only call for shared religious experience, but it will *enable* us to share that experience. To have acted and struggled together will clarify, vivify, direct our shared meditations, prayers, rituals. I would venture to say that to sit together after having acted together is notably different from just sitting together. Sharing religious experience after sharing the struggle for eco-human justice is, I suggest, a deeper, more effective sharing.

To summarize this section, we can look on the three forms of dialogue—action, study, prayer—as three spokes of a wheel. All are necessary for the wheel to be sturdy and to turn. We begin the turning of the wheel by pushing on the spoke of action or liberative praxis, but if the other two spokes do not turn with it, there will be no real movement. Or, to change images, every interreligious conversation must involve the voices of three participants from the various religions: the prophet, the mystic, and the scholar. It is the prophets' role to begin the conversation and to provide it with an essential content as it unfolds. But once the conversation begins, unless the voices of the mystic and the scholar are also heard, the conversation will lose its religious content or it will be turned into a tool for purposes that can only discredit all the participants.

•

Can all this really work? Can communities of different religions be formed around a core of shared praxis? Can such praxis lead to deeper understanding and spiritual sharing? Can we oppose others in this community without excluding them? It all sounds so grand, so idealistic. If the proof of the pudding is in the eating thereof, we have to admit that this pudding of globally responsible dialogue has not yet been eaten. But there are those who have begun to taste. We will look at just how they are doing that and what we can learn from them in the next chapter.

9

IT'S WORKING

Examples of a Globally Responsible Dialogue

The practical directives on how to carry out a liberative, correlational dialogue that I offered in the previous chapter really have been, despite their practical intent, quite theoretical and general. In the hope of being more down-to-earth, I want in this chapter to share and reflect on the examples and insights I have gained from people who actually are attempting to practice this kind of interfaith cooperation for eco-human well-being. I am speaking primarily about persons, groups, and movements in India and Sri Lanka that I have met and read about. Here, on a subcontinent that is perhaps the richest in the world, both in the number and diversity of its religions and in the number and diversity of its poor, one would expect to find religious people joining hands and hearts to overcome the widespread suffering of the poor and of the land. What I found as I met with individuals and groups—Christians, Hindus, Muslims, Buddhists—committed to dialogue in India and Sri Lanka was much more complex, ambiguous, tenuous, and at the same time hopeful than I ever expected.[1]

INDIA: LABORATORY FOR DIALOGUE

THE NECESSITY OF A LIBERATIVE DIALOGUE IN INDIA

As I traveled through India and met with Christians, Hindus, and Muslims concerned about the religious diversity of their country, I heard the almost unanimous refrain: For interreligious dialogue to be relevant and authentic in India today it must be concerned with human (and many added, ecological) liberation. From those Indians directly involved in efforts to transform the awesome economic inequity and the culture-crusted forms of exploitation, I heard, not with equal unanimity but still strongly, that if socioeconomic liberation is going to succeed in India, it must be a multireligious undertaking. On the one hand, there is the spreading sense among believers and nonbelievers in India that if the traditional religions of India do not have a word to speak to the task of nation-building and to the challenge of removing the divisions and disparities that have increased since Independence in 1947, then such religions will not find a place within the struggling nation. Thus I found, even among the traditional proponents of dialogue and leaders of Catholic ashrams, an ever-present suspicion and uneasiness about traditional forms of dialogue that are purely religious or totally removed from the sprawling poverty in villages and cities.[2]

On the other hand, I found even among hardened secularists and organizers of social action groups an awareness, sometimes fully articulate and sometimes just forming, that if the masses of India are going to see their social situation of exploitation with clear eyes and if they are to be steeled with the courage to demand and act for change, they must be sustained and nourished by their traditional religious beliefs. Here is where Marxist analysis in India shows its limitations— its inability to broaden its class analysis to include the realities of caste and religion. Simply, there will be no social revolution unless it is also a religious revolution. As a group of Indian Jesuits meeting in April 1989 in Pune put it:

> In India no effective social change can take place which does not tap the power of religiosity of the masses. The only successful social movements in concrete have been religious in inspiration. The Bhakti movement was a mighty revolution that overtook the country and was stifled only by the colonial intervention in favour of the Brahmins; the freedom movement was successful when Gandhi gave it religious overtones. Another example at a different level is the tribal Christian movement (Irudayaraj 1989, 120).

Walter Fernandes of the Indian Social Institute in Delhi echoes what I heard repeatedly throughout India:

> A liberation theology in India cannot be Christian. It would have to be interreligious. Hindus, Sikhs, Muslims, and Christians would have to search together each one finding his/her inspiration in his/her own religious tradition and respecting one another's expression. . . . The same scriptures, for example, have been used as support by the subordinate classes in their struggle to be equal as well as by the ruling classes to assert their domination. The dividing line was the class option. This is the challenge in India. It would have to be an inter-religious option. To evolve a libera-

tion theology, persons of different religious traditions would have to search for the prophetic elements in the context of their common option to support those who are struggling to free themselves from oppression (Fernandes 1992, 62).

And so, the Roman Catholic Indian Theological Association, in its 1988 and 1989 annual meetings, drew up concluding statements that take an anthropocentric approach to the reality of other religions and to the challenge of interreligious dialogue: "We became convinced that any authentic and living theology of religious pluralism can emerge only from the context of an interreligious praxis of liberation, dialogue, and inculturation" (Indian Theological Association 1989, no. 4). "We in India are aware that this liberation process cannot be successfully achieved by only one community or ideological group alone. The different communities have to come together for the transformation of society and for the betterment of 'Man' who is their common centre as well as their rallying point" (Indian Theological Association 1988, no. 25).[3]

Though perhaps not as well orchestrated as the Christians, there are spokespersons from the other religious traditions of India who are equally resolute and even passionate in calling for a meeting of religions that will have as its starting point and focus the widespread social and economic pain of the majority of Indians. One of the clearest and most provocative voices within the Hindu community is that of Swami Agnivesh, who, from his work with the outcasts, was personally transformed from a staunch opponent of interfaith dialogue to one of the most prophetic voices for a liberative revision of traditional Hinduism and for a "liberative ecumenism" among India's religions (see Swami Agnivesh, 1995). Using the example of Gandhi, S. Jeyapragasam, of the Centre for Gandhian Studies in Madurai, challenges all Hindus and religious persons of India to follow Gandhi in forming a collaborative community of differing religions for the well-being of all Indians (Pushparajan 1990). From his personal and scholarly identification with the tradition of Saiva Siddhanta, S. Gangadaran is calling his fellow Saivites of South India to respond to the call for authentic, transformative love of neighbor in collaboration with other religious communities (Gangadaran 1991). And from the Muslim community, speaking to all the other religious communities, Asghar Ali Engineer offers his socioreligious analysis of India's divisiveness and his call to his fellow Muslims and religious neighbors to develop an intercommunal "theology of liberation" (Engineer 1990, 1988b; also Singh 1991).

The Roman Catholic bishops of Asia, meeting in Madras in 1982, gave voice to a consensus that finds echoes of agreement among many of the religious leaders of India: "Since the religions, as the Church, are at the service of the world, inter-religious dialogue cannot be confined to the religious sphere but must embrace all dimensions of life: economic, socio-political, cultural and religious. It is in their common commitment to the fuller life of the human community that they discover their complementarity and the urgency and relevance of dialogue at all levels" (quoted in Amaladoss 1992a, 168).

THE COMPLEXITY/IMPOSSIBILITY OF A LIBERATIVE DIALOGUE IN INDIA

But all is not as consensual and clear as it may sound. As adamant and coherent as were the voices I heard in India calling for a multifaith liberative dialogue, just as somber and pained were these same voices as they spoke of the complexity, even apparent impossibility, of such a dialogue in India. The Jesuit Community of St. Joseph's High School and College in Bangalore pinpointed the problem that I heard referred to by scholars and grassroots promoters of dialogue in both northern and southern India: on the macro level one can talk about how the religions can come together for the welfare of society, but on the micro level—in the villages, the urban slums, and among social activists—this is not how religion is *felt*.[4] The much more evident, if not actual, role of religion in India today (some would argue, in the world today) is as a dynamo of division and conflict rather than of unity and cooperation.

The historical track record of religion in India, I heard from many Indian analysts, seems to be that of an agent of animosity rather than of amity. From the earliest records of Indian history, when the invading light-skinned Aryans overwhelmed and subjected the dark-skinned Dravidians, it was in the name of their superior, warring gods that the Aryans justified their victory, and it was with religion that they elaborated the caste system as the enduring seal of their victory. Centuries later, when the Muslims launched their invasion (from the ninth to the sixteenth centuries), it was again in the name of the one, all-powerful Allah that so much of the devastation was wrought. And when the Portuguese and then the British came to impose their colonial rules or raj, their sense of superiority and ownership was nurtured by the superiority of their one true religion over the aberrations of paganism.[5] Finally today, when the tables have been turned and the indigenous cultures of India are free to take their legitimate place in the sun, calls are resounding to reinstate "Hindutva"—the Hinduness of India—which all too often means the subordination or suppression of other religious communities. Against the background of both history and the daily newspapers, religion in India appears to be much more of an intercommunal weapon than an intercommunal bond.

That's the word one hears over and over again in discussions of India's present plight and of the role of religion in that plight: *communalism* (Engineer 1984, 1988b; Arokiasamy 1988). The word indicates not the cohesion of communities but their conflict. A land teeming with ethnic, linguistic, and cultural differences, India has not been able to turn the rich diversity of its ethnic ores into the precious gold of national unity. Some would argue that one of the principal reasons the high hopes of such unity, which blew so strongly after Independence in 1947, have not borne fruit is precisely because those in power have not respected the vibrant, incorrigible plurality that is India. Instead of unification, the goal has been centralization, and centralization can come about only when one economic or cultural group assumes and exercises domination over the others (Wilfred 1994). Centralization boils diversity into oneness; unity respects the diversity and forms it into connectedness. And it would seem to many that this drive to centralize the other under one's own power and thus to incite the response of communalism (every group either refusing to be absorbed or seeking to absorb) is either *caused* or at least *promoted* by religious identities. In the name of Ram, the mosque in Ayodhya had to be destroyed by the Hindus; in the name of Allah, it had to be defended. Communalism and religion are, in the experience of many in India, synonymous.

Here we encounter another paradox. It is precisely the difficulty or apparent impossibility of a liberative dialogue among religions in India that becomes the reason, or at least the pressing occasion, for its *necessity*! This, too, I experienced repeatedly in my travels throughout the subcontinent: the anguish that I heard in the voices and saw on the faces of Hindus, Muslims, and Christians as they described how people were battling and killing each other in the name of religious identity usually became the emboldened, impassioned resolve on their part to put an end to such use or abuse of religion. Precisely because religion is being used so effectively and extensively as a tool of communal violence, we *must* make counter efforts to use it as a tool of dialogical cooperation.

Such a counter-response, calling for a correlational, cooperative dialogue of religions, was explained to me as a necessity both in the name of hard-nosed political analysis and of deep religious faith. The political analysis is, first of all, coldly pragmatic: fight fire with fire. If people are using religion to divide, we must use it to unite. This claim is grounded in a multitude of sociological-political studies arguing that in the vast majority of cases of interreligious violence, the issue or the fundamental cause is not at all religious. Rather, politicians or economic blocs make use of religion to stir up group fears or passions; under the banner of religious identity, competing electoral votes or economic parties are attacked and driven from one's locale. To proclaim a vote for a particular party as a vote to protect or reinstate one's religious dignity is a highly effective political ploy (Swamy 1991; Lourdusamy 1990; Engineer 1988b; Pulsfort 1991).

In the minds of those in India intent on maintaining or securing their economic-political power, there is no doubt: they cannot do so without making use of religion—usually a fundamentalistic type of religion—as part of their political platform. Walter Fernandes tellingly contrasts this clarity of the dominant powers with the uncertainty of the diverse groups of dominated: "While the subordinate sections are divided on the role of religion either as a tool in the hands of their oppressors or as a prophetic element which can help them reacquire their identity, the dominant sections are, by and large, clear on the role religion can play. In order to protect their economic interests, they use religion regularly against the subordinate classes" (Fernandes 1989, 36).

This is where religious faith adds its voice: the unanimity and clarity among the politicians in their abuse of religion in India must be met by an equally unanimous and committed resolve on the part of the religious communities to promote what their religious convictions tell them is the authentic use of religion. Yes, religion can be used as either a tool of oppression *or* a power for transformation, but the former is an abuse of the nature of religion, while the latter is its fulfillment. And in the horrible specter of so much abuse, responsible, committed religious people must respond, more resolutely and courageously than ever, to foster and insist on the unitive, collaborative, healing powers of religious experience. The difficulty of doing this is all the more reason for its necessity.

In India Dialogue Is a Second Step

I found widespread agreement among many Indians that when groups of Hindus and Muslims and Christians come together, dialogue, as it has traditionally been understood, is not the first order of the day. It must come second, maybe third. The reason for this insistence is not the hermeneutical considerations I gave earlier—that shared praxis prepares the soil in which understanding can grow. Rather, historical and present sociological realities convince Indians that without preparatory conditioning, the soil of dialogue in India is barren. The history of the abuse of religion—the history of Muslims killing Hindus and Hindus murdering Muslims and Christian colonialists exploiting both—must be faced, accepted, mourned, and repented. Especially in India, for multifaith dialogue to get off the ground, it needs the strong winds of what we called a hermeneutical suspicion of religion. Individuals must be suspicious of and sincerely resolved to amend the way their religions have been used to belittle and besmirch others. As Samuel Rayan summarizes his experience of attempted dialogue in India: "Dialogue is not authentic unless it leads to reinterpretation or rejection of all oppressive aspects of the religious heritage of both partners" (Rayan 1989, 70).

In India, this first step of hermeneutical suspicion and of confession of sin cannot be properly carried out unless the primary victims of religion's abusive power have a clear and preferential voice in the interreligious encounters. The experience of many Indians, I found, confirms my theoretical arguments for the hermeneutical priority of the oppressed. Only the abused can truly paint the picture of abuse. Therefore, in outlining a program for liberative dialogue in India, Felix Wilfred reminds us:

> Millions of Dalits [outcasts] and oppressed . . . would repudiate (and in fact have repudiated) the religion of their experience because their history and social experience have demonstrated that it has been one of the chief sources of their enslavement. . . . We [therefore] cannot today meaningfully enter into a discourse of praxis of liberating dialogue without taking into serious account the colossal fact of the ideological critique of Indian religious traditions, especially Hinduism, on the part of the marginalized, especially the Dalits. Any liberating dialogue has to settle score with the religious experience of the marginalized. . . . Liberating dialogue is possible only among the victims in the various religious traditions of India—Hindu, Islamic, Christian, etc.—who dare such a radical critique of their religion and their religious sources. . . . The victims themselves are the active subjects of liberating dialogue. This and nothing short of this deserves to be named as liberating dialogue (Wilfred 1994, 37).

As part, or a consequence, of the active participation of the victims in the dialogue and the critique of religion that results from this participation, there will follow the concrete working together for a shared project of human or ecological justice. Some such praxis—extended over time, fully shared, and calling for the commitment and compassion of all involved—will serve as further salve for the wounds caused by the abuse of religion. Such praxis will create the atmosphere of trust and solidarity that will enable Hindus, Christians, Muslims to be together religiously and to share their beliefs and experiences. Again, Samuel Rayan speaks of his own experience of dialogue in India: "Working together for liberation and for a community of justice, equality and peace, the religions enter a process of self-discovery and inter-fecundation" (Rayan 1990, 130).

Ashrams vs. Base Human Communities

There is another area which lays bare tensions between the practical advice I gave in the previous chapter and the actual situation in India. The suggestions that I made for balancing and yet setting priorities for the different types of dialogue (action, prayer, study) don't seem to work that smoothly in India; in fact, there seem to be insurmountable difficulties. In the Christian communities of India, these problems are spotlighted mainly in the conversations going on between the contemplatives and the liberationists—or between those who turn to *ashrams* (centers of contemplation, open to all religions)[6] and those who prefer *base human communities* as the most appropriate way to respond to the signs of the times in India.[7] From eavesdropping on these often animated conversations, I have learned, I think, to be both more cautious and more clear in speaking about the priority of a liberative or globally responsible model for dialogue.[8]

The differences between the ashramites who practice a dialogue of contemplation and the liberationists who urge a dialogue of action are certainly not a matter of either-or. With Christian tradition (and with many other religious traditions), both sides agree that the spiritual life generally must move like a pendulum between action and contemplation, between efforts at personal and societal transformation. For the most part, the contemplatives of the ashrams readily agree that given both the demands of the gospel and the situation of poverty and suffering in India, an active commitment to working for social justice claims a priority for the churches in India. They also readily admit that life in an ashram must include, in some way and to some degree, an active concern for the plight of the Dalits, the scheduled castes and tribal peoples, and the exploitation of Indian women (Vandana 1982). But they also remind those whose priority is a liberative dialogue in base human communities, that there will always be, as there always must be, those individuals who receive a special calling to the life of contemplation; while not excluding a concern for societal suffering and transformation, these people will give priority to a life of silence and withdrawal.

The reasons, as I understood them, why there will always be the need for ashramites or contemplatives to give a priority to the "dialogue of prayer," are twofold—theological and psycho-spiritual. Theologically, according to the beliefs of Christianity (and I again suspect that there would be widespread interreligious agreement on this), while in the practical order our first response must be to help our neighbor, in the deeper or ontological order, that response needs to be grounded in our oneness with the Divine. More directly, while love of neighbor and love of God cannot be separated, and usually God wants us to love our neighbor first, the love we spill over our neighbor must flow from a love of God if it is to be authentic and enduring. The role of contemplatives is to live this truth and so to remind all people of it. As Sister Vandana, 1991 president of the Catholic Ashramites of India, puts it: "The human race needs men and women who embody the absolute claims of God on his creatures in a strictly contemplative life, and this has to be recognized as an authentic vocation, not only for the sake of the individual's concerns but for all humans who need to be reminded of this essential dimension of their own being" (Vandana 1993, 158).

This theological reality of the "priority of the Divine" is reflected practically in a psycho-spiritual truth that the ashramites feel does not need proving. It is evident all too often in social or ecological movements or agents: their successes are short-lived or cause as many problems of discrimination or power as they started with. Why? Sister Sarah Grant, another veteran ashramite of India, offers a sharply clear response in her contribution to a conference on liberative dialogue in India: "I came to see more and more clearly that real liberation has to take place first of all within the human psyche. . . . A liberation theology for India, or anywhere else for that matter, must in fact start from this basic conviction that freedom must first take root in the human heart" (Grant 1994, 72-73; also Grant 1987). And so she delivers this powerful assertion: "The ineradicable conviction, born of experience, that the inner freedom of every human person ultimately depends on a certain awareness, however obscure, of being thus 'rooted in the Eternal' is, it seems to me, the most distinctive contribution of the ashram tradition to the theology of liberation" (Grant 1994, 75).

These creative tensions between ashrams and basic human communities are essential for a life-giving balance and interplay between a dialogue of action and a dialogue of contemplation. Even though, as Sister Grant herself would admit, we cannot wait to be truly liberated internally before we take up the interreligious work for eco-human justice, still, if we go about this work without constant contemplative efforts to be "rooted in the Eternal," our work will ultimately be to no one's avail. Thus there will be those—I would consider them to be specially chosen and so not the majority—whose role is to give a priority to the dialogue of contemplation in order to make sure that the task of struggling for eco-human well-being—given to *all* religious persons—will not be without roots. So when I insist that for the most part our interreligious encounters must begin with some kind of globally responsible praxis, I now have to add that such a beginning needs to have its roots in the individual's spirituality. Later, as the liberative praxis intensifies, those spiritual roots will become more evident and will be shared—and thus, will be deepened.

But the "dialogue" in India between ashramites and liberationists has revealed a more tangled knot in efforts to balance the claimed *priority* of liberative dialogue with the recognized *necessity* of other forms of dialogue. There seem to be situations in which the dialogue of contemplation can actually become an obstacle to the dialogue of liberation. More precisely, proponents of liberation-oriented religion and dialogue point out to the ashramites that in dialoguing with spokespersons of traditional Hinduism (as has been the case for most of the history of Christian ashrams), they are often praying and meditating with the guardians of a religious structure that continues to maintain a caste and social system that keeps Dalits, tribals, and women in a well-guarded prison of exploitation and bondage. As the record seems to show, efforts on the part of Christian ashramites to bring up these matters of caste and dowry-deaths[9] all too often meet with polite, religious silence; nothing really changes.

As George Soares-Prabhu, a liberationist critic of ashrams, puts it: "At inter-religious dialogue [with spokespersons of Brahmanic Hinduism] I have found that any attempt to bring up social issues invariably meets the standard response: 'but that is not religion'" (quoted in Vandana 1993, 154). Therefore, in the estimation of the liberationists, to continue such a dialogue is not just to avoid the issue of eco-human suffering, but to continue to recognize and indirectly give approval to a form of religion that is a cause or abettor of this suffering. Especially as a Christian committed to Jesus' God of the poor, one cannot go on with such a dialogue; indeed, one must replace it with resistance and opposition! (Rayan 1989, 69-70; Ayrookuzhiel 1989, 96-99; Soares-Prabhu in Vandana 1993, 153-56).

The depth and power of the ashramites' response to this criticism gently slapped me in the face when I had the opportunity to discuss just this issue with the participants of a meeting of Catholic Ashramites of India at Anjali Ashram in Mysore, November 11-17, 1991. Foreigner though I was, they received me graciously and listened quietly as I posed my problem: "If I were in dialogue with a Brahmin who supported caste or the subordination of women and who refused to discuss my objections to his understanding of these aspects of Hinduism, I would have to shake the dust from my feet and move on to another dialogue." After a moment of silence, Sister Vandana, with the nodding approval of others such as Bede Griffiths, Sarah Grant, and Iswar Prasad, responded: "I would not. I would continue, tactfully and appropriately, to voice my objections, but I would not stop talking and meditating with such a Brahmin. And I would do so in the hope that our rootedness in the Eternal, and in the Dharma of love and unity in the depth of Hindu tradition, would eventually enable this Brahmin to see such evils."[10]

I did not have an answer. Though I am uncomfortable with her response, it is telling me something I, and all those given to the priority of liberative praxis and dialogue, need to hear. It is pushing even further a challenge I tried to articulate in the previous chapter: in all our liberative dialogues, we must learn to *resist without excluding, to resist and at the same time embrace*. As necessary and morally imperative as our resistance and opposition may be, they must also always be "connected" and nonviolent. This, I believe, is one of the most complex and difficult challenges for a globally responsible multifaith dialogue.

SOME MODELS OF GLOBALLY RESPONSIBLE DIALOGUE

Taking heart and guidance from the old Scholastic adage, *ab esse ad posse valet illatio*—"from existence you can conclude to possibility" (or, more casually, "if something's happening, you know it is possible")—I'd like to describe, briefly but I hope adequately, a few concrete examples of what I've been calling a correlational, globally responsible dialogue. All of these examples are fledgling, still taking their "baby steps" toward reversing the exploitative or incendiary bad name that religions have in South Asia and toward linking religious communities in a shared project of social-economic transformation. Amid uncertainties, experiments, and mistakes, they're doing it. And so they are showing the possibility and promise of a liberative dialogue.

DALIT DIALOGUE—LIBERATIVE DIALOGUE

One of the most encouraging signs of such possibility and promise I found in the Dalit movements and consciousness throughout India, and in particular in the projects and vision of the Christian Institute for the Study of Religion and Society (CISRS) in Bangalore and the Department of Dalit Theology at Gurukul Theological Seminary in Madras. The multitudinous and diverse Dalits of India—the outcastes and "scheduled castes" at the bottom of (or better, buried under) the social heap, are coming to realize, slowly but inevitably, that what they have in common is much more immediate and unitive than all their social and religious differences (see, e.g., Ayrookuzhiel 1990). Whatever their social or geographical location, whatever their religious practices, they are coming to comprehend that the suffering and oppression that each of them experiences has three basic qualities in common with the experience of every other Dalit: the oppression they all suffer is essentially the same; it has basically the same cause in the cultural-economic structures of Indian reality; and its remedy will call for the efforts of more than just their own Dalit group. According to M. E. Prabhakar and A. Ayrookuzhiel of CISRS, social workers among the Dalits and poor of Bangalore are discovering that the common experiences of suffering and the shared experience of raised social consciousness are enabling Dalit men and women to *feel* that they are lost family members finding each other once again; they share a common brotherhood and sisterhood in their plight as victims of injustice.

Even though most of the so-called secular Dalit movements are still generally wary of making use of religion as an added glue to bind the various forms of Dalit experience, many of them are starting to come to a different sense of what religion is or can be: not only a culturally given that they have to deal with but also a neglected font of transformative, subversive power. Community organizers among the poor in Bangalore are discovering that when oppressed people who are also religious come together to do something about their oppression, they generally want to and need to talk about their religious motivations and ideals.[11] What Christian Dalit theologians are urging is also finding a new and clear echo among leaders from other Dalit religious communities[12]:

> In the Indian context, characterized by its religious pluralism and ethnic diversity, the vision of a just social order must be accountable to many religious traditions (Prabhakar 1989, 2-3).

> Therefore, Dalit theology should go beyond the frontiers of Christianity. *Dalits include a larger religious framework*. In our country they form a large bulk of people. A common heritage of oppression is one of the factors that should enable us to include people of other faiths. . . . The Christian and the non-Christian Dalits are both a people with a future longing (Clarke 1989, 32-33, emphasis mine).

As the Dalit groups open to each other, first in a shared praxis for the human well-being of all Dalits and then in a shared religious dialogue, they are also discovering that there is much they have in common in their forms of spirituality and even in the sacred texts or oral traditions that have guided their ancestors. What has taken place in Christian base communities is assuming form in various Dalit communities: when the oppressed are enabled to read their own scriptures or hear their own stories, they see and hear what the religious establishment seems to have been blind and deaf to. Proclamations criticizing the exploiters and empowering the exploited are resounding from new readings of the Bhagavad Gita or the story of Buddha or the message of the Upanishads.[13] Also, a hidden or simply neglected tradition (usually oral) is being discovered among Dalit societies; it portrays deities taking the side of the poor or tells dramas of how the little people were affirmed, guided, and emboldened to proclaim their dignity and throw off the shackles of oppression.[14] This very different kind of popular religion—apparently within the Hindu fold but staunchly and courageously critical of its Brahmin hierarchs—was "preached by the untouchable and lower-caste saints—many of whom were wandering ascetics without any economic base and political support" (Ayrookuzhiel 1994, 18).[15] They clearly condemned caste practices and preached a religion of interiority and common humanity. In the words of Kapila, a saint of South India:

> Oh, Brahmans, list to me!
> In all this blessed land
> There is but one great caste,
> One tribe and brotherhood
> One God does dwell above,
> And he hath made us one
> In birth and frame and tongue.[16]

Or, as a Telugu folk song puts it:

> Food or caste or place of birth
> Cannot alter human worth
> Why let caste be so supreme?
> 'tis but folly's passing stream.[17]

In the interreligious dialogue among Dalits that is getting under way in India, these are the kind of texts and narratives that are discussed and interpreted.[18]

In speaking with those involved in these first forms of interreligious dialogue among Dalits,[19] I marveled at how, in a sense, such discussions burst my familiar categories of "exclusivism, inclusivism, pluralism" (see chapter 2). The interaction among the Dalits, arising from their differing religious perspectives, swings back and forth among these classifications, always directed by their central criterion: Does a particular religious tenet or practice further the full humanity of Dalits? If a particular religion or religious community does this, it is readily admitted, no matter how different or foreign, into the pluralistic character of the Dalit conversation. In this conversation all are ready to learn—to be "included" by—the other, so that the cause of Dalit liberation may be fostered. Yet, at the same time, such a conversation among Dalits can be staunchly exclusivistic and in opposition to any form of religion that promotes the manipulation or extortion of the outcastes, whether Brahmanical Hinduism or the politics of the local Catholic bishop (see Antony Raj 1990, Japhet 1989).

With A.M. Abraham Ayrookuzhiel, "One may wonder whether this emerging historical situation of the Dalits with their increasing conscientization, decisive political importance, and growing economic base may not lead to a renaissance of all Indian religious traditions" (1994, 19). I expect that in this next decade those of us in the West who are committed to the dialogue of world religions will have much to learn from Christian Dalit theology and from the interreligious Dalit dialogue in India (see Prabhakar 1989, Nirmal 1990, Nirmal n.d., Devasahayam 1992, Irudayaraj 1990).

BASIC GANDHIAN COMMUNITIES

On the southernmost tip of India, in the district of Kanyakumari, I came across a group of people involved in a movement that proved to me that real-life praxis is indeed always a step ahead of the kind of theory that books such as this one seek to promote. They call themselves *basic* or *grassroot Gandhian communities*. They're basic or grassroot insofar as they consist of ordinary Indian folk, mainly working people from villages or small urban communities with a variety of religious backgrounds and practices. They're Gandhian insofar as what brings them together is the vision of the Mahatma that *all* Indians from *all* social levels, castes, and religions can take personal responsibility for building a united nation that will still allow for diversity, a nation grounded in justice for all. So, in their defining statement the communities describe themselves as "consisting of people from various religious affiliations and background coming together under the banner of Gandhism" (Palerasu 1991, 1).

The first stirrings of such a grand vision were enkindled in the fires of religious and communal strife that seemed to destroy such hopes. Again, the paradox: the impossibility of interreligious cooperation moved people to affirm its necessity. Communal clashes in the town of Manavalakurichi in 1982 horrified and catalyzed religious people who looked upon such conflict in the name of Hinduism or Islam as a violation of their own religious convictions. So they met, in order, as it were, to fight fire with fire. In this situation, in this concrete crisis, it worked. People were inspired to carry on this effort of using their specific community needs as the stimulus for interreligious cooperation and understanding. By 1987 these communities in Manavalakurichi were meeting regularly. In 1989, a community was formed in nearby Aloor. Today, there are about eight such communities meeting regularly, each with between twenty and thirty families; the goal is to boost the number of communities in the district to about sixty.

The early organization of these communities was itself the result of interreligious conversations. Mr. N. Palerasu, a Hindu and Gandhian scholar, provided the "Gandhian dreams of Gram Raj" (a "village nation") as one which all Indians of all religions could affirm; Father A. Tobias of the Nagercoil Catholic Diocese, affirmed the dream and provided a suggestion for structural organization. In the diocese, Catholics were experimenting with the Latin American model of basic Christian communities. Why not apply this model to India's interreligious reality and needs as Gandhi would want? The idea, though still in its infancy, grew into acting, deliberating, praying communities. Basic Gandhian communities hold as their aims and objectives to:

1. Foster fraternity among people of different faiths and an understanding of each other.

2. Celebrate all religious and national festivals jointly by people of all communities and faiths.

3. Prevent events that tend to disturb religious tolerance and take active steps to avert communal clashes.

4. Achieve social justice by actively devising constructive approaches to social problems (Tibursius 1991, 1).

These gatherings of "commoners" hope to realize the Gandhian vision of forming face-to-face communities that would give the small people a sense of empowerment in their local villages. Drawing on the religious richness of India, these communities would "also be a way of bringing interreligious and inter-ideological dialogue down from armchair experts to people at the grassroots" (Palerasu 1991, 11-13).

The practical plan was to find interested villages and to establish communities of no more than thirty families; members are to receive training in leadership and community organization. Through their example the idea will spread, it is hoped, to other villages and eventually—way down the road—become a "network of grassroot structures formed throughout the nation," thus providing "the basic infrastructure for a new social order" (Palerasu 1991, 3, 12). Grandiose dreams, indeed, but to be built on small, solid beginnings. Such an infrastructure would grow out of a sense of interreligious and inter-class community rooted in a common commitment to and cooperation for specific concerns that affect the entire community "like health, development, women's rights, youth formation" (Palerasu 1991, 3).

In the meetings of the BGCs (they use that acronym in their correspondence) that I attended in Aloor and Manavalakurichi, I saw how the dynamic of a "globally responsible, correlational" interreligious dialogue can work. In Aloor, at the Sri Krishna Ashram, on November 20, 1991, the meeting was attended by about twenty participants— Hindus, Muslims, Christian, Jains. (There were no women, but this, they informed me, was not usually the case.) After some general chit-chat and catching up on each others' families and activities, the meeting opened with reports and discussions on the two main issues for that day: conflict between Hindus and Christians in a nearby village about the village's name, and the environmental problem of contamination of the local tank or source of potable water. Concrete steps for dealing with these concerns were deliberated and selected; in the case of the village conflict, the Basic Gandhian Community of Aloor would send a three-person team—a Hindu, a Christian, and a Muslim—who had some training in the Gandhian technique of conflict resolution.[20] After about an hour of this kind of praxis-oriented interchange, everyone refolded his legs into a more comfortable sitting position and listened to readings from different sacred scriptures; communal reflec-

tion followed and then some final, spontaneous prayers. Tea and bis-
cuits prepared everyone for the journey home.

The meeting I attended at Manavalakurichi followed a similar pattern, though it was open to the general public and was less informal.
One of the community issues that had focused this Basic Gandhian
Community had already been achieved—the construction of a dam
across the Vallyar river in order to prevent the inflow of sea water.
Projects still on the drawing board for interreligious effort were a
much-needed bridge across the river and, once again, how to protect
the local water supply from contamination. As part of the interfaith
dialogue that grew out of and sustained such undertakings, the BGC
of Manavalakurichi had already organized "joint celebrations" of
Christmas in 1988, Deepavali in 1989, and Ramzan in 1991. From
what I was told and could see, this small basic community was an
agent of change in the broader village community and a microcosmic
model of what India will have to become if it is to survive. Can our
world of differing religions and cultures become a Gandhian community?

SRI LANKAN APOSTLES OF DIALOGUE AND LIBERATION

In a visit to Sri Lanka, I found that one of Asia's principal proponents of basic human communities, Aloysius Pieris, S.J., practices what
he preaches. In his research and dialogue center of Tulana on the outskirts of Colombo, a concern for and engagement with the life-struggles
of the nation and of the local communities are a major part of the
energy that draws a constant flow of Christians and Buddhists to the
center. Scholars, activists, teachers, prelates, politicians, and just ordinary people come to study, to talk to each other, to strategize. As "Aloy"
himself explains, such basic human communities form naturally in a
context such as that of Sri Lanka; whether you are Christian or Buddhist, if you are serious about your religion and concerned about the
sufferings of your people, you will respond naturally to anyone who
provides a religious context for coming together to confront and do
something about such suffering. The widespread and enduring success
of Pieris's popular courses on "Liberation in the Buddhist and Christian Scriptures," taught at the center and at other locations in the area,
attests to the people's eagerness and delight in exploring their differing
religious perspectives on their common commitment to justice.

Among the most inspiring, and yet at the same time most ordinary,
examples of how basic human communities have taken shape around
the Tulana Centre is the Association for Hearing Impaired Children.
Born from the commitment, professional training, and dreams of Sister Greta Nalawatta, nurtured through the spiritual and material counsel of Pieris, a small pre-school program for hearing-impaired children
began in 1983. Given the drastic lack of any such programs in the Sri

Lankan educational system, parents responded, and the numbers of students in the program grew and soon outstripped the facility's equipment and space. In such a situation, a community of shared concern and cooperation was born; it consisted mainly of the parents of hearing impaired children, and they represented the religious coloring of Sri Lanka: Buddhists, Hindus, Christians, Muslims. Problems grew apace with successes, and the community tightened as it struggled to secure funds, buy equipment, find a new building. When more space was needed, an elderly Buddhist woman contributed a room in her large house, and then the entire house. When that proved inadequate, a Muslim parent offered part of his land and a building on it for a new school. Over the years of success, as the Association has become established, so has the basic community of parents and supporters. They have met regularly to plan together, work together, and also to celebrate together; as they have grown close on these levels, they have deepened in respect for and mutual understanding of their different religious ideals and practices. Acting together has led to believing together.

Much of the same kind of globally responsible—which means socially, politically, economically responsible—dialogue that Pieris nurtures at his Tulana Research Center is also being fostered at the Centre for Religion and Society in Colombo, mainly under the inspiration of Tissa Balasuriya, O.M.I. The CRS staff is larger and its programs more diversified—but the central intent is clear: to call upon all religious persons to recognize and realize together the essential links between religion and society. Pieris and Balasuriya are two of the most prominent and provocative Christian voices calling for a coordination of responses to the reality of the many poor and the many religions in Sri Lanka and throughout Asia. Thanks in large part to their vision and example, basic human communities (whether they bear this name or not) are growing throughout Sri Lanka, despite and because of the civil war that has been ravaging this beautiful island.[21]

A "CHRISTIAN WORKERS FELLOWSHIP" THAT IS NOT JUST CHRISTIAN

On the national level in Sri Lanka, one of the most astounding and promising examples of how shared commitment to social justice can enable people from different religious communities not only to cooperate socio-politically but to share their religious identities and rituals is the Christian Workers Fellowship. Christian in its origins and vision, the Fellowship was formed in 1958 in the aftermath of the social and economic unrest resulting from the elections of 1956. It was to be a Christian ecumenical initiative that would help bring justice to the working classes and heal the animosity growing between the Buddhist Sinhala majority and the Hindu Tamil minority.[22]

In the late '50s and early '60s, the CWF in many ways anticipated the *communidades de base* of Latin America and the liberation theol-

ogy that grew out of them. In the following statement taken from the
CWF's initial declaration, in November 1958, we see the first steps of
a new-born Asian theology of liberation ten years before a similar
birth in Latin America:

> Christianity is not just "pie in the sky" as some folks imagine. It
> has very much to do with the living of our daily lives here and
> now. Nor is Christianity merely an individualistic religion, in-
> tensely personal but with little or nothing to say about social and
> secular matters. On the contrary, to a Christian, the claim of
> Christ is a total claim. It is valid over the whole of life, whether
> public or private, spiritual or material, religious or secular. The
> Redeemer of the soul is also the Saviour of the Body (*The Chris-
> tian Worker and the Trade Union*, quoted in Balasuriya 1993,
> 124).

From the beginning, CWF members met in small groups, led by lay
people, with bible study as an essential ingredient to their discussions.
But the Bible was studied from the perspective of a social-political
analysis of what was going on in the workers' lives; the experience of
the struggling workers became the interpretative lens by which they
read and lived the biblical message. But in Sri Lanka, these communities, if they were truly going to represent the cause and experience of
the workers, could not remain simply Christian. When the CWF decided during the 1960s to move into and live amid the working classes
of the Ratmalana area, they soon found, like the early Christian community as it moved out of Jerusalem, that "Gentile/Buddhist" workers
wanted to join their ranks. But they also wanted to remain Buddhist!
Religious differences did not remove the undergirding unity that the
workers felt in their shared economic sufferings and their common
cause for social liberation. Indeed, Buddhists and Christians soon came
to sense that the Dharma of Buddha and the gospel of Christ were
calling them to act for the removal of greed and oppression.[23] This
multifaith coloring of the CWF meetings increased as the organization
found a presence among plantation workers. What Pieris came to call
basic human communities were taking spontaneous and exuberant form
within the CWF—groups of Christians and Buddhists, sharing a common plight, a common program, and sharing, too, their different religious traditions.

The practical and spiritual communion that Christians found themselves entering into with their Buddhist sisters and brothers did not fit
snugly into the theology that the European missionaries had brought.
Thus lay and clerical members from the various Christian denominations began to develop a theology and pastoral practice that would
better explain their experience both to themselves *and* to their Bud-

dhist colleagues. They sought to reread the gospel message with new questions and insights, and they developed forms of teaching and worship that would "meet their needs of inter-Christian communion, social relevance, lay participation or initiative, and inter-religious relations" (Balasuriya 1993, 127).

They elaborated a theology of the Logos which affirmed that the Word proclaimed by Jesus and the Dharma realized by Buddha were both expressions of the "Dynamic of history," which "provides all human beings coming into existence with the means of salvation, the path of liberation in their own religio-cultural contexts. . . . It is through the sacraments of Buddhism and Hinduism, through the message of morality and the self-giving life, that such salvation is normally transmitted and received" (*The Christian Worker and the Trade Union*, quoted in Balasuriya 1993, 126).

Realizing that the liberative-transformative power of the Dharma-Logos was a universal reality, CWF members also came to recognize that the "church" that is called to realize the Reign of God is much broader than Christianity or Judaism. Within their differences, because of their common commitment to bringing greater justice and unity to Sri Lankan society, Buddhist and Hindus and Christians could form one community, a basic human community that preserved and connected their religious differences.

Today the Christian Workers Fellowship has branches in all the provinces of Sri Lanka. Its communities find their focus and nourishment around whatever happen to be issues of eco-human well-being in their area. From its base among the industrial workers of Colombo the CWF has established communities among plantation workers, free-trade-zone workers, and especially, farmers. Among its more recent projects: the CWF community in Hatton has organized health seminars on AIDS; the CWF branch in Wattala has helped poor families coordinate efforts to oppose government attempts to use local farm lands for a tourist complex; in Badulla the CWF has succeeded in offsetting the exploitation of local farmers by middle-men and large companies by establishing the Organization for the Marketing of Small Farmer's Produce ("Fellowship in Action" 1994). Even more significantly and hopefully, the CWF has been able for the most part to maintain contact and cooperation among its Sinhala and Tamil members throughout a civil war that has divided most other groups along ethnic-religious lines (Balasuriya 1993, 130). Thus it provides Sri Lanka as a source of hope that peace is possible and that religion can unite just as much as it can divide.

The CWF is also an example of how ritual, one of the most particular and "incommensurable" ingredients of religion, can become a "communing" of differences. CWF has developed a ritual, the CWF May Day Mass, that embodies the full meaning of liturgy—*leitourgia*: work (*ergon*) of the people (*laos*). Because it comes forth from and expresses the people's shared *work* or praxis toward liberation, CWF liturgy becomes a ritual-work that persons of differing religions can share in. This ceremony is the central and largest of the movement's public celebrations, and as a Mass, it clearly has a religious content and purpose. While that content, in the beginning, was predominantly Christian, that too soon changed. As the CWF became multireligious, so did its ritual. Soon more than half of the workers attending the Mass were Buddhists.

Then it happened. A Buddhist went up for communion. He was not refused, but an interreligious dialogue about what happened followed immediately. Christians commented that Buddhists would never have done this at a standard Roman or Anglican Mass; this Mass was different. The Buddhists explained how it differed: this was a Mass honoring Christ the Worker, for all workers. One Buddhist expressed the sense of many others: "I feel Jesus represents who I am and what I strive for; here I feel filled with life to work for justice. Why should I not eat with all the others?" As Mr. Vijaya Vidyasagara, one of the original founders of the CWF, put it succinctly: "How could we, as fellow workers and as Christians, refuse them?"[24] In the eucharistic theology of the CWF, the table at which people continue to break bread with Jesus and feel his presence must be open to "all persons of good will who opt for the values of the reign of righteousness preached by Jesus" (Balasuriya 1993, 128).

The CWF's May Day Mass has been celebrated every year since 1960, even during the two years (1971 and 1989) when tensions brought the government to ban all other May Day processions and gatherings. Today, 60 to 70 percent of the participants at the annual Mass are Buddhists. The liturgy is held in a secular setting or hall to show that this Christ and what he represents are not confined to a Christian community or church. Buddhists help prepare the liturgy, which includes Buddhist-Hindu texts for its readings, and many Sinhala and Hindu-Buddhist elements such as silence, drums, use of the conch shell, fire, incense, and veneration through profound bowing.[25] *All* are invited to the table. The Mass remains a Christian ritual primarily, but in the dialogue that has gone on in these interfaith communities committed to justice, Buddhists and Hindus have come to grasp and feel this ritual in such a way that they feel able to participate in it—as Buddhists and Hindus.[26]

THE VILLAGE OF KATCHUR—RESISTING YET EMBRACING

From the diverse, but limited, palette of examples of liberative dialogue that I gathered in India, I must mention one more, for it embodies a necessary though difficult dynamic not always present, or present clearly, in attempts at such dialogue. In the little village of Katchur, on

the outskirts of Madras, is an organization called Share and Care
Children's Welfare Society. It is directed by a Roman Catholic married
couple, Carmel and Steven Arokiasamy. There I found in seedling form
a basic human community that marvelously combined a passionate
preferential option for the oppressed with the ability to reach out to
and love the oppressors. Steven and Carmel imbibed both their passion for justice and their commitment to nonviolence as lay participants in the Aikiya Alayam Ashram and Dialogue Centre in Madras,
established and guided by Ignatius Hirudayam, S.J. From this
"ashramite" spirituality, they developed their theology and program
of liberation.

In Katchur (which is just one of their many social-economic and
medical projects, most of them in the slums and among the poor of
Madras), the Arokiasamys have set up an orphanage, school, and medical center mainly for the Dalits and lower castes of the village and its
surroundings. Typical of thousands of villages throughout India,
Katchur is clearly demarcated between the stately residences of the
high-caste landowners on one side and the tiny, often squalid huts of
the Dalits who work the land for the wealthy on the other. Dalits are
allowed in the high-caste section only to work during the day; wells
and drinking water are strictly segregated. Naturally, from the start
the work of Share and Care was seen by the upper castes as both a
disruption of the social order and a proselytizing maneuver to win
converts from Hinduism. From the kind of social analysis they had
learned, the Arokiasamys saw the wealthy landowners as the sustaining muscle of the oppressive system in Katchur.

From the start, they grounded and focused their work on an always
prior and central commitment to promote the well-being of the Dalits
and the entire village. Theirs was a primacy of liberative praxis. But it
was also a multireligious praxis, for they enlisted the help of both
Hindus and Christians and were ready to work with anyone who was
committed to improving the quality of life for all in the village. Also,
the religious practices of their school and orphanage were both Hindu
and Christian. While Mass was celebrated every Sunday, so were the
Hindu festivals; Hindus and Christians were welcome in the celebration of every feast. For Christmas and Divali sweets were exchanged
between Hindus and Christians. Hindus placed the "bindi" (the red
dot on the forehead) on the statue of Mary. Christians took part in the
Hindu Ayudha Puja (the blessing of implements of labor).

From this primacy of liberative praxis, an atmosphere of trust and
dialogue gradually took shape. Hindus, including high-caste Hindus,
came to see that the intent of this work was not to convert to a new
religion but to a new cooperation for human well-being. In this atmosphere, the high-caste people began to respond to the invitations that
Steven and Carmel extended to them from the beginning—to partici-

pate, often to take a place of prestige, in all the official functions and festivals celebrated at the orphanage. On one of the national holidays, for instance, the local high-caste leader was asked to hoist the flag and give the formal address for all the community; the following year, an elder from the Dalits carried out the same privileged role of raising the flag and addressing the community.

Naturally, not everything went smoothly. Yet potential conflicts, though not avoided, were not provoked or fomented. When some of the high-caste landowners, for example, shut off the water supply in the Dalit part of the village, the poor protested, but then, with aid from Share and Care, dug their own water supply. When many of the Dalits, experiencing a new sense of self-dignity, demanded higher wages for their work in the fields, the landowners resisted; but the conflict was solved—and wages were raised—through discussion and compromise. Gradually a new kind of community has been forming between the two parts of the village; in this community and in their conversations with those in power, the poor have been often and clearly *opposed* to the wealthy, but they have, for the most part, continued to *embrace* the wealthy. One of the most hopeful indications of what this can lead to was the decision of the wealthiest landowner in the village to sell land for further expansion of the school and orphanage. Such a transaction and cooperative gesture had never happened before in Katchur. The nonviolence that characterizes the interreligious praxis and dialogue in this community is bearing fruits of conversion (not to Christianity) and socioeconomic betterment.

The Broad but Hidden Liberative Dialogue

The examples I have described of a liberative dialogue between religions in India and Sri Lanka are for me, and I hope for others, a source of enlightenment and inspiration; they show that such dialogue is taking place and what its further promise might be. But the inspiration and the enlightenment can be even deeper. For I was told by a number of Indian "experts" who have lived their religious and dialogical lives immersed in the struggle of modern India, that the kinds of explicit, organized interfaith cooperation that I have described are but the protruding tip of a larger reality hidden not far beneath the surface of Indian history and Indian everyday life.[27] Among ordinary people, especially in the villages, a "dialogue of action" or a "dialogue of life" is very often simply part of the Indian and Sri Lankan way of existing, even though it is not consciously recognized as such. In most villages, life is marked and molded by two dominant realities: a) the daily effort to live in a society where simply to eat, have a roof over one's head, and keep one's family healthy is a wrenching struggle; life is hard, problems abound, many of the cultural-social structures are blatantly oppressive. Ordinary people, the poor, know this and feel this daily; and b) ordinary people belong to a variety of religious communities as part of the village community.

Real life, in other words, is for most Indians a daily dealing with poverty and religious pluralism. In dealing with the struggle of life, they do, because they have to, cooperate—not always amicably, not without recurrent tensions, but if village life is to function, people do find themselves working with their neighbors. And they do this as devoutly religious people. Religion, for the most part, marks all that they do. So the daily give-and-take of village life in India and Sri Lanka is also, generally, an interreligious give and take. This is expressed in something I heard so often in my travels throughout the subcontinent—that in the villages, despite the recent outbursts of communalism, there is a history of celebrating religious feasts together, or at least of Hindus and Muslims and Christians helping each other and joining at least partially in celebrations of Divali or Christmas or the end of Ramadan.

As Samuel Rayan explained to me, although in so much of this kind of interreligious cooperation and living together there is usually not much of what we would call formal dialogue—a discussion of religious beliefs and experiences—still, such acting together as devout religious believers is already an implicit dialogue; it is, as it were, the "prime matter" or the inner reality or heart of such dialogue. For even though the Hindu villager may not be talking about the Christian notion of grace and the Christian may not be asking about the Hindu belief in karma, still these people, by acting together to deal with their common social problems, are *sharing* their religious lives with each other; they are coming to "know" by practice and feeling what Christians or Muslims or Hindus are like and what they hold valuable. And so they can celebrate or share their festivals with each other.

This is a real, living dialogue that has not yet taken a fully reflective, or a theological, form. It is something like the kind of liberation conversations and action that were already present and active in the basic Christian communities of Latin America and which became the object of reflection and learning for theologians like Gustavo Gutiérrez and Leonardo Boff, who developed a theology of liberation out of this community living of liberation. Theologians and religious "experts" need to immerse themselves more in this living reality of village dialogue in India in order to develop more fully and securely their theologies of religion and of dialogue. Such reflection, it is hoped, will deepen the lived reality of dialogue in the villages, and the lived reality will nourish and guide the reflection.

•

This chapter was intended to be a source of instruction, but more so, of hope. The examples we have reviewed and reflected upon can assure us, I trust, that despite the complexities, dangers, and some-times opposition involved in launching and sustaining globally respon-sible dialogue among religious communities, such new ways for reli-gious peoples to come together *are possible* and they can bear much needed fruit. There is much to learn from these examples about *how* such multifaith encounters work, but their primary significance is that they show that this kind of dialogue *can* work. One has to believe in the possibility of a program before one works out its pragmatics.

Our case studies have been limited to India and Sri Lanka. The limitation was deliberate. Here are two countries where some kind of liberating, transforming dialogue among their many religious commu-nities is as urgent as it is problematic. My sense was that if a globally responsible dialogue can succeed here, it can succeed anywhere. The Indian subcontinent, I suspect and I hope, is called upon today to make another major contribution to the religious history of humankind. Just as in ages past it has been the birthplace, and then the nourishing mother, of some of the world's richest religious traditions, so today it can pro-vide the world with new models of how the different members of the religious family can live and act together. Burdened as they are, India and Sri Lanka have much to teach the world.

10

AN INTRODUCTORY CONCLUSION

Theological Left-overs

Our conversations and discussions in this book have dealt mainly with *dialogue*—with a correlational (the usual but problematic term is *pluralistic*), globally responsible (or liberative) dialogue. I've tried to make a case that the best way to carry on a multifaith dialogue that will encourage all the participants to relate to each other in a conversation in which everyone genuinely speaks and listens to each other is to base such a dialogue on a shared commitment to promoting the eco-human well-being of Earth and humanity. After an autobiographical introduction in which I described how I have come to be claimed by such a dialogue, I tried to outline what a correlational/globally responsible meeting of religions entails (chapter 2), why it is necessary (chapters 2, 4), why many people think it won't work (chapter 3), and how this kind of a dialogue can respect the diversity of religious communities but at the same time connect and evaluate that diversity in light of the needs of our "one Earth" (chapters 5-7). Then I tried to provide a practical finale with concrete advice and examples of how this kind of dialogue can be and is being practiced (chapters 8-9).

If my efforts find some measure of success in encouraging religious people to take up a correlational, globally responsible dialogue, this success, I'm afraid, will be only half-measured. For most religious people, certainly for Christians, the prospect of such a dialogue raises all kinds of theological questions and calls for theological foundations. How does a correlational or pluralistic dialogue square with religious beliefs, with an understanding of the Ultimate and the human condition? How does a globally responsible dialogue fit with a traditional understanding of "salvation" or "the last things"? How do we deal with discrepancies or out-and-out clashes between what seem to be the prerequisites of a "dialogue of equals" and our inherited religious convictions? These are all theological questions. In this book, for the most part, I may have noted such questions, but I haven't taken them up.

They need to be taken up; at least for me, and for most of the Christians I know, they need to be. If my fellow-Christians are going to get behind the correlational, globally responsible interfaith dialogue proposed in this book, they are going to have to wrestle with—better, embrace—the questions, challenges, and opportunities that such a dialogue presents, especially for traditional Christian beliefs in the role of Jesus, the meaning of the church, and the purpose of Christian mission. Any measure of success this book may have is only half-measured until those questions are accepted and to some extent resolved by the Christian community.

That's why this conclusion is also an introduction. In another book, I've tried to embrace the theological challenges a correlational, globally responsible dialogue poses. This other book, titled *Jesus and the Other Names: Christian Mission and Global Responsibility,* should follow fast on the heels of this one, also from Orbis Books. In it, I try to take up the urgent theological left-overs from this book: how engagement in a genuine, globally responsible dialogue with other religious communities can help Christians come to a clearer, deeper, and more engaging understanding of the uniqueness of Jesus, the role of the church, and the purpose of mission. Just as in this book I tried to show that the cultural or philosophical critics of a correlational dialogue can best be answered by making that dialogue globally responsible, so in this sister-book I attempt to show that we can best respond to the Christian theological criticisms of a pluralistic dialogue by seeking first the Kingdom of God in our following of Jesus and our carrying out of his mission. In other words, a globally responsible understanding of Jesus' uniqueness and the church's mission will enable, and require, Christians to carry out a correlational dialogue with persons of other faiths.

You readers who have made it through this book with basic sympathy for its argument but *without* any theological qualms need not bother with the second book; at the most it would be an interesting curiosity for you. But for you readers whose resonance (partial or full) with this book has caused a few theological headaches, I hope that the other book might not only remove the headaches but help promote a greater sense of Christian health.

Finally, because I've spent a good deal of my life associating with Jesuits, I can express the hope that this entire project may be *ad majorem Dei gloriam*—"to the greater glory of God." But as one of the most exemplary Jesuits I know, Jon Sobrino, has reminded me (quoting Irenaeus), "*Gloria Dei, Vivens Homo*"—"God's glory is in the life of God's creatures." If religions and religious books are to promote God's glory, they will promote the well-being of creation. To that I can say amen!

NOTES

1 MY DIALOGICAL ODYSSEY

1. As I will explain later in this chapter, I do not think the term *pluralism* properly expresses what this approach is reacting against and trying to achieve.

2. Brahman is the Hindu symbol for the Universal Spirit or Ultimate Reality; Atman indicates the expression of that Universal Spirit in the individual spirit of creatures. This seemed to me to richly illuminate Rahner's efforts to explain that our existence or existential situation as humans is thoroughly supernatural—that our "nature" is imbued with "supernature" or the divine life.

3. Especially in the Faith and Justice Base Community of Bellarmine Parish at Xavier University.

4. See especially his response to my article in a volume edited by him and Jürgen Moltmann (Küng 1986b).

2 TALKING ABOUT WHAT REALLY MATTERS

1. As has often been pointed out by critics, the differences among the team of pluralists that came together for the publication of *The Myth of Christian Uniqueness* in 1986 were evident and often surprising (see Hick 1987).

2. See for instance the frustrations that John Hick has experienced when critics try to hold him to views that he held in the past but later revised or abandoned (see his response to Loughlin in Hick 1990).

3. What such a comparative theology implies and how it can be carried out will be taken up in chapter 8.

4. Approaches that do not fit neatly into these categories have recently been taking shape. Below we will talk more about the "postliberal" model for a theology of religions (Lindbeck 1984; Placher 1989) and of Schubert Ogden's "pluralistic inclusivism" (1992, p. x).

5. The mainline Protestant model can be classified, really, as either exclusivist or inclusivist. It is exclusivist insofar as it allows for salvation to be mediated only through Christ and through the Christian churches, for there is no salvation outside of the proclaimed Word, outside of some explicit contact with the saving deed of Jesus Christ; it can also be called inclusivist in that it allows for authentic knowledge of God in other religions, though that knowledge will have to be brought to its true clarity and fulfillment in Christianity.

6. Some helpful overviews include Race, Knitter, Drummond, D'Costa, M. Barnes, Ogden, Dupuis.

7. For clear, engaging presentations of the inclusivist position see D'Costa, Hillman, Dupuis, Lochhead.

8. I would disagree with Ogden when he maintains that the real difference between inclusivists and pluralists is in their christology: inclusivists, according to Ogden, hold to a constitutive christology, whereas pluralists (or "pluralistic inclusivists" like Ogden) prefer a representative understanding of Christ's role. The dividing lines proposed by Ogden do not seem to fit the line-up of theologians on this issue. Although such inclusivist theologians as John Cobb and Hans Küng hold to a representative or at least non-constitutive christology, neither of them would want to be numbered among the pluralists. (For Cobb and Küng, see my summary of their christologies in Knitter 1985, 133-34, 189-92; for a still helpful classification of models for a theology of religions that recognizes the presence of a representative christology among true-blue inclusivists, see Peter Schineller 1976.)

9. Perhaps the best known and most controversial advocate for a Copernican revolution in Christian theology of religions has been John Hick. See especially his early, exploratory *God and the Universe of Faiths* (1973) and his more recent *Interpretation of Religion* (1989). Other recommendations for something like pluralism have been: Race 1983, Knitter 1985, Samartha 1987; Krieger 1991; Swidler 1990.

10. Perhaps the main offenders in this regard are John Hick, especially in his earlier writings (Hick 1973), Leonard Swidler with his calls for an "ecumenical esperanto" (Swidler 1990b, 56-60), and myself in certain sections of *No Other Name?* While I spent the first third of this 1985 book summarizing but then pointing out the inadequacies and dangers of perspectives that hold that "all religions are limited" (Troeltsch and relativism), or that "all are the same" (Toynbee and common essence) or that "all are expressions of the same psychic experience" (Jung and common experience), I was not careful enough in the last part of the book when I took up the need for common ground as a presupposition for dialogue (see Knitter 1985, 208-9).

11. With his critique, Ogden has done a great service to those searching for a more pluralistic view of other religions. If, as has been suggested, there is a Rubicon running between the new and traditional views of religions, Ogden applauds the pluralists for pointing out the inadequacies of the exclusivists and inclusivists on this side of the Rubicon, but reproves them for too hastily crossing the river to set up their pluralistic forts. Ogden, it seems, wants to find a middle ground (an island in the middle of the Rubicon?) between the exclusivists/inclusivists and the pluralists. Pluralism, he announces, is not the only alternative to exclusivism or inclusivism. He proposes what he calls a "pluralistic inclusivism." Just as exclusivists and inclusivists lack sufficient grounds to claim that Christianity is the *only* true religion, so pluralists lack sufficient grounds (at least at the moment) to claim that there are *many* true religions. In a sense, Ogden, with David Tracy, admonishes pluralists not to jump to conclusions (Ogden 1992, chaps. 3-4; Tracy 1990a, 95-97).

It seems to me, however, that Ogden is more of a pluralist than he cares to admit. He recognizes that his position is "closest to pluralism, somewhat as inclusivism, in a way, is closest to exclusivism" (1992, p. x). His bottom-line evaluation of the pluralist model is, he admits, "skeptical rather than negative" (p. 79). It seems to me that a better name for Ogden's position would be not a "pluralistic inclusivism" (p. x), but rather a "cautious pluralism"; he is calling on pluralists to be much more careful. Even more appropriately, his position might be called a "methodological pluralism" or a "foundational pluralism," for he lays the foundations for the pluralist shift and then suggests the way in which data may be gathered in order to verify this shift.

Also, I think that Ogden would be more consistent with his own theology if he would recognize more than the mere *possibility* of other true religions. If, as he has expounded powerfully in other writings, God is indeed pure unbounded love, then he should expect to find that love active in other religious communities; otherwise such love cannot be real and effective. And from his own experience of interreligious dialogue, in which he admits to having found much truth and beauty and new insights in Buddhism (1992, 60-66), he should be able to attest not only to the possibility but to the reality of other true religions.

So to Ogden's question, "Are there many true religions?" Christians have good reasons to answer, "Yes!" But he reminds such Christians that to say many religions are true does not mean that all of them are.

12. Even when Christian theologians, especially since the Council of Trent, admitted that saving grace is operative outside the visible borders of the church, they never allowed this grace to work through other religions.

13. *Jesus and the Other Names,* chapter 3, forthcoming from Orbis Books.

14. In chapter 3 of the forthcoming *Jesus and the Other Names,* I review such critical assessments. Among the toughest christological critics are Braaten (1992), Newbigin (1990), Molnar (1991).

15. See Hick 1977. In *The Metaphor of God Incarnate* (1993) Hick explores further how the divinity of Jesus might be understood and personally appropriated; Hick interprets the divinity along the lines of a Spirit christology (Hick 1987).

16. These issues in christology, ecclesiology, and missiology are explored in *Jesus and the Other Names* (Knitter, forthcoming).

17. As will become evident in the next chapter, I am using the Greek word *soteria* as a heuristic or direction-pointing term to suggest that a concern for human and ecological well-being (salvation)—however different that may be understood and sought after by each religion—can serve as a starting or gathering point for the dialogue. In using the term *soteria* I do not make any claims that I have a neat, complete, "absolute" knowledge of just what it means.

18. As I hope that the forthcoming *Jesus and the Other Names* will make clear, I want to say that church and Christ are *necessary* for the salvation of the world.

3   PROBLEMS AND PITFALLS

1. Ihab Hassan's oft-cited description contrasts the schematic differences between modernity and postmodernity: "Purpose becomes play, hierarchy is replaced by anarchy and semantics by rhetoric. Absence displaces presence, metonymy takes the place of metaphor, and instead of metaphysics we now have only irony." See, "The Culture of Postmodernism," in *Theory, Culture, and Society,* vol. 2/3 (Hassan 1982, 119-32).

One of the clearest and most engaging descriptions and analyses of postmodern thinking is William Placher's *An Unapologetic Theology* (1989). Charlene Spretnak also offers both a clear description and an environmental-feminist response to the postmodern program in *States of Grace* (Spretnak 1991, chap. 1 [appendices A and B]).

2. This was the reminder that the English philosopher Peter Winch expressed when the much-accredited anthropologist Evans Pritchard, in his otherwise culturally sensitive studies of the Sudanese tribe the Azande, concluded that some of the tribal beliefs and practices were "irrational." "Criteria of logic," admonished Winch, "are not a direct gift of God, but arise out of, and are only intelligible in the context of, ways of living or modes of social life [read: filters]" (Winch 1958, 100-101). What seems irrational through one filter might be solid common sense through another.

3. Quoted in Placher 1989, 34. William Placher's bottom-line commentary on the strengths and weaknesses of the scientific method are balanced: "Good arguments *can* be offered in favor of or against a theory or a research program. Feyerabend and Kuhn, however, seem to me to make a persuasive case that 1) those arguments will in turn always rest on assumptions that can be challenged, and 2) their results can often not be quantified, so that deciding among theories will always involve factors more like aesthetic judgment than like adding up a column of numbers" (Placher 1989, 51).

4. Theological discussions of postmodernity abound. Some helpful examples are Devaney 1991; Burnham 1989. Two recent works that provide both a realistic acceptance of and yet a critical, creative response to postmodernity are Tracy 1987a and Fiorenza 1984, part 4.

5. John Milbank makes much the same case with an even sharper edge; he holds, rather pessimistically in my estimation, that any attempt at dialogue is an imperialistic gesture aimed at bending the other to one's own criterion of truth (Milbank 1990, 174-81).

6. This kind of imperialism, or imposition of one's own filter on others, can extend beyond the world of religions and cultures. It can also become an attempted imperialism over God. Raimon Panikkar, himself a pioneer of radical pluralism, warns his fellow pluralists that in referring to "God" as the center of all religions, in trying to universalize God as the one Reality which each religion names differently, they become so lost in universal abstractions that they miss the real and the irreducible differences not only among the religions but within Deity itself! God is not simply one universal reality that reveals itself differently; rather, God is a multifaceted Reality that must *be* and *remain* different among the different religions. Panikkar rejects the notion that God is "a 'thing in itself' unknowable but which we later name differently or indifferently.... The living God has never wished to be a universal God. This is the great abstraction of philosophers—or many of them. ... The living God who speaks through a people, who suffers, who yells or sings or dances is no common denominator. The Christian experience of 'God' through Christ is not the same as the *vishnuita* experience through Krishna. God is unique— therefore incomparable. ... It is a distortion of thought to seek something wider, more inclusive which would allow us to compare different notions of Divinity. Only a pretentiously deluded Reason would dare attempt it" (Panikkar 1986, 109-10).

7. Such a dialogue will embody Jürgen Habermas's call for "communicative praxis" based on the creation of "ideal speech situations." The requirements for such situations are, according to Habermas, self-evident to anyone

of any culture who is sincerely committed to conversation: that we do not adopt any kind of violence, physical or moral in our discussions, that we listen openly and honestly, that we do not appeal to any absolute norms but only to the persuasive force of our arguments, and that we keep the conversation open to anyone who wants to join it (Habermas 1979, 1984). Such "ideal speech situations" reflect what pluralist theologians are striving for and presuming as the common method for interreligious dialogue.

8. Milbank also adduces what seem to me to be highly dubious historical arguments for the radical difference in the notions of justice or social order in the East and the West. He claims that the rule of society in the East is grounded in the absolute, authoritarian king, while the ideals of justice and freedom in the West are due to the Greek notion of the universal Good. Thus, we have an incommensurable clash of social models (Milbank 1990).

9. Rawls spelled out what conditions for a fair chance would require: "First, each person is to have an equal right to the most extensive basic liberty compatible with the similar liberty for others. Second, social and economic inequalities are to be arranged so that they are both a) reasonably expected to be to everyone's advantage, and b) attached to positions and offices open to all" (Rawls 1971, 60).

10. This was basically the ethos and state of affairs under the governments of Reagan and Thatcher. Such broad notions of justice, without any particular content but calling for the freedom of the individual, prepare the ground for the exploitation of the many by the powerful.

11. Other critics are not as gentle as Ogden in pointing out the irony of pluralists who reject the absolutism of traditional christological claims about Jesus but then accept, perhaps unconsciously, the absolutism of claims about justice made by liberation theology. "It is impossible," says Lesslie Newbigin, paraphrasing the liberationists, "to make absolute claims for Jesus or any other particular name in the history of religions. But it is possible and necessary to claim absolute validity for the praxis of justice and liberation" (Newbigin 1990, 146). Or more sarcastically, in the words of Indian theologian Subhash Anand: "These theologians who refuse to swear by Jesus Christ are ready to swear by liberation theology" (Anand 1991, 404). Despite the irony or sarcasm, the criticism is appropriate. Speaking personally, I must admit that the commitment to social or ecological justice that I want to place at the heart of our interreligious dialogue does have a resolute, decisive, yes even exclusive quality about it. I feel obliged to press or "impose" this concern for justice, as I understand it, on others. But doesn't this sense of obligation offend against my pluralist identity?—This is a question I hope to face squarely in the coming chapters.

12. See Knitter 1987, 199, n.41.

13. The philosopher Mikhail Bakhtin helps us understand this political import of all words: "There are no 'neutral' words and forms—words and forms that belong to 'no one'; language has been completely taken over, shot through with intentions and accents. . . . All words have the 'taste' of a profession, a genre, a tendency, a party, a particular work, a particular person, a generation, an age group, the day and hour. Each word tastes of the context and contexts in which it has lived its socially charged life; all words and forms are populated by intentions" (Bakhtin 1981, 293, see also 346, 354).

14. Critics of literary theory help give voice and substance to the political critics of pluralistic interreligious dialogue. The title of Ellen Rooney's book *Seductive Reasoning: Pluralism as Problematic of Contemporary Literary Theory* might have substituted "Interreligious Dialogue" for the last two words of her subtitle. She reveals how "pluralism is the method employed by the *central* authorities to neutralize opposition by seeming to accept it" (Rooney 1989, 242). The strategy of pluralism, Rooney explains, is to exclude such interests as gender, race, class, sexual orientation, or national identity as peripheral to the process of interpreting a text or carrying on a conversation; rather, the process of pluralistic discourse calls on all interpreters to speak a "common language" or to adopt a basic methodology or to follow "right reason" rather than to introduce "interested rhetoric" or provincial concerns (see Lindsey 1992, 62-65). The discourse becomes "managerial"—it manages what will be discussed, the method for discussion, and the goals of the discussion. What doesn't fit these determinations is judged, in the political discourse, as a disruptive "interest group"; in the religious dialogue it might be called a "closed" or "primitive" or "fundamentalist" or "polytheistic" or a "feminist" perspective.

15. For a moderate, well-researched description of the growing inequalities and dangers within the new world order, see Paul Kennedy, *Preparing for the Twenty-First Century* (New York: Random House, 1993); also, Richard J. Barnet and John Cavanagh, *Global Dreams: Imperial Corporations and the New World Order* (New York: Simon & Schuster, 1994).

16. On these provisional plots, we carry on a conversation in which we open ourselves to the very real possibility of learning something from our dialogue partner. Lindbeck admits that although Christians must affirm the *solus Christus* and insist that "only in Christ" do we have a truly authentic way of speaking about ultimate reality and the goal of history, still other religions may reveal truths by which Christians can be "greatly enriched" (Lindbeck 1984, 56-61). Placher would step to the dialogue table more readily and boldly than Lindbeck; he recognizes the dangers of self-isolation in Lindbeck's cultural-linguistic model; he also affirms the reasons internal to Christian belief that urge Christians to speak with others. Still, even for Placher, postliberal convictions seem to rein him in and remind him that in the dialogue it is more important for the Christian to preserve and announce the gospel than to learn any new good news. "Postliberal theologians note ad hoc conjunctions and analogies with the questions and beliefs of non-Christians, but their primary concern is to preserve the Christian vision free of distortion and they must mistrust systematic efforts to correlate Christian beliefs with more general claims of human experience" (Placher 1989, 154). "Christians must remain faithful to their own vision of things for reasons internal to Christian faith, and if, in some contexts, this means intellectual isolation, so be it" (Placher 1989, 13).

4 GLOBAL SUFFERING CALLING FOR GLOBAL RESPONSIBILITY

1. Edward T. Oakes points out the same dangers of individualism and isolation in the postmodern and postliberal convictions: such views imply "that historicity means isolation and not membership in a single drama, that on the lonely 'I' hangs the fate of all that could possibly be meaningful in

what is otherwise a cold and mechanical universe" (Oakes 1992, 48; see also Dean 1991). Spretnak goes on to describe how "many of its [postmodern deconstructionism] thematic concerns and conclusions have always been central to patriarchal philosophy and culture." In some of the more extreme deconstructionists she sees a shift from the modern "patriarchal model of control to the patriarchal notions of autonomy" (Spretnak 1991, 245).

2. Spretnak makes the same disturbing point: "The aggressive surge of denial called for by deconstructionism . . . leads to a flattened valuelessness in which nothing is left but the will to power. The preferences of an individual or group can then carry the day through political manipulations and displays of power, control, and forceful domination. Hence some observers conclude that the extreme relativism of deconstructive postmodernism leads to a societal model of ruthless power plays and perhaps fascism" (Spretnak 1991, 260).

3. Some postmodernists themselves are recognizing that their view of the human condition needs some ethical place to stand, some source of moral muscle. "A few deconstructive postmodernists themselves have admitted that free negotiation among multiple centers of interests needs an overarching principle, or, as they would say, a 'valorized universal' perspective" (Spretnak 1991, 221). Steven Connor concludes his careful study, *Postmodernist Culture*, with the suggestion that postmodernism needs "new and more inclusive forms of ethical collectivity" (in Spretnak 1991, 222).

4. The figure of thirty million is some ten years ago; according to recent United Nations statistics the number is now forty million (see Nelson-Pallmeyer 1992, xiii).

5. Francis Schüssler Fiorenza refers to this situation as providing a "hermeneutical key" by which religions can communicate across their religious and cultural divides and understand each other as never before (Fiorenza 1991, 136-37).

6. *National Catholic Reporter* (May 6, 1994), p. 28, citing figures given in a lecture by Dr. Peter Raven, biologist, botanist, and member of the Pontifical Academy of Sciences.

7. See the United Nations Development Report for 1992; also, Nelson-Pallmeyer 1992, xiii.

8. Ruth Leger-Sivard, *World Military and Social Expenditures*, 1993 ed., cited in the *National Catholic Reporter* (December 3, 1993), p. 9.

9. Leger-Sivard, *World Military and Social Expenditures;* see also, *Publik Forum* (Germany) (June 21, 1991).

10. *The New York Times*, May 5, 1992, p. B5.

11. Ibid.

12. *State of the World 1991* (New York: W. W. Norton, 1991), pp. 4-5.

13. The General Secretary went on to give special attention to the primal religions which have always believed that the Earth has a soul and that we must live in spiritual relationship with it (reported in Granberg-Michaelson 1992, 32).

14. "The North, with about one fourth of the world's population, consumes 70% of the world's energy, 75% of its metals, 85% of its wood, and 60% of its food" (United Nations Development Report [1993], p. 35). Such lopsided consumption has amazing environmental effects: "The average

American baby represents twice the environmental damage of a Swedish child, three times that of an Italian, thirteen times that of a Brazilian, thirty-five times that of an Indian, and 280 (!) times that of a Chadian or Haitian. . . . This is not a comfortable statistic for anyone with a conscience" (Kennedy 1993, 32-33).

15. The United Nations Development Report for 1993, as summarized in *The National Catholic Reporter* (December 17, 1993). See basically the same statistic in the 1992 United Nations Development Report, p. 34.

16. See *Publik Forum* (June 21, 1991); Nelson-Pallmayer 1992, 10-14; *Food First Action Alert* ("Creating a Wasteland") (Winter 1993), p. 2.

17. The hidden injustice of the economic system in the United States is also revealed in its system of taxation. The Tax Reform Act of 1986 was supposed to bring across-the-board advantages. But by 1989 it was evident (though not known) that the rich were reaping far greater benefits. The 1989 tax gain of an income earner in the $10,000 to $20,000 bracket was $69; in the $30,000 to $40,000 bracket $467; in the $500,000 to $1 million category $86,084; and in the over $1 million category $281,033! Also painfully revealing is the fact that from the 1950s to the 1980s, taxes paid by corporations increased 26 percent, while those of individuals rose by 1,041 percent. Such insightful figures can be found in Barlett and Steele (1992) and in Greider (1992).

18. In the United States, family income of blacks in 1987 was only 56 percent of whites (the biggest gap since the 60s), while child and infant mortality rates were twice as high. Women, between 1974 and 1988, were able to narrow the income gap between men and women only slightly—from 59 cents to 70 cents per dollar, but at the same time, the proportion of women who were poor increased by 13 percent. See the study done by Fordham University's Institute for Innovation in Social Policy (January 1991).

19. Back in 1981, the Ecumenical Association of Third World Theologians (EATWOT) in New Delhi described what it termed a "new consciousness" among the victims; today it is "old," but nonetheless robust and determined: "Over against this dramatic picture of poverty, oppression, and the threat of total destruction, a new consciousness has arisen among the downtrodden. This growing consciousness of the tragic reality of the Third World has caused the irruption of exploited classes, marginalized cultures, and humiliated races. They are burst from the underside of history into the world long dominated by the West. It is an irruption expressed in revolutionary struggles, political uprisings, and liberation movements. It is an irruption of religious and ethnic groups looking for affirmation of their authentic identity, of women demanding recognition and equality, of youth protesting dominant systems and values. It is an irruption of all those who struggle for full humanity and for their rightful place in history" (Torres and Fabella 1983, 195).

20. See Ramsey Clark, *The Fire This Time: U.S. War Crimes in the Gulf* (New York: Thunder's Mouth Press, 1992); Thomas C. Fox, *Iraq: Military Victory, Moral Defeat* (Kansas City, Mo.: Sheed & Ward, 1991); Alan F. Geyer and Barbara G. Green, *Lines in the Sand: Justice and the Gulf War* (Louisville: Westminster/John Knox, 1991).

21. This was the cautious but clear message of the Roman Catholic Bishops' pastoral letter *The Challenge of Peace: God's Promise and Our Response* (May 1983).

22. Timothy Ferris offers a sobering reflection on whether the nuclear threat is qualitatively different just because it has been quantitatively reduced: "At this writing, owing to a welcome thaw in the cold war, the perception is becoming widespread that the threat of nuclear disaster has abated. The correct way to assess a hazard, however, is to multiply the probability of its occurring by the severity of the prospective outcome, and since the severity of nuclear war is for all practical purposes infinite, little comfort is to be taken in marginally reducing the odds that it will happen at a given time and place. For nuclear deterrence to work it must *never* fail, and never is a long time. Imagine that every day of your life you are required to bet on one spin of a roulette wheel. If a certain number comes up, the world will be destroyed; otherwise nothing will happen, and life will go on for another day. Imagine, further, that twenty years ago there were three fatal numbers, and that today there is but one. That means you are statistically safer than you used to be, in that the daily odds of annihilation have dropped from three in thirty-eight (there are thirty-eight numbers on an American roulette wheel) to only one in thirty-eight. Nevertheless, you cannot expect to keep winning forever; sooner or later your number is going to come up, and when it does the penalty will be horrible enough to overshadow whatever satisfaction you may have garnered from living on borrowed time. That is the predicament in which the human species remains, so long as we have anything like our present arsenal of fifty thousand nuclear warheads" (*The Mind's Sky: Human Intelligence in a Cosmic Context* [New York, Bantam Books, 1992], pp. 176-77).

23. For a chilling account of the enduring danger of nuclear conflict, not among superpowers, but among mini-powers who want to settle age-old racial, ethnic, or religious scores and for whom the restraints of Mutually Assured Destruction are less important than the appeal of Mutually Assured Annihilation, see Burrows and Windrem 1994. The authors show that although the end of the Cold War has lessened chances of global nuclear war, the proliferation of nuclear weapons and the expertise to build them have accelerated dangerously. They underscore the astonishing ease with which third-world nations, and even terrorist groups, can acquire the requisite technology to build nuclear weapons.

24. From "Two Trillion Dollars in Seven Years," *The Defense Monitor* 16, no. 7 (1987) and "Militarism in America," *The Defense Monitor* 15, no. 3 (1987).

25. According to the War Resisters League (339 Lafayette St., NY, NY 10012), of the $1,144 billion in the 1993 USA federal budget, $317 billion went into current military expenditures, $285 billion paid for past military costs, and only $298 billion went into human resources and services.

26. Paul Kennedy comes to the same conclusion at the end of his study of the world on the brink of the twenty-first century: "Because we are all members of a world citizenry, we also need to equip ourselves with a system of ethics, a sense of fairness, *and* a sense of proportion as we consider the various ways in which, collectively or individually, we can better prepare for the twenty-first century" (Kennedy 1993, 341).

27. When Küng, for instance, announces that today Westerners are aware of Eurocentrism and are ready to endorse a "polycentric constellation of different regions," and when he holds that the world today is conscious of the

need to remove the economic dichotomies of North and South (Küng 1991, 11-22), he is either too naive or too hasty in his assessments of geo-political realities in the new world order and of what is really going on in the political and economic chambers of Washington, Berlin, and Tokyo. His cultural and theological assessments and vision would benefit, I think, from a more thorough economic analysis as is being done in the so-called developing world.

28. John Hick, for instance, believes that unconditioned moral obligations can just as well be explained and lived out as "a function of our human nature." We are social beings who are happily dependent on each other; we need to be in relationship if we are to grow and survive. "It is this interpersonal nature of personality that gives rise to the sense of mutual moral obligation. . . . Ethics, I suggest, is grounded in this de-facto character of human nature as essentially inter-personal, in virtue of which we have a deep need for one another and feel . . . a natural tendency to mutual sympathy" (Hick 1989, 97-98).

29. Ralph Wendell Burhoe and Donald Campbell have offered a more scientific or biological argument for the important contribution that religions must make to assuring the advancement of evolution. They hold that biological evolution, which for the most part has been motored by the so-called "selfish gene" and sought the survival of the fittest, has arrived at *cultural evolution*, which must be motored by new values that will seek the survival of the most cooperative. Whereas previously only the strong could survive—and so competition and even aggression were genetically programmed into our species—today, in our global village armed with nuclear weapons, only the cooperative will survive. Evolution, in other words, must move forward based on new values, not of competition and aggression, but of mutuality and cooperation. But where do we find such new values? How do we make the quantum leap from "nature red in tooth and claw" to culture concerned with love and justice?

Burhoe turns to the religions and argues that they can serve as the "missing link between ape-man's selfish genes and civilized altruism" (Burhoe 1979, 135). He holds that only the religious traditions of the world can provide the "'cultural genes' of love, unity, justice, self-sacrifice necessary to overcome the weight of our biologically selfish genes and so to insure the continued evolution of the species." Of course to do this Burhoe adds that the religions will have to give up their absolute, competitive claims and enter into a new era of dialogue and cooperation (Burhoe 1976; 1986; Campbell 1976).

Burhoe's case may be overstated, both in its biological and religious claims. And yet there are two elements in his position that are hard to deny: 1) that the religions of the world, in the original messages of their founders and in their scriptures, do hold up a vision that there is a unifying force or presence within the universe and that human beings are called and empowered to live in unity, love, and justice; and 2) that our contemporary world, given the devastating dangers of its ethical confusion, stands in need of hearing and believing and acting upon such a message.

30. Küng's, as well as Swidler's, practical, next-step proposals are to call for new research centers and meetings among religious and cultural leaders, who will work out a "theoretical" agreement for a world ethics among religions. As necessary as such endeavors are, if they are not sustained and car-

ried out in constant contact with similar efforts on the grassroots level, they will wither in the thin air of academic mountaintops.

5   GLOBAL RESPONSIBILITY: COMMON GROUND FOR INTERFAITH DIALOGUE

1. Mark Taylor would agree with this priority of responsibility over diversity. In his proposal that theology today must work out a balance among the postmodern trilemma of identity, diversity, and emancipation, he recognizes that a perfect equilibrium between the three is neither possible nor admissible. Emancipation, in the final analysis, bears a greater weight: "Difference [plurality] and the critiques by the oppressed [emancipation] are always thought together. They are inseparably so. Although inseparable, however, they are not equal. . . . The problematics of plurality and emancipation do not have an equal standing" (Mark Taylor 1990, 66). "A celebration of plurality . . . is possible only through limiting that celebration by commitment to the emancipation of dominated groups" (Mark Taylor 1990, 56).

2. If Gadamer's image of melting horizons seems a little too placid, Rolston's "harder" image may be more meaningful: "Perhaps the better way to say this is that although we cannot get outside our systems, what is outside our system can nevertheless hit us hard enough to make dents in our system" (Rolston 1985, 244). Joseph van Beeck tries to ground Gadamer's notion of a fusion of horizons in a natural order we can all recognize, one which tells us that "the world and humanity are basically intelligible and we humans are one at least in the sense that we recognize each other as essentially equipped for the kind of intelligent, interpretative communication, that can lead to growth in shared participative understanding of truth" (van Beeck 1991, 557).

3. This is especially the case in Wittgenstein's *Philosophical Investigations* (1958). See David Krieger's review and interpretation of this aspect of Wittgenstein's thought (Krieger 1991, 102-32); William Placher is in essential agreement with Krieger (see Placher 1989, 65).

4. Pieris goes on to insist that Christians in particular are called upon to be multilinguists. "The obligation to understand the language that the Spirit speaks in a neighboring faith-community is not an academic luxury of scholars but a pneumatological imperative constituting the ecclesial nature of the Christian *koinonia*, the implication being that no language, not even the Christian one, exhausts the totality of the Spirit's liberative self-communication" (Pieris 1989, 199).

5. Placher himself, in a different context, acknowledges the impropriety of expecting all religions to affirm the value of the Western insistence on openness and conversation (Placher 1989, 147).

6. See the *Nichomachean Ethics,* Books 2-5.

7. "The phrase *practical philosophy* refers to a loosely associated group of philosophical positions that emphasize the importance of practical wisdom or *phronesis* in contrast to theoretical reason *(theoria)* or technical reason *(techne)*" (Browning 1991, 34).

8. "Praxis is, positively stated, the realization that humans make history and, negatively stated, the realization that humans cannot rely on any ahistorical, universal truths to guide life. In recent years we have come to understand praxis as foundational, recognizing ideology critique, relativism,

and pluralism as appealing to human praxis for criteria of both reflection and action" (Chopp 1986, 36-37).

9. See also Lane's excellent review of the central hermeneutical role of praxis in contemporary philosophy and theology, in 1984, chapters 2 and 3.

10. With Dermot Lane I would note the certain tension—though not opposition—between David Tracy's seeming preference for a conversation with classics as "the primary source of knowledge," whereas liberationists find that "the actual experience of liberating praxis is the central source of knowledge and understanding." While Tracy would argue for manifestative *and* transformative models of truth, liberation theologians would hold to the primacy of "knowing by doing" over "knowing by reflecting" (see Lane 1991, 35-36).

11. Julius Lipner makes the same claims in an essay on what he calls the primary challenge for Christianity and all religions—how to reach beyond the incommensurability gap that separates cultures and religions. After proposing a dialogue based on "constructive empathy," Lipner turns to the gnarled question of where to find criteria for cross-cultural, empathetic judgments on truth and value. He finds the material for such criteria in what he terms "foundational experiences"—experiences that are foundational to what it is to be human. Central to such experiences are the reality of suffering and the need to confront it: "In this enterprise [of dialogue] such experiences as joy, pleasure, grief, pain, hunger, thirst, deprivation, anger, frustration, etc. especially in their 'foundational' forms, i.e. with minimal interpretative content, as shared reference-points for living, cannot be overestimated" (Lipner 1993, 163).

12. "To understand the difference between an error and a systemic distortion is to understand a central difference between modernity and post-modernity" (Tracy 1987a, 73).

13. John O'Brien invites us to look into our own self-awareness to identify, maybe only glimmeringly, the pervasiveness of such systemic distortions: "Each of us knows that she or he has internalized structures of marginalization, whether as oppressor or oppressed. We know, too, how insight dawns on us that our own discourse, whether theological or otherwise, is distorted through being unconsciously—in the very structure of the grammar, one might say—either a justification of our privilege or a reinforcement of our oppression" (O'Brien 1992, 136).

14. David Tracy uses the language of the academy to make the same point: "We can develop new and more complex narratives that elicit the subversive memories of those individuals and peoples whose stories have been distorted by the compulsive narratives of the Faustian victors" (Tracy 1987a, 72).

6 WHOSE JUSTICE? WHOSE LIBERATION?

1. I well realize that such talk of the *divinum* or the transcendent will not sit comfortably with some religious traditions, especially with some Buddhists. Delicate and controversial though this issue may be, I think a case can be made that the experience of enlightenment or satori is precisely that "added ingredient" (though already/always given) which the Buddhist brings to the effort to promote the welfare of all sentient beings. What I in my Christian-Western terminology call the Divine, Buddhists would want to refer to as the Dharma or the Buddha-nature or Emptiness. Our differing terms are not de-

fining the very same Reality, but pointing in the same direction. My sense is that there are many practicing Buddhists who would be basically comfortable with what I have just stated (See Eppsteiner 1988).

2. Roger Haight agrees with Kaufman but makes the same point more broadly: "Without the question of salvation, there would be no religion at all, because salvation simply gives specific content to the religious question" (Haight 1994, 243-44).

3. Stanley Samartha, a Christian surrounded by Hindu neighbors, chides his follow Christians and reminds them that such neat classifications between mystical and prophetic religions "need to be corrected. Very often the manner in which such observations are made and the conclusions drawn are historically untrue and theologically wrong. To perpetuate this notion would amount to bearing false witness against our neighbours" (Samartha 1983, 113).

4. Tracy goes on to explain why every religious tradition and person must foster a mutually sustaining, clarifying, and criticizing flow between the mystical and prophetic: "Only the mystic understands what the prophet really meant, for only the mystic knows both the basic structure of the whole and its radically de-structuring actuality. But even the mystic may eventually find it necessary to adopt a prophetic rhetoric and proclaim the word of the Other. Otherwise, the others in their secure institutions will trivialize and reify the words of the Other once again" (Tracy 1990a, 26).

5. This is the realization that Thomas Merton seems to have reached in his struggles to reconcile Christian expectation of the coming Reign of God with Zen's exclusive concern for the present (see Merton 1968, 116-33).

6. Hick's formulation and proposal have been the target of widespread criticisms (see, D'Costa 1987, Gillis 1989, DiNoia 1992, Griffiths 1991). What the critics seem to miss is that Hick is offering a heuristic device to understand differing religious traditions; he is not describing the actual content of what those religions are saying.

7. Maura O'Neill believes that even in his response to feminist criticisms of his proposal for a shift from self to Reality-centeredness, Hick does not get the point (see O'Neill 1990, 27-29).

8. Ralph Burhoe may be overstepping his biological data when he argues that the human species has been able to evolve beyond its genetically limited altruism mainly because the religions of the world have inspired and motivated humans to love not only their genetically-related kin but also members of their broader family of nation or religion; Burhoe may be even more idyllic when he goes on to suggest that today, without the combined contribution of the religions, humanity will not really be able to carry out the next necessary and breath-taking stage of evolution—from national altruism to universal altruism, toward "a single worldwide ingroup of mutual concern" (Burhoe 1986, esp. 462). Though he may give too much past and future credit to the religions, Burhoe is in essential agreement with David Tracy's conclusion: "Despite their often radical differences, as John Hick suggests, all these ways [i.e., religions] do demand a singular transformation of the self; from self-centeredness to Reality-centeredness. In any religious way, we must shift our center from the ego, by means of that new relationship with Ultimate Reality" (Tracy 1987a, 89-90).

9. This appeal to how people feel or act provides the basis for a corrective response to the emphasis that Joseph DiNoia places on the diversity of religious views of salvation. His emphasis is so heavy that it seems to exclude any genuine possibility of analogous similarities such as Hick and Tracy are proposing (see DiNoia 1992).

10. Ruether goes on to contrast this sacred canopy theology with its theological opposite: "The theology of prophetic critique located God and the spokespersons for God on the side of those victimized or despised by the social and political elites. The word of God comes as a critique of these social and political elites, calling them to reform their ways in order to be faithful to divine justice or else threatening them with a revolutionary intervention of God in history that will overthrow their power and bring in a new world, where justice and peace will be established" (Ruether 1990, 73).

11. Juan Luis Segundo calls such "pre-religious" experiences "anthropological faith," which for him is a commitment to this world and to overcoming its limitations; out of such human faith, for Segundo, religious faith is born (Segundo 1985, 23). Roger Haight is even broader in his claims; he holds that all religion takes its origin in "the question of salvation"—that is, in the struggle to understand and do something about the "negativities of existence." "Some form of negativity in human experience is the very condition for religious understanding and theological interpretation" (Haight 1990, 195, see 196-98).)

12. Final report of the Consultation organized by the Indian regional committee of EATWOT, February 27-March 2, 1989, in Madras. Privately distributed.

7   THE ONE EARTH AND OUR MANY STORIES

1. Thus, Thomas Berry, one of the earliest and most creative contributors to this Earth-centered way of approaching religion, today prefers to call himself a "geologian" rather than a "theologian." To try to understand *Theos* without understanding *Gaia* or the spirit of the Earth is to produce a denatured and denaturing theology.

2. The document was distributed by the International Coordinating Committee on Religion and the Earth, Wainwright House, 260 Stuyvesant Ave., Rye, NY 10580.

3. One such set of general norms was suggested by the International Coordinating Committee on Religion and the Earth for the Rio Conference. The Committee formulated a statement of "Ethics for Living" which called on all people to live: sustainably (with a concern for the present *and* for the future), justly, frugally, peacefully, interdependently, knowledgeably (recognizing the need for ecological education), and holistically (fostering the whole person, spiritually, physically, intellectually). See "An Earth Charter," mentioned in the previous note.

4. "It must be admitted that there is little agreement among religious traditions on conceptions of the human or on the understanding of what constitutes human fulfillment. But the formulation I am proposing makes that an issue which can now be directly debated and argued, each part invoking in its own support whatever experiential and other evidence is available publicly in our present human existence" (Kaufman 1981, 199).

5. Our experience of truth as a paradoxical relative-absolute can also be more clearly understood and accepted on the basis of Bernard Lonergan's view of our cognitional structures. After describing truth as the result of a dynamic movement in our consciousness by which we proceed from experience to understanding to judgment, he describes the final act of judgment—that stage by which truth is really known—as "virtually unconditioned." It's never "absolutely unconditioned." But even though the absolute quality is missing, our judgment can still be unconditioned. "The judgment is unconditioned, since it answers the questions relevant to the subject, the criteria, and the evidence now available to competent inquirers. Such judgment, as dependent upon the present community's available evidence and modes of inquiry, is also only virtually unconditioned, since every judgment is by definition open to further revision as further questions emerge" (Tracy 1989, 567).

6. In proposing a globally responsible dialogue among religions based on eco-human well-being as a relative-absolute norm for the dialogue, I believe I am in essential agreement with the model of "orientational pluralism" that S. Mark Heim urges as a way of understanding religious pluralism and interaction. Following the philosophical proposal of Nicholas Rescher (Rescher 1985) (and, I would suggest, leaning heavily on the postliberal theology of George Lindbeck), Heim urges all religious persons to recognize that every person takes up the voyage of truth with a definite orientational compass or perspective; within each perspective, one can use rational argumentation and personal values in order to assert the one or superior truth. But there are other orientations, other perspectives that can make similar claims. While one will feel the possibility and the obligation to hold that one's own truth is universal and normative, one must always be open to such claims from others. Indeed, openness to and dialogue with these other claims are for Rescher and Heim essential to carrying on the search for truth from within one's own perspective. To me this seems to indicate that while one is called on to make absolute claims for one's own perspective, there is always the possibility of it being relativized in the encounter with other perspectives (Heim 1994; 1995, 144-56).

7. The "worldly" conversion I am privileging is not really opposed to the "religious" conversion Lonergan speaks about. Indeed, in light of what I said above about the world as a context for religious expression, I understand such a conversion to the well-being of the world and others to be a conversion to the Great Mystery. Thus, such a conversion is not really a "pre-religious priority"; it is deeply religious, for it is in the experience of loving our neighbor that we discover the God who animates and grounds such "worldly" love.

8. What George Lindbeck said of the "norms of reasonableness" fits nicely with what I am trying to say of the norms of global responsibility: "the norms of reasonableness are too rich and subtle to be adequately specified in any general theory of reason or knowledge. . . . The norms . . . are like the rules of depth grammar, which linguists search for and may at times approximate but never grasp. The reasonable [or, the globally responsible] in religion and theory, as in other domains, has something of that aesthetic character, that quality of unformalizable skill, which we usually associate with the artist or the linguistically competent" (Lindbeck 1984, 130).

9. But I would ask Burrows: What makes it possible for the religions to respond to the future as they are doing? It must be something in their past and in their given identity that is retrieved, revisioned, and reaffirmed and then used as their response to the future. Peter Donovan agrees essentially with Burrows when he points out that although we cannot maintain that the different religions have the same answers to the global questions of our times, we do see that they have the ability to respond to the same questions and provide answers that are more compatible than contradictory: "Pronouncements like that of the Dalai Lama ('All religions teach common moral precepts') are not to be taken, then, as descriptions of an actual state of affairs. They are, rather, pleas for religions to make common cause (in the interests, in this case, of world peace), interpreting and adjusting their traditions of belief so as to be able intentionally to affirm such common concerns as moral" (Donovan 1986, 375).

10. Some recent examples of such efforts to reinterpret and rehear the religious messages of social and ecological justice include the following:

Badiner, Allan Hunt, ed., *Dharma Gaia: A Harvest of Essays in Buddhism and Society* (Berkeley: Parallax Press, 1990).

Callicott, J. Baird, *Earth's Insights* (Berkeley: University of California Press, 1994).

Callicott, J. Baird, and Roger T. Ames, eds., *Nature in Asian Traditions of Thought: Essays in Environmental Philosophy* (Albany: State University Press of America, 1989).

Cohn-Sherbok, Dan. ed., *World Religions and Human Liberation* (Maryknoll, N.Y.: Orbis Books. 1992).

Dwivedi, O.P., ed., *World Religions and the Environment* (New Delhi: Gitanjali Publishing House, 1989).

Engineer, Asghar Ali, ed., *Religion and Liberation*, special issue of *Islamic Perspective*, vol. 4/2 (1990), *Islam and Liberation Theology: Essays on Liberative Elements in Islam* (New Delhi: Sterling Publishers, 1990).

Eppsteiner, Fred, ed., *The Path of Compassion: Writings on Socially Engaged Buddhism* (Berkeley: Parallax Press, 1988).

Jones, Ken, *The Social Face of Buddhism: An Approach to Political and Social Activism* (London: Wisdom Publications, 1989).

Küng, Hans, and Jürgen Moltmann, eds., *The Ethics of World Religions and Human Rights*, *Concilium* 1990/2 (Philadelphia: Trinity Press International, 1990).

Rockefeller, Steven C., and John C. Elder, *Spirit and Nature: Why the Environment Is a Religious Issue* (Boston: Beacon Press, 1992).

Sivaraksa, Sulak, *A Socially Engaged Buddhism* (Bangkok: Thai Inter-Religious Commission for Development, 1988).

8 HOW DOES IT WORK?

1. Gort believes that this mutual comprehension is based on a deeper mutual religious experience: "This mutual cooperation with the poor can itself become mediatory of shared religious experience of the *presentia realis Dei* [the real presence of God] in and among the poor, i.e., can lead to a shared vision of God *semper minor, semper major*, [always smaller, always greater] the God who in becoming ever smaller becomes ever greater and

who announces to all religious believers: *les amis de mes amis sont mes amis* [the friends of my friends are my friends]" (1991, 73).

2. Some Christians even use the term *multifaith parishes*. "My definition . . . of a multifaith parish will include, in addition to the givenness of the particular Christian community, the people who are politically oppressed, economically exploited, culturally despised, and socially marginalized, people who happen to be not merely the majority but also the devotees of Buddhism, Hinduism, and Islam" (Perera 1986, 90).

3. As has so often happened in Latin America, Father Rodrigo, who spent his last years organizing base human communities in the villages of Sri Lanka, threatened those in power. He was assassinated while saying Mass in November 1987 (see *Father Mike: The Prophet and Martyr* [Colombo: Centre for Society and Religion, 1989]).

4. In 1984 it was called the Vatican Secretariate for Non-Christian Religions. The 1991 document was issued together with the Congregation for the Evangelization of Peoples.

9   IT'S WORKING

1. Besides drawing on my general study of the South Asian context, I base the contents of this chapter on an extended visit there in 1991 and on continuing communication with my Indian and Sri Lankan dialogue partners. The persons or centers that have influenced me most have been the theological communities of United Theological College and Dharmaram College in Bangalore, Tamilnadu Theological Seminary in Madurai, Vidyajyoti School of Theology in Delhi, and Gurukul Theological Seminary in Madras; I also learned much at the dialogue centers/ashrams of Ashirvad (Bangalore), Aikiya Alayam (Madras), Shantivanam (Tiruchirappalli), Christa Prema Seva (Pune), Centre for the Promotion of Communal Harmony and Inter-Religious Amity (Madurai), and the Gandhian Base Communities (Kanyakumari), Maitri Bhavan (Varanasi). Among the Hindus who were most helpful for me were Professor S. Gangadaran (Tamilnadu Theological Seminary), Professor S. Jeyapragasm (Madurai Kamaraj University), Mr. N. Palarasu (Kanyakumari), Professor K. N. Mishra (Hindu Banares University), Professor Veena Daas (University of Delhi), Dr. Ashis Nandy (Center for the Study of Developing Societies, Delhi), and Purushottam Agrawal (Jawaharlal Nehru University). Muslim friends and experts who have overwhelmed me with insights and questions are especially, Asghar Ali Engineer (Institute of Islamic Studies, Bombay), Riffat Hassan (Pakistan, now at the University of Louisville), and Khalid Duran. In Sri Lanka, I was introduced into the exciting arena of dialogue there primarily by Aloysius Pieris (Tulana Research Centre), Tissa Balasuriya (Centre for Society and Religion), and Vijaya Vidyasagara (Christian Workers Fellowship).

2. This was especially clear to me at a meeting of Catholic ashramites from all over India in Mysore, November 1991.

3. In an article on these statements of the ITA, J. Kottukapally places in even clearer relief the tight bonds between dialogue and liberation among Indian theologians; he also refers to some of my earlier writings and comments: "The Statement of the Indian Theological Association . . . follows a line that is nearly identical in substance and style with Knitter's." Given the

lack of direct influence between the ITA and myself in the years previous to 1989, I find this resonance extremely reassuring; what I thought I saw from my theological watchtower at an American university proves to be among the most urgent signs of the time in the actual situation of India (Kottukapally 1991, 544; see also 536).

4. In a conversation with the Jesuit community of St. Joseph's, October 1991.

5. Certainly in the case of Muslim, Portuguese, and British colonial expansion, the primary motivation came from "the god of wealth" rather than religious convictions. Still, what lingers in historical memory is the way this god of wealth was able to dictate to, or make use of, religious beliefs. All too often, religion became another weapon in the arsenal of conquest.

6. Ashrams have a long history in India. Originating in Vedic times (1200 BCE) in the custom of a man leaving home after he has reared his family to retreat into the forest to seek after deeper spiritual truths, they have been taken up in the first part of this century by Catholics, and subsequently Protestants, as centers where Christians can retreat in order to delve into and appropriate the mystical riches of Hinduism. The emphasis is on contemplation in an interreligious context. See Ralston 1987; Vandana 1993; Pulsfort 1990.

7. These same tensions are evident, though not as sharply, within the Hindu community of India—between those who would stress the *marga* of knowledge (*jnana*) or contemplation (*raja*) over the *margas* of action (*karma*) or love (*bhakti*). Often these differences are played out under the rubrics of a Hinduism that is more "Brahminical" or "sanskritic" and one that is more popular and active.

8. I had a particularly insightful and inspiring opportunity to listen in on these conversations when I was invited to participate in the Ashram Aikiya Satssang VII—the seventh annual meeting of Roman Catholic ashramites from all over India, held at the Anjali Ashram in Mysore, November 11-17, 1991.

9. Wives who are "accidentally" murdered by their husbands or husband's family when an increase in the dowry demanded by the husband's family is not met.

10. These are not Sister Vandana's exact words but do represent the basic point she was making.

11. As reported to me in conversations with M.E. Prabhakar on August 29, 1991, and with A. Ayrookuzhiel on September 20, 1991, at the CISRS office in Bangalore.

12. Such as Swami Agnivesh (Hindu, Delhi), Venerable Bhikku Lolopalo (Neo-Buddhist, Bangalore), Sri S.R. Ramaswamy (Hindu, Dharwad Karnataka), Pandurang Shashtri Athavale (Hindu, Bombay), and Asghar Ali Engineer (Muslim, Bombay)

13. For an overview of such liberative reinterpretations within Hinduism, see Wilfred 1992; see also Dwivedi 1980, Dinakaran 1988, Mukerji 1990, Pattery 1991, Sivaraman 1985.

14. A. Ayrookuzhiel is assembling a collection of liberative stories and poems from written and especially oral traditions among various Dalit groups. See also Appavdo 1986, Joshi 1986, and Nirmal 1989.

15. Among the groups in India who carry on and follow the message from low-caste or untouchable saints are the Ravidasis, Kabir Panthis, Dadu Panthis, Satnamis, and Valmikis (see Ayrookuzhiel 1994, 15; more generally on this point, see Sontheimer and Kulke 1991).

16. From "The Brotherhood of Man" as given in *The Folk Songs of Southern India* (Madras: Higginbothams and Co. 1971), pp. 168-69, quoted in Ayrookuzhiel 1994, 16.

17. From "The Brotherhood of Man" as given in *The Folk Songs of Southern India*, p. 275, quoted in Ayrookuzhiel 1994, 17.

18. Some Dalit spokespersons are claiming that there is a pre-Aryan and pre-Vedic religious tradition, preserved especially in forms of devotion to Shiva (Saivism), that is one of "the most ancient living faiths in the world . . . a democratic, ethical, humanistic, egalitarian and tolerant religion." The words are those of Sir John Marshall, quoted in Prabhakar 1989, 40-41.

19. Especially with Dr. V. Devasahayam of the Department of Dalit Theology at Gurukul Theological Seminary, Madras, October 31, 1991.

20. In a subsequent letter the community informed me that the conflict resolution worked and the village is at peace; as for the drinking water problem, there is improvement but still not a satisfying solution.

21. There are BHCs in Kandy, in Galaha, and in Devasaranaramaya.

22. The Tamils had received preferential treatment by the British colonialists in education and government jobs. After independence, the Sinhala-dominated new government attempted to settle the balance (or settle the score), but many of its measures only increased the rift between the two groups. That rift led to civil war in 1983.

23. As reported to me by Mr. Vijaya Vidyasagara, one of the founders of the CWF, in a conversation in Colombo on September 7, 1991.

24. Vidyasagara discussed this theological-liturgical case with Bishop John A.T. Robinson when he visited the CWF. The bishop felt that the Buddhists exhibited sufficient faith in the "real presence" of Christ to warrant their full eucharistic participation in this multireligious Mass.

25. Excerpts from the Eucharistic Prayer used at the 1994 May Day Mass provide a sense of how this liturgy has become an interreligious ritual:

> Cleansing Fire of the Universe
> Preserver and Life-giver
> O Holy God, we worship you . . .
> Of all reality the heart,
> O Dharma eternal and true
> Sat-Chit-Ananda are You!
>
> Accept, O God, this sacrifice of thanksgiving and
>   praise.
> Quicken and awaken with your Spirit's dower
> This people, bread and cup
> That they truly all become
> In flesh and in blood, the very Dharma
> Transformed by your mighty power.

> Awakened are we, arisen are we.
> The Dharma and we are now one.
> United now with the oppressed ones
> And in their struggle to birth the new age
> We declare freedom for all and a common weal
> In partaking now of this freedom meal.
>
> —*The Christian Worker,*
> 1st and 2nd Quarters, 1994, pp. 76-77

26. There are other CWF rituals that have been adapted for multifaith participation, especially during the Christian Holy Week. Part of these celebrations is a program of Holy Week Studies. During the three-day gathering, the study sessions are held in the mornings, while the liturgies take place in the evenings. For 1994, the studies focused on death and life as seen from Hindu, Buddhist, Muslim, and Christian perspectives (see "Fellowship in Action" 1994, 72).

27. I am thinking especially of conversations with Samuel Rayan, S.J., of Vidyajyoti in Delhi; Aloysius Pieris, S.J., and Anto Poruthur, SVD of the Divine Word Dialogue Centre in New Delhi; S. Gangadaran of Tamilnadu Theological Seminary; and Asghar Ali Engineer of the Islamic Centre in Bombay.

WORKS CITED

Abhishiktananda. 1984. *Saccidananda: A Christian Approach to Advaitic Experience.* Delhi: ISPCK.

Amaladoss, Michael. 1992a. "Liberation as an Interreligious Project." In *Leave the Temple: Indian Paths to Human Liberation.* Ed. Felix Wilfred. Maryknoll, N.Y.: Orbis Books, pp. 158-74.

_____ . 1992b. "Mission and Missioners in Today's Global Context," *Discovery: Jesuit International Ministries* 1: 1-14.

Anand, Subhash. 1991. "Universally Unique and Uniquely Universal," *Vidyajyoti* 55: 393-424.

Appavdo, James Theophilus. 1986. *Folklore for Change.* Madurai: T.T.S. Publications.

Arendt, Hannah. 1961. "The Crisis in Culture." In *Between Past and Future: Six Exercises in Political Thought.* New York: Meridian, pp. 197-227.

Arokiasamy, S. 1987. "Sarvodaya through Antyodaya: The Liberation of the Poor in the Contextualization of Morals." *Vidyajyoti* 51: 545-64.

_____ . 1988. *Communalism in India: A Challenge to Theologizing.* Bangalore: Claretian Publications.

Assmann, Hugo. 1974. *Theology for a Nomad Church.* Maryknoll, N.Y.: Orbis Books.

"Attitude of the Church toward the Followers of Other Religions." 1984. Issued by the Vatican Council for Inter-religious Dialogue. In *Bulletin of the Pontifical Council on Interreligious Dialogue,* vol. 56, no. 2.

Ayrookuzhiel, A.M. Abraham. 1989. "Dalit Theology: A Movement of Counter-Culture." In Prabhakar 1989, pp. 83-103.

_____ , ed. 1990. *The Dalit Desiyata: The Kerala Experience in Development and Class Struggle.* Delhi: ISPCK.

_____ . 1994. "The Dalits, Religions, and Interfaith Dialogue." *Hindu-Christian Studies Bulletin* 7: 13-19.

Bakhtin, Mikhail. 1981. *The Dialogic Imagination.* Ed. Michael Holquist. Austin: University of Texas Press.

Balasuriya, Tissa. 1993. "The Christian Workers Fellowship of Sri Lanka." In *Any Room for Christ in Asia?* Ed. Leonardo Boff and Virgil Elizondo (Concilium 1993/2). Maryknoll, N.Y.: Orbis Books, pp. 121-30.

Barlett, Donald L., and James B. Steele. 1992. *America: What Went Wrong?* Kansas City: Andrews and McMeel.

Barnes, Michael. 1989. *Christian Identity and Religious Pluralism: Religions in Conversation.* Nashville: Abingdon Press.

Barnet, Richard J., and John Cavanagh. 1994. *Global Dreams: Imperial Corporations and the New World Order.* New York: Simon & Schuster.

Baum, Gregory. 1986. "The Social Context of American Catholic Theology." In *Catholic Theology in North American Context: Current Issues in Theology* (CTSA Proceedings). Ed. George Kilkourse. Macon: Mercer University Press, pp. 83-100.

———. 1991. "Radical Pluralism and Liberation Theology." In *Radical Pluralism and Truth: David Tracy and the Hermeneutics of Religion*. Ed. W. G. Jeanrond and J. L. Rike. New York: Crossroad, pp. 1-17.

———. 1994. "Religious Pluralism and Common Values." *The Journal of Religious Pluralism* 4: 1-16.

Benhabib, Seyla. 1992. *Situating the Self: Gender, Community, and Postmodernism in Contemporary Ethics*. New York: Routledge.

Berger, Peter. 1969. *A Rumor of Angels: Modern Society and the Rediscovery of the Supernatural*. New York: Doubleday.

Bernstein, Richard. 1983. *Beyond Objectivism and Relativism*. Philadephia: University of Pennsylvania Press.

Berry, Thomas. 1988. *The Dream of the Earth*. San Francisco: Sierra Club Books.

Berry, Thomas, and Brian Swimme. 1992. *The Universe Story*. San Francisco: Harper SanFrancisco.

Biallas, Leonard J. 1991. *World Religions: A Story Approach*. Mystic, Conn.: Twenty-Third Publications.

Boff, Leonardo, and Clodovis Boff. 1987. *Introducing Liberation Theology*. Maryknoll, N.Y.: Orbis Books.

Boulding, Elise. 1986. "Two Cultures of Religion as Obstacles to Peace." *Zygon* 21: 501-18.

Braaten, Carl. 1992. *No Other Gospel! Christianity among the World's Religions*. Minneapolis: Augsburg Fortress Press.

Browning, Don S. 1991. *A Fundamental Practical Theology: Descriptive and Strategic Proposals*. Minneapolis: Fortress Press.

Buck, David B. 1991. "Forum on Universalism and Relativism in Asian Studies." *Asian Studies Journal* 50: 29-34.

Burhoe, Ralph Wendell. 1976. "The Source of Civilization in the Natural Selection of Coadapted Information in Genes and Cultures." *Zygon* 11: 263-303.

———. 1979. "Religion's Role in Human Evolution: The Missing Link between Ape-Man's Selfish Genes and Civilized Altruism." *Zygon* 21: 135-62.

———. 1986. "War, Peace, and Religion's Biocultural Evolution." *Zygon* 21: 439-72.

Burnham, Frederic B., ed. 1989. *Postmodern Theology: Christian Faith in a Pluralistic World*. San Francisco: Harper & Row.

Burrows, William. 1992. "Commensurability and Ambiguity: Liberation as an Interreligiously Usable Concept." In *World Religions and Human Liberation*. Ed. Dan Cohn-Sherbok. Maryknoll, N.Y.: Orbis Books, pp. 127-42.

Burrows, William E., and Robert Windrem. 1994. *Critical Mass: The Dangerous Race for Superweapons in a Fragmenting World*. New York: Simon & Schuster.

Cady, Linnell. 1987. "Foundation or Scaffolding: The Possibility of Justification in an Historical Approach to Ethics." *Union Seminary Quarterly*

Review 41: 45-62.

Campbell, Donald T. 1976. "On the Conflicts between Biological and Social Evolution and between Psychology and Moral Tradition." *Zygon* 11: 167-208.

Capra, Fritjof. 1982. *The Turning Point: Science, Society, and the Rising Culture*. New York: Simon & Schuster.

Carmody, Denise Lardner, and John Carmody. 1988. *The Story of World Religions*. Mountain View, Cal.: Mayfield Publishing Company.

Chopp, Rebecca. 1986. *The Praxis of Suffering: An Interpretation of Liberation and Political Theologies*. Maryknoll, N.Y.: Orbis Books.

Clarke, Sundar. 1989. "Dalit Movements—Need for a Theology." In Prabhakar 1989, pp. 30-34.

Clooney, Francis X. 1993. *Theology after Vedanta: An Experiment in Comparative Theology*. Albany: State University of New York Press.

Cobb, John B., Jr. 1990. "Beyond 'Pluralism.'" In D'Costa 1990, pp. 81-95.

Cohn-Sherbok, Dan, ed. 1992. *World Religions and Human Liberation*. Maryknoll, N.Y.: Orbis Books.

Cone, James. 1975. *God of the Oppressed*. New York: Seabury Press.

Cragg, Kenneth. 1984. *Muhammad and the Christian: A Question of Response*. Maryknoll, N.Y.: Orbis Books.

D'Costa, Gavin. 1987. *John Hick's Theology of Religions: A Critical Evaluation*. Lanham, Md.: University Press of America.

——————, ed. 1990. *Christian Uniqueness Reconsidered: The Myth of a Pluralistic Theology of Religions*. Maryknoll, N.Y.: Orbis Books.

——————. 1990. "Christ, the Trinity, and Religious Plurality." In D'Costa 1990, pp. 16-29.

——————. 1993. "Creating Confusion: A Response to Markham." *New Blackfriars* 74: 41-47.

Dean, Thomas. 1987. "The Conflict of Christologies: A Response to S. Mark Heim." *Journal of Ecumenical Studies* 24: 24-31.

Dean, William. 1991. "Humanistic Historicism and Naturalistic Historicism." In Devaney 1991, pp.41-60.

Demarest, Bruce A. 1992. "General and Special Revelation: Epistemological Foundations of Religious Pluralism." In *One God, One Lord: Christianity in a World of Religious Pluralism*. Ed. Andrew D. Clarke and Bruce W. Winters. Grand Rapids, Mich.: Baker Book House, pp. 189-206.

Devaney, Sheila Greeve, ed. 1991. *Theology at the End of Modernity*. Philadelphia: Trinity Press International.

Devasahayam, V., ed. 1992. *Dalits and Women: Quest for Humanity*. Madras: Gurukul Lutheran Theological College and Research Institute.

"Dialogue and Proclamation." 1991. Issued by the Vatican Council for Interreligious Dialogue and the Congregation for the Evangelization of Peoples. In *Bulletin of the Pontifical Council on Interreligious Dialogue*, vol. 26, no. 2.

Dinakaran, M.C. 1988. "Liberative Undercurrents in Hindu Thought: A Preliminary Inquiry." In Engineer 1988a, pp. 25-46.

DiNoia, J. A. 1990. "Pluralist Theology of Religions: Pluralistic or Non-Pluralistic?" In D'Costa 1990, pp. 119-34.

——————. 1992. *The Diversity of Religions: A Christian Perspective*. Washington, D.C.: The Catholic University Press of America.

Donovan, Peter J. 1986. "Do Different Religions Share Moral Common Ground?" *Religious Studies* 22: 367-76.

Drummond, Richard Henry. 1985. *Toward a New Age in Christian Theology.* Maryknoll, N.Y.: Orbis Books.

Dunne, John. 1972. *The Way of All the Earth.* Notre Dame, Ind.: University of Notre Dame Press.

Dupuis, Jacques. 1991. *Jesus Christ at the Encounter of World Religions.* Maryknoll, N.Y.: Orbis Books.

Dwivedi, Kanak. 1980. "The Concept of Social Justice in Traditional Hindu Thought." *Religion and Society* 27: 5-12.

EATWOT. 1988. "Statement of EATWOT Consultation on Religion and Liberation." New Delhi, December 1-5, 1987. In *From Dar Es Salaam to Mexico: Third World Theologians in Dialogue—Voices from the Third World* 11: 152-71.

Engineer, Asghar Ali. 1984. *On Developing Theory of Communal Riots.* Bombay: Institute of Islamic Studies.

————. 1988a. *Communalism and Communal Violence in India.* (*Islamic Perspective*, vol. 4, July).

————, ed. 1988b. *Religion and Liberation* (*Islamic Perspective*, vol. 4, December).

————. 1990. *Islam and Liberation Theology: Essays on Liberative Elements in Islam.* New Delhi: Sterling Publishers.

Eppsteiner, Fred, ed. 1988. *The Path of Compassion: Writings on Socially Engaged Buddhism.* Berkeley: Parallax Press.

Falk, Richard. 1988. "Religion and Politics: Verging on the Postmodern." *Alternatives* 13: 379-94.

"Fellowship in Action." 1994. *Christian Worker: Quarterly of the Christian Workers Fellowship* (1st and 2d quarters), pp. 72-75.

Fernandes, Walter. 1989. "Social Action and Inter-Religious Dialogue." In Irudayaraj 1989, pp. 29-44.

————. 1992. "Bhakti and Liberation Theology for India." In Wilfred 1992, pp. 47-65.

Feyerabend, Paul. 1978. *Against Method.* London: Verso.

Fiorenza, Francis Schüssler. 1984. *Foundational Theology: Jesus and Church.* New York: Crossroad.

————. 1991. "Theological and Religious Studies: The Contest of the Faculties." In *Shifting Boundaries: Contextual Approaches to the Structure of Theological Education.* Ed. Barbara G. Wheeler and Edward Farley. Louisville: Westminster/John Knox Press, pp. 119-50.

Foucault, Michel. 1980. *Power/Knowledge: Selected Interviews and Other Writings, 1972-1977.* New York: Pantheon Books.

————. 1984. "Le souci de la verité." *Magazine Littéraire* (May).

Frei, Hans. 1974. *The Eclipse of Biblical Narrative.* New Haven: Yale University Press.

————. 1975. *The Identity of Jesus Christ.* Philadelphia: Fortress Press.

Gadamer, Hans-Georg. 1982. *Truth and Method.* New York: Seabury.

Gandhi, M. K. 1957. *My Autobiography.* Boston: Beacon Press.

Gangadaran, S. 1991. "A Hindu View of Dialogue from Saiva Siddhanta and Gandhian Perspectives." *Indian Missiological Review* (June), pp. 7-25.

Gilkey, Langdon. 1987. "Plurality and Its Theological Implications." In Hick and Knitter 1987, pp. 37-53.

Gillis, Chester. 1989. *A Question of Final Belief: John Hick's Pluralistic Theory of Salvation.* New York: St. Martin's Press.

Gort, John. 1991. "Liberative Ecumenism: Gateway to the Sharing of Religious Experience Today." *Mission Studies* 8: 57-76.

Granberg-Michaelson, Wesley. 1992. "On Behalf of the Earth." *Sojourners* (September), pp. 28-32.

Grant, Sarah, 1987. "Toward an Indian Theology of Liberation." In *Lord of the Dance.* Bangalore: Asian Trading Corporation, pp. 137-57.

_____ . 1994. "Awareness of Rootedness in the Eternal: A Potential Contribution of Ashrams to Liberation Theology," German translation in *Befreiender Dialog—Befreite Gesellschaft: Politische Theologie und Begegnung der Religionen in Indien und Europa.* Ed. Sybille Fritsch-Oppermann. Loccum: Evangelische Akademie, pp. 65-76.

Greider, William. 1992. *Who Will Tell the People? The Betrayal of American Democracy.* New York: Simon & Schuster.

Griffiths, Bede. 1976. *Return to the Center.* Springfield, Ill.: Templegate.

Griffiths, Paul. 1990. "The Uniqueness of Christian Doctrine Defended." In D'Costa 1990, pp. 157-73.

_____ . 1991. *An Apology for Apologetics: A Study in the Logic of Interreligious Dialogue.* Maryknoll, N.Y.: Orbis Books.

Guarino, Thomas. 1990. "Revelation and Foundationalism: Toward Hermeneutical and Ontological Appropriateness." *Modern Theology* 6: 221-35.

Gutiérrez, Gustavo. 1973. *A Theology of Liberation.* Maryknoll, N.Y.: Orbis Books.

_____ . 1979. "Liberation Praxis and Christian Faith." In *Frontiers of Theology in Latin America.* Ed. Rosino Gibellini. Maryknoll, N.Y.: Orbis Books, pp. 1-33.

_____ . 1984. *We Drink from Our Own Wells: The Spiritual Journey of a People.* Maryknoll, N.Y.: Orbis Books.

Habermas, Jürgen. 1979. *Communication and the Evolution of Society.* Boston: Beacon Press.

_____ . 1984. *The Theory of Communicative Action,* vol. 1. Boston: Beacon Press.

Haight, Roger. 1990. *Dynamics of Theology.* New York: Paulist Press.

_____ . 1994. "Jesus and Salvation: An Essay in Interpretation." *Theological Studies* 55: 225-51.

Hassan, Ihab. 1982. "The Culture of Postmodernism." *Theory, Culture, and Society* 2/3: 119-32.

Hauerwas, Stanley. 1985. *Against the Nations.* Minneapolis: Winston Press.

Heim, S. Mark. 1985. *Is Christ the Only Way? Christian Faith in a Pluralistic World.* Valley Forge, Penn.: Judson Press.

_____ . 1994. "Salvations: A More Pluralistic Hypothesis." *Modern Theology* 10: 341-60.

_____ . 1995. *Salvations: Truth and Difference in Religion.* Maryknoll, N.Y.: Orbis Books.

Hick, John. 1973. *God and the Universe of Faiths.* New York: St. Martin's Press.

_____ . 1977. "Jesus and the World Religions." In *The Myth of Incarnation*. Ed. John Hick. London: SCM Press, pp. 167-85.

_____ . 1980. "Whatever Path Men Choose Is Mine." In *Christianity and Other Religions*. Ed. John Hick and Brian Hebblethwaite. Philadelphia: Fortress Press, pp. 171-90.

_____ . 1983. "On Grading Religions." *Religious Studies* 17: 451-67.

_____ . 1987. "The Non-Absoluteness of Christianity." In Hick and Knitter 1987, pp. 16-36.

_____ . 1989. *An Interpretation of Religion*. New Haven: Yale University Press.

_____ . 1990. "A Response to Gerard Loughlin." *Modern Theology* 7: 57-66.

_____ . 1993. *The Metaphor of God Incarnate*. London: SCM Press.

_____ , and Paul F. Knitter, eds. 1987. *The Myth of Christian Uniqueness: Toward a Pluralistic Theology of Religions*. Maryknoll, N.Y.: Orbis Books.

Hillman, Eugene. 1989. *Many Paths: A Catholic Approach to Religious Pluralism*. Maryknoll, N.Y.: Orbis Books.

Indian Theological Association. 1988. "Towards a Theology of Religions: An Indian Christian Perspective." In *Religious Pluralism: An Indian Christian Perspective*. Ed. Kuncheria Pathil. Delhi: ISPCK, 1991, pp. 324-37.

Indian Theological Association. 1989. "Towards an Indian Christian Theology of Religious Pluralism." In *Religious Pluralism: An Indian Christian Perspective*. Ed. Kuncheria Pathil. Delhi: ISPCK, 1991, pp. 338-49.

Irudayaraj, Xavier, ed. 1989. *Liberation and Dialogue*. Bangalore: Claretian Publications.

_____ , ed. 1990. *Emerging Dalit Theology*. Madras: Jesuit Theological Secretariate/Madurai: Tamilnadu Theological Seminary.

Japhet, S. 1989. "Caste Oppression in the Catholic Church." In Prabhakar 1989, pp. 176-80.

John, T. K. 1989. "Interfaith Dialogue in Justice Perspective." In Irudayaraj 1989, pp. 45-63.

Joshi, Barbara, ed. 1986. *Untouchable Voices of Dalit Liberation Movement*. New Delhi: Select Book Services Syndicate.

Katz, Steven T. 1978. "Language, Epistemology, and Mysticism." In *Mysticism and Philosophical Analysis*. Ed. S. T. Katz. New York: Oxford University Press, pp. 22-74.

Kaufman, Gordon. D. 1981. *The Theological Imagination: Constructing the Concept of God*. Philadelphia: Westminster Press.

Keller, Catherine. 1986. *From a Broken Web: Separation, Sexism, and Self*. Boston: Beacon Press.

Kennedy, Paul. 1993. *Preparing for the Twenty-First Century*. New York: Random House.

King, Sallie. 1988. "Two Epistemological Models for the Interpretation of Mysticism." *Journal of the American Academy of Religion* 56: 257-79.

Knitter, Paul. F. 1975. *Toward a Protestant Theology of Religions: A Case Study of Paul Althaus and Contemporary Attitudes*. Marburg: N.G. Elwert Verlag.

_____ . 1978. "World Religions and the Finality of Christ: A Critique of Hans Küng's *On Being a Christian*." *Horizons* 5: 151-64.

_____ . 1983. "Theocentric Christology." *Theology Today* 40: 130-49.

_____ . 1985. *No Other Name? A Critical Survey of Christian Attitudes toward World Religions.* Maryknoll, N.Y.: Orbis Books.

_____ . 1987. "Toward a Liberation Theology of Religions." In Hick and Knitter 1987, pp. 178-200.

_____ . 1988. "Dialogue and Liberation: Foundations for a Pluralist Theology of Religions." *The Drew Gateway* 58: 1-53.

_____ . 1990. "Interreligious Dialogue: What? Why? How?" In *Death or Dialogue: From the Age of Monologue to the Age of Dialogue.* With L. Swidler, J. B. Cobb, M. Hellwig. Philadelphia: Trinity Press International, pp. 19-44.

Kottukapally, Joseph. 1991. "Mission and Dialogue in Conflict." In *Emerging India and the Word of God.* Ed. Paul Puthanangady. Bangalore: NBCLC, pp. 536-54.

Krieger, David. 1990. "Conversion: On the Possibility of Global Thinking in an Age of Particularism." *Journal of the American Academy of Religion* 58: 223-243.

_____ . 1991. *The New Universalism: Foundations for a Global Theology.* Maryknoll, N.Y.: Orbis Books.

Kuhn, Thomas S. 1970. *The Structure of Scientific Revolutions.* 2d ed. Chicago: University of Chicago Press.

Küng, Hans. 1976. *On Being a Christian.* New York: Doubleday.

_____ . 1986a. *Christianity and the World Religions: Paths of Dialogue with Islam, Hinduism, and Buddhism.* New York: Doubleday.

_____ . 1986b. "Towards an Ecumenical Theology of Religions: Some Theses for Clarification." *Concilium,* vol. 183, pp. 119-25.

_____ . 1991. *Global Responsibility: In Search of a New World Ethic.* New York: Crossroad.

Lakatos, Imre. 1978. *The Methodology of Scientific Research Programmes.* Ed. John Worral and Gregory Currie. Cambridge University Press.

Lane, Dermot A. 1984. *Foundations for a Social Theology: Praxis, Process and Salvation.* New York: Paulist Press.

_____ . 1991. "David Tracy and the Debate about Praxis." In *Radical Pluralism and Truth: David Tracy and the Hermeneutics of Religion.* Ed. W. G. Jeanrond and J. L. Rike. New York: Crossroad, pp. 18-37.

Lefebure, Leo D. 1993. *The Buddha and the Christ: Explorations in Buddhist and Christian Dialogue.* Maryknoll, N.Y.: Orbis Books.

Lindbeck, George. 1984. *The Nature of Doctrine: Religion and Theology in a Postliberal Age.* Philadelphia: Westminster Press.

Lindsey, William D. 1992. "Public Theology as Civil Discourse: What Are We Talking About?" *Horizons* 19: 125-47.

Lipner, Julius J. 1993. "Seeking Others in their Otherness." *New Blackfriars* 74: 152-65.

Lochhead, David. 1988. *The Dialogical Imperative: A Christian Reflection on Interfaith Encounter.* Maryknoll, N.Y.: Orbis Books.

Lonergan, Bernard. 1972. *Method in Theology.* New York: Herder & Herder.

Lourdusamy, Stan. 1990. "Religious Fundamentalism as Political Weapon: Socio-Economic and Political Factors." *Journal of Dharma* 15: 125-47.

Lukas, Steven. 1977. *Essays in Social Theory.* London: Macmillan & Co.

Lyotard, Jean-Francois. 1984. *The Postmodern Condition.* Minneapolis: Minnesota University Press.

MacIntyre. Alasdair C. 1988. *Whose Justice? Whose Rationality?* Notre Dame, Ind.: University of Notre Dame Press.

Maguire, Daniel C. 1993. *The Moral Core of Judaism and Christianity: Reclaiming the Revolution.* Minneapolis: Fortress Press.

Markham, Ian. 1993. "Creating Options: Shattering the 'Exclusivist, Inclusivist, and Pluralist' Paradigm." *New Blackfriars* 74: 33-41.

McFague, Sallie. 1987. *Models of God: Theology for an Ecological, Nuclear Age.* Philadelphia: Fortress Press.

_____ . 1991. "Cosmology and Christianity: Implications of the Common Creation Story for Theology." In Devaney 1991, pp. 19-40.

Merton, Thomas. 1968. *Zen and the Birds of Appetite.* New York: New Directions.

Milbank, John. 1990. "The End of Dialogue." In D'Costa 1990, pp. 174-91.

Mitchell, Donald W. 1991. *Spirituality and Emptiness: The Dynamics of Spiritual Life in Buddhism and Christianity.* New York: Paulist Press.

Molnar, Paul. 1991. "Some Consequences of Paul F. Knitter's Unitarian Theocentrism." *The Thomist* 55: 449-96.

Morrison, Toni. 1987. *Beloved.* New York: Alfred Knopf.

Mukerji, Bithika. 1990. "The Foundations of Unity and Equality: A Hindu Understanding of Human Rights." In *The Ethics of World Religions and Human Rights.* Ed. Hans Küng and Jürgen Moltmann. *Concilium* 1990/ 92. Philadelphia: Trinity Press International, pp. 70-78.

Nasr, Seyyed Hossein. 1992. "Islam and the Environmental Crisis." In *Spirit and Nature: Why the Environment Is a Religious Issue.* Ed. Steven C. Rockefeller and John C. Elder. Boston: Beacon Press, pp. 83-108.

Nelson-Pallmeyer, Jack. 1992. *Brave New World Order.* Maryknoll, N.Y.: Orbis Books.

Neville, Robert. 1991. *Behind the Masks of God: An Essay toward Comparative Theology.* Albany: State University of New York Press.

Newbigin, Lesslie. 1990. "Religion for the Marketplace." In D'Costa 1990, pp. 135-48.

Nirmal, Arvind P. 1989. "A Dialogue with Dalit Literature." In Prabhakar 1989, pp. 64-82.

_____ , ed. 1990. *Towards a Common Dalit Ideology.* Madras: Gurukul Lutheran Theological College.

_____ , ed. n.d. *A Reader in Dalit Theology.* Madras: Gurukul Lutheran Theological College.

Oakes, Edward T. 1992. "Apologetics and the Pathos of Narrative Theology." *Journal of Religion* 72: 37-58.

O'Brien, John. 1992. *Theology and the Option for the Poor.* Collegeville, Minn.: Liturgical Press.

O'Neill, Maura. 1990. *Women Speaking, Women Listening: Women in Interreligious Dialogue.* Maryknoll, N.Y.: Orbis Books.

Ogden, Schubert. 1972. "What Is Theology?" *The Journal of Religion* 52: 22-40.

_____ . 1992. *Is There Only One True Religion or Are There Many?* Dallas: Southern Methodist Press.

"Opting for the Poor—Challenge to the Universal Religions." 1988. Conference of World Religions, Colombo, Sri Lanka, August 23-29, 1987. Reported in *East-Asian Pastoral Review* 25: 75-79.

Palerasu, N. 1991. "Gandhian Grassroot Communities." Non-published project description formulated in October 1991.

Panikkar, Raimon. 1978. *The Intrareligious Dialogue*. New York: Paulist Press.

_____ . 1983. "Religion or Politics: The Western Dilemma." In *Religion and Politics in the Modern World*. Ed. Peter H. Merkle and Ninian Smart. New York: New York University Press, pp. 44-60.

_____ . 1986. "God of Life, Idols of Death." *Monastic Studies* 17: 101-20.

_____ . 1990. "The Christian Challenge to the Third Millenium." In *Christian Mission and Interreligious Dialogue*. Ed. Paul Mojzes and Leonard Swidler. Lewiston: Edwin Mellen Press, pp. 113-25.

_____ . 1993. *The Cosmotheandric Experience: Emerging Religious Consciousness*. Maryknoll, N.Y.: Orbis Books.

Pattery, George. 1991. "Satyagraha-Religiousness: A Dialogical Way of Liberation." *Vidyajyoti* 155: 7-21.

Perera, Rienzie. 1986. "Ministerial Formation in a Multifaith Parish." In *Ministerial Formation in a Multifaith Milieu*. Ed. Sam Amirtham and S. Wesley Ariarajah. Geneva: WCC, pp. 88-99.

Phillips, W. Gary. 1992. "Evangelicals and Pluralism: Current Opinions." In *Proceedings of the Wheaton Theology Conference*. Wheaton: Ill., pp. 174-89.

Pieris, Aloysius. 1987. "Jesus and Buddha: Mediators of Liberation" in Hick and Knitter 1987, pp. 162-77.

_____ . 1988a. *An Asian Theology of Liberation*. Maryknoll, N.Y.: Orbis Books.

_____ . 1988b. *Love Meets Wisdom: A Christian Experience of Buddhism*. Maryknoll, New York: Orbis Books.

_____ . 1989. "Faith-Communities and Communalism." *East Asian Pastoral Review*, vols. 3 and 4: 294-309.

Placher, William. 1989. *Unapologetic Theology: A Christian Voice in a Pluralistic Conversation*. Louisville: Westminster/John Knox Press.

Plaskow, Judith. 1980. *Sex, Sin, and Grace: Women's Experience and the Theologies of Reinhold Niebuhr and Paul Tillich*. Landham, Md.: University Press of America.

Popper, Karl. 1959. *The Logic of Scientific Discovery*. New York: Basic Books.

Prabhakar, M. E., ed. 1989. *Towards a Dalit Theology*. Delhi: ISPCK.

_____ . 1989. "The Search for a Dalit Theology" in Prabhakar 1989, pp. 35-47.

Pulsfort, Ernst. 1990. *Christliche Ashrams in Indien: Zwischen dem religiösen Erbe Indiens und der christlichen Tradition des Abendlands*. Altenberge: Oros Verlag.

_____ . 1991. *Indien am Scheideweg zwischen Säkularismus und Fundamentalismus*. Würzburg: Echter Verlag.

Pushparajan, A. 1990. "A Gandhian Blueprint for Interreligious Cooperation in India." *Kristu Jyoti* 6: 16-43.

Rabinow, Paul, ed. 1984. *The Foucault Reader*. New York: Pantheon Books.

Rabinow, Paul. 1979. *Reflections on Fieldwork in Morocco*. Berkeley and Los Angeles: University of California Press.

Race, Alan. 1983. *Christian and Religious Pluralism: Patterns in Christian Theology of Religions*. Maryknoll, N.Y.: Orbis Books.

Rahner, Karl. 1966. "Christianity and the Non-Christian Religions." In *Theological Investigations*, vol. 5. Baltimore: Helicon, pp. 115-34.

Raj, Antony. 1990. "Disobedience: A Legitimate Act for Dalit Liberation." In Nirmal 1990, pp. 39-52.

Raj, Joseph Jaswant. 1989. *Grace in the Saiva Siddhantham and in St. Paul*. Madras: South Indian Salesian Society.

Ralston, Helen. 1987. *Christian Ashrams: A New Religious Movement in Contemporary India*. Lewiston, N.Y.: Edwin Mellen Press.

Rapp, R. 1985. "Cultural Disarmament." *Interculture* 89: 14-33.

Rawls, John. 1971. *A Theory of Justice*. Cambridge: Harvard University Press.

Rayan, Samuel. 1989. "Spirituality for Inter-faith Social Action." In Irudayaraj 1989, pp. 64-73.

———. 1990. "Religions, Salvation, Mission." in *Christian Mission and Interreligious Dialogue*. Ed. Paul Mojzes and Leonard Swidler. Lewiston: Edwin Mellen Press, pp. 126-39.

Rescher, Nicholas. 1985. *The Strife of Systems*. Pittsburgh: Pittsburgh University Press.

Robinson, John A.T. 1979. *Truth Is Two Eyed*. London: SCM Press.

Rodrigo, Michael. 1988. "Buddhism and Christianity: Towards the Human Future." *Logos* (Sri Lanka) 27: 19-29.

Rolston, Holmes III. 1985. *Religious Inquiry-Participation and Detachment*. New York: Philosophical Library.

Rooney, Ellen. 1989. *Seductive Reasoning: Pluralism as Problematic of Contemporary Literary Theory*. Ithaca, N.Y.: Cornell University Press.

Ruether, Rosemary Radford. 1990. "Religion and Society: Sacred Canopy vs. Prophetic Critique." In *Expanding the View: Gustavo Gutiérrez and the Future of Liberation Theology*. Ed. Marc H. Ellis and Otto Maduro. Maryknoll, N.Y.: Orbis Books, pp. 72-76.

Saiving, Valerie. 1979. "The Human Situation: A Feminine View." In *Womanspirit Rising: A Feminist Reader in Religion*." Ed. Carol Christ and Judith Plaskow. San Francisco: Harper & Row, pp. 25-42.

Samartha, Stanley J. 1983. "Religions and the Aspirations of the People." *Religion and Society* 30: 102-14.

———. 1987. "The Cross and the Rainbow: Christ in a Multireligious Culture." In Hick and Knitter 1987, pp. 69-88.

Schillebeeckx, Edward. 1990. *The Church: The Human Story of God*. New York: Crossroad.

Schineller, J. Peter. 1976. "Christ and the Church: A Spectrum of Views." *Theological Studies* 37: 545-66.

Segundo, Juan Luis. 1975. *The Liberation of Theology*. Maryknoll, N.Y.: Orbis Books.

———. 1985. *Faith and Ideologies*. Maryknoll, N.Y.: Orbis Books.

Singh, Dharam. 1991. *Sikh Theology of Liberation*. New Delhi: Harman Publishing House.

Sivaraman, S. K. 1985. "The Hindu Vision and World Problems." *Journal of Dharma* 10: 34-41.

Smith, Wilfred Cantwell. 1993. *What Is Scripture? A Comparative Approach*. Minneapolis: Fortress Press.

Sobrino, Jon. 1987. *Spirituality of Liberation: Toward a Political Holiness.* Maryknoll, N.Y.: Orbis Books.

Sontheimer, Gunther D., and Hermann Kulke, eds. 1991. *Hinduism Reconsidered.* Manohar, Delhi.

Spretnak, Charlene. 1991. *States of Grace: The Recovery of Meaning in the Postmodern Age.* Harper SanFrancisco.

Suchocki, Marjorie. 1987. "In Search of Justice: Religious Pluralism from a Feminist Perspective." In Hick and Knitter 1987, pp. 149-61.

Surin, Kenneth. 1990. "A 'Politics of Speech': Religious Pluralism in the Age of the McDonald's Hamburger." In D'Costa 1990, pp. 192-212.

"Swami Agnivesh on Religion as a Weapon for the Poor." 1995. Third World Network Features. In *Vidyajyoti* 59: 337-40.

Swamy, Dalip S. 1991. "Communal Violence." *Mainstream.* Annual 1991, pp. 19-21.

Swidler, Leonard. 1990. *After the Absolute: The Dialogical Future of Religious Reflection.* Minneapolis: Augsburg-Fortress Press.

_____. 1991. "Toward a 'Universal Declaration of Global Ethos'" (press release).

Swimme, Brian. 1988. "Science: A Partner in Creating the Vision." In *Thomas Berry and the New Cosmology.* Ed. Anne Lonergan and Caroline Richards. Mystic, Conn.: Twenty-Third Publications, pp. 81-90.

Taylor, John. 1981. "The Theological Basis of Interfaith Dialogue." In *Mission Trends No. 5: Faith Meets Faith.* Ed. G. Anderson and T. Stranskey. New York: Paulist Press, pp. 93-110.

Taylor, Mark Kline. 1986. "In Praise of Shaky Ground: The Liminal Christ and Cultural Pluralism." *Theology Today* 43: 36-51.

_____. 1990. *Remembering Esperanza: A Cultural-Political Theology for North American Praxis.* Maryknoll, N.Y.: Orbis Books.

_____. 1991. "Religion, Cultural Pluralism, and Liberating Praxis: In Conversation with the Work of Langdon Gilkey." *Journal of Religion* 71:145-66.

Tibursius, A. 1991. "Fifth Annual Report of the Interreligious Fellowship Society, Manavalakurichi, Kanyakumari." Non-published document.

Torres, Sergio, and Virginia Fabella, eds. 1983. *The Irruption of the Third World: A Challenge to Theology.* Maryknoll, N.Y.: Orbis Books.

Tracy, David. 1975. *Blessed Rage for Order: The New Pluralism in Theology.* New York: Seabury.

_____. 1987a. *Plurality and Ambiguity: Hermeneutics, Religion, Hope.* New York: Harper & Row.

_____. 1987b. "Practical Theology in the Situation of Global Pluralism." In *Formation and Reflection: The Promise of Practical Theology.* Ed. Lewis S. Mudge and James N. Poling. Philadelphia: Fortress Press, pp. 139-54.

_____. 1989. "The Uneasy Alliance Reconceived: Catholic Theological Method, Modernity, and Postmodernity." *Theological Studies* 50: 548-70.

_____. 1990a. *Dialogue with the Other: The Inter-Religious Dialogue.* Grand Rapids: Eerdmans.

_____. 1990b. "God, Dialogue and Solidarity: A Theologian's Refrain." *The Christian Century,* October 10, pp. 900-04.

Vachon, Robert. 1985. "Cultural Disarmament and Peace." *Interculture* 18: 34-39.

van Beeck, Joseph. 1991. "Professing the Creed among the World's Religions." *The Thomist* 55: 539-568.

Vandana, Mataji, ed. 1982. *Social Justice and Ashrams*. Bangalore: Asian Trading Corporation.

_____ , ed. 1993. *Christian Ashrams: A Movement with a Future?* Delhi: ISPCK.

VanderWerff, Lyle. 1992. "Religious Pluralism and the Uniqueness of Christ." In *Proceedings of the Wheaton Theology Conference*. Wheaton, Ill., pp. 111-18.

Vempeny, Ishanand. 1988. *Krisna and Christ*. Pune: Ishvani Kendra.

Volf, Miroslav. 1992. "Exclusion and Embrace: Theological Reflections in the Wake of 'Ethnic Cleansing.'" *Journal of Ecumenical Studies* 29: 230-48.

_____ . 1994. "Justice, Exclusion, Difference." Paper delivered at the Concilium Conference, "Ecumenism and Justice: Toward the Twenty-First Century." Princeton Theological Seminary, May 23, 1994.

Werpehowski, William. 1986. "Ad Hoc Apologetics." *Journal of Religion* 66: 282-301.

Whitehead, Alfred North. 1957. *Process and Reality: An Essay in Cosmology*. New York: Free Press (Original: 1929).

Wilfred, Felix. 1986. "Sunset in the East? The Asian Realities Challenging the Church and Its Laity Today." FABC Papers, no. 45, July 1986.

_____ , ed. 1992. *Leave the Temple: Indian Paths to Human Liberation*. Maryknoll, N.Y.: Orbis Books.

_____ . 1994. "Liberating Dialogue in India," German translation in *Befreiender Dialog—Befreite Gesellschaft: Politische Theologie und Begegnung der Religionen in Indien und Europa*. Ed. Sybille Fritsch-Oppermann. Loccum: Evangelische Akademie, pp. 29-40.

Williams, Raymond. 1977. *Marxism and Literature*. New York: Oxford University Press.

Wilson, Edward O. 1993. "Is Humanity Suicidal?" *The New York Times Magazine*, May 30, pp. 24-29.

Winch, Peter. 1958. *The Idea of a Social Science*. London: Routledge & Kegan Paul.

Wittgenstein, Ludwig. 1958. *Philosophical Investigations*. New York: Macmillan.

INDEX